GROUPS, RULES AND LEGAL PRACTICE

Law and Philosophy Library

VOLUME 89

For further volumes:
http://www.springer.com/series/6210

GROUPS, RULES AND LEGAL PRACTICE

by

RODRIGO E. SÁNCHEZ BRIGIDO

Universidad Nacional de Córdoba

Springer

Rodrigo Eduardo Sánchez Brigido
Caseros 628
5000 Cordoba
Argentina
rodrigosanchezb@uolsinectis.com.ar

ISSN 1572-4395
ISBN 978-94-007-3200-1 ISBN 978-90-481-8770-6(eBook)
DOI 10.1007/978-90-481-8770-6
Springer Dordrecht Heidelberg London New York

Printed on acid-free paper

Springer is part of Springer Science+Business Media (www.springer.com)

To Benjamín and Catalina

Preface

It is generally accepted that, if there is law, there are norm-applying officials engaged in a particular practice. Yet there is no agreement as to what the nature of this practice is. The thesis focuses on that issue.

The first part of the study is critical. It examines three of the main accounts of the practice of norm-applying officials, namely: the account, suggested by Hart and further developed by others, that claims that it is a conventional practice; Raz's account, according to which this practice is, more generally, the practice that obtains when there is a particular type of social rule; and one sophisticated version (Shapiro's) of the account that claims that it is a collective intentional activity. It is argued that these accounts, despite containing important insights, are unsuccessful. Firstly, the practice is an institutional practice. It is the practice of members of an institution. These theories do not capture that feature. In particular, they do not capture the fact that members think that they have a duty, qua members, to apply certain norms. Secondly, members sometimes disagree about what the norms to be applied are and yet think of themselves as involved in the same practice (a point raised by Dworkin). These theories cannot capture that feature either.

The second part of the study is constructive. It suggests an account of certain institutional practices in general, and of the institutional practice of norm-applying officials in particular, in terms of a model of collective intentional activities. This account retains the insights of the theories assessed, but it explains in what sense the practice is the practice of members of an institution. In particular, it captures the fact that members consider themselves, qua members, under a duty. And it explains how members can disagree in the way described.

Córdoba, Argentina R.E. Sánchez Brigido

Acknowledgements

This book is the result of my investigations as a Dphil student in the University of Oxford. I am enormously grateful to Nicos Stavropoulos, my supervisor, for his incredible patience. His insightful comments and objections have been of invaluable help. I have learnt a great deal for him, but I have the impression that I could (and should) have learnt much more. I am also greatly thankful to Timothy Endicott, my College Tutor, for his constant support and encouragement.

I am particularly indebted to Ricardo Caracciolo and Pablo Navarro. They have supported me unconditionally, each in his own way, ever since we met, and I would not have had the chance of publishing this book without them. Special thanks to Paolo Comanducci and Jose Juan Moreso for their assistance too.

Hernán Bouvier, Richard Ekins, Maris Köpcke-Tinturé, Guillermo Lariguet, James Lee, Santiago Legarre, Cristina Redondo, Hugo Seleme, Scott Shapiro and Paul Yowell have helped me a lot with their observations to (some of) the drafts that ended up becoming part of the work. The comments by two anonymous referees have been of great importance as well. So special thanks to them.

My stance in Oxford was made possible by the generous support provided by Clarendon Fund and by the Kulke's Fund. The Chaplaincy at Balliol has also provided assistance in times of financial difficulty.

My deepest thanks go to my family. And to Carolina. Without her this work could not have been done.

Contents

1 Three Tests 1
- 1.1 Overview of the Chapter 1
- 1.2 The First Test 1
- 1.3 The Second Test 1
  - 1.3.1 Institutions: Preliminary Remarks 3
  - 1.3.2 Institutions: Further Remarks 9
  - 1.3.3 A Distinction 13
  - 1.3.4 Legal Practice 14
  - 1.3.5 Bringing the Second Test into Sharper Focus 15
- 1.4 The Third Test 17
- 1.5 Conclusion 23

2 Accounts Based on the Idea of a Social Rule (I): Hart's Account and the Coordinative-Convention Approach 25
- 2.1 Overview of the Chapter 25
- 2.2 Elaborating the First Test: Social Rules and Conventions 25
- 2.3 Hart's Account 29
- 2.4 Assessing Hart's Conception 33
  - 2.4.1 Meeting the First Test 33
  - 2.4.2 Meeting the Second Test 36
  - 2.4.3 Meeting the Third Test 39
- 2.5 The Coordinative-Convention Approach 40
- 2.6 Conclusion 44

3 Accounts Based on the Idea of a Social Rule (II): Raz's Account 45
- 3.1 Overview of the Chapter 45
- 3.2 Raz on Legal Practice 45
- 3.3 Assessing Raz's Model: Meeting the First Test 49
- 3.4 Meeting the Second Test 50
- 3.5 Meeting the Third Test 54
- 3.6 Conclusion 55

4 Collective Intentional Activities: Shapiro's Model . . . 57
4.1 Overview of the Chapter . . . 57
4.2 Collective Intentional Activities . . . 57
4.3 Shapiro's Account . . . 62
4.3.1 Shapiro on Collective Intentional Activities . . . 62
4.3.2 Some Difficulties with Shapiro's Model: Meeting the First Test . . . 66
4.3.3 Shapiro's Conception of Legal Practice . . . 70
4.3.4 Assessing Shapiro's Model: Meeting the Second Test . . . 72
4.3.5 Meeting the Third Test . . . 77
4.4 Conclusion . . . 78

5 Kutz on Collective Intentional Activities. Building an Alternative Model: Groups Which Act with No Normative Unity . . . 79
5.1 Overview of the Chapter . . . 79
5.2 Kutz's Model . . . 79
5.3 Assessing Kutz's Model . . . 82
5.3.1 Meeting Condition (a) of the Test . . . 83
5.3.2 Meeting Condition (b): Groups Which Act with No Normative Unity . . . 87
5.3.3 Meeting Condition (b): Groups Which Act with a Normative Unity . . . 89
5.4 Conclusion . . . 89

6 The Activities of Groups with a Normative Unity of Type (I). Non-developed Instances of Legal Practice . . . 91
6.1 Overview of the Chapter . . . 91
6.2 The Alternative Account and the Activities of Groups with a Normative Unity of Type (I) . . . 91
6.3 Other-Regarding, Non-developed Institutions . . . 95
6.4 Non-developed Instances of the Judiciary . . . 103
6.5 Meeting the Tests . . . 107
6.6 Conclusion . . . 108

7 Gilbert's Account of Collective Activities . . . 111
7.1 Overview of the Chapter . . . 111
7.2 Gilbert's Account . . . 111
7.3 Assessing Gilbert's Account . . . 113
7.4 Conclusion . . . 118

8 On Agreements . . . 121
8.1 Overview of the Chapter . . . 121
8.2 The Standard Model . . . 121
8.2.1 The Practice View . . . 123
8.2.2 The Intention Conception . . . 124
8.3 Assessing the Standard Model: Agreements Reconsidered . . . 133

8.4 The Content of Agreements 137
8.5 Conclusion 139

9 The Activities of Groups with a Normative Unity of Type II. Other-Regarding, Developed Institutions. Developed Instances of the Judiciary 141
9.1 Overview of the Chapter 141
9.2 The Activities of Groups with a Normative Unity of Type (II) . 141
9.3 Other-Regarding, Developed Institutions 150
9.4 Developed Instances of the Judiciary 158
9.5 Conclusion 160

10 Developed Instances of Legal Practice. Meeting the Tests 163
10.1 Overview of the Chapter 163
10.2 Meeting the First Test 163
10.3 Meeting the Second Test 163
10.4 Meeting the Third Test 171
10.5 Conclusion 183

Bibliography 185

Index 189

List of Abbreviations

FI	Bratman, M. *Faces of Intention: Selected Essays on Intention and Agency.* Cambridge: CUP, 1999
TRS	Dworkin, R. *Taking Rights Seriously.* London, Duckworth, 1977
OSF	Gilbert, M. *On Social Facts.* London: Routledge, 1989
LT	Gilbert, M. *Living Together: Rationality, Sociality and Obligation.* Lanham: Rowman & Littlefield Publishers, 1996
CJC	Gilbert, M. "Considerations on Joint Commitment: Responses to Various Comments." In *Social Facts & Collective Intentionality*, edited by G Meggle. Frankfurt: Dr Hansel-Hohenhausen AG, 2002
CL	Hart, HLA. *The Concept of Law* (2nd ed). Oxford: Clarendon Press, 1994
C	Kutz, C. *Complicity: Ethics and Law for a Collective Age.* Cambridge: CUP, 2000
CLS	Raz, J. *The Concept of a Legal System* (2nd ed). Oxford: Clarendon Press, 1980
VONP	Raz, J. "Voluntary Obligations and Normative Powers." *Proceedings of the Aristotelian Society* Supp 46 (1972): 79
AL	Raz, J. *The Authority of Law: Essays on Law and Morality.* Oxford: Clarendon Press, 1979
PRN	Raz, J. *Practical Reason and Norms.* Oxford: OUP, 1990
PO	Raz, J. "Promises and Obligations." In *Law, Morality and Society: Essays in Honour of H.L.A. Hart*, edited by PMS Hacker and J Raz. Oxford: Clarendon Press, 1977
ONR	Raz, J. "On the Nature of Rights." *Mind* 93 (1984): 194
MF	Raz, J. *The Morality of Freedom.* Oxford: Clarendon Press, 1986
TVNL	Raz, J. "Two Views of the Nature of the Theory of Law: A Partial Comparison." *Legal Theory* 4 (1998): 249
LPPR	Shapiro, S. "Law, Plans, and Practical Reason." *Legal Theory* 8 (2002): 387

Introduction

1 The Problem

It is a truism that, if there is law, there is a social practice. We can label it "legal practice". Legal practice, as any social practice, takes place in a group. It is the practice, we can say very abstractly, of a political community.

Most contemporary legal theorists understand this practice as constituted by a complex set of interrelated practices among different subgroups within a political community. They claim that this practice is constituted by the practice of those members of the community who create the relevant norms (norm-creating officials), of those who apply the relevant norms (norm-applying officials), and of whose conduct is evaluated according to the relevant norms (ordinary citizens).[1]

So most theorists agree at least on this: if there is an instance of legal practice, there are officials involved in the practice of applying the relevant norms (norm-applying officials). This view is, I believe, correct. The practice of norm-applying officials is distinctive of legal practice. This is what distinguishes, in part, legal practice from other rule-governed social practices. For instance, the practice of a group playing a game is also a rule-governed social practice. But it is not of its essence that there be norm-applying officials. Not so with legal practice. Yet despite this agreement among contemporary legal theorists to the effect that the practice of norm-applying officials is a necessary condition for there to be law, there is no consensus (and in fact there is a long standing dispute) about how to understand such practice.

In this study I shall focus on the practice of norm-applying officials. I shall be concerned with the problem of elucidating its nature. The problem is important. Solving it is not, of course, elucidating the nature of legal practice as a whole. But since the practice of norm-applying officials is a necessary (and a distinctive) aspect of legal practice, then a satisfactory response to the problem will contribute to our understanding of legal practice as a whole.

---

[1] Some version of this view is held by HLA Hart (*CL* 114–117); *PRN* 130–154; MacCormick (1981, 22); Coleman (2001a, 74–77); Shapiro (LLPR 417–437); Postema (1982, 165, 166); Marmor (2001, 212–217); Sartorious (1987, 51–52), among many others. Dworkin's (1986) doctrine, as outlined in *Law's Empire*, and Finnis'(1980) doctrine, as outlined in *Natural Law and Natural Rights*, may be interpreted as upholding some version of this view, but this is not altogether clear.

2 Two Questions

Let us bring our problem into sharper focus. It seems plausible to think, and there is no particular reason to deny, that the practice of norm-applying officials belongs to a category of social practices with which we are familiar. So we can rephrase our problem thus: To what category of social practices does it belong? And what distinguishes this practice from other social practices within that same category?

In fact, we can phrase these questions more precisely by introducing some distinctions that, though coarse, will be helpful to that end.

A social practice can be characterized in terms of its *structure*. From this point of view, any social practice seems to consist in part of a group of people regularly doing something. Let us label the idea of doing something (whatever that may be) "J-ing". That a group regularly J seems necessary for there to be a social practice. But it is clearly not enough. For instance, there would not be a social practice if J-ing occurred regularly but members of the group J-ed inadvertently, or accidentally. It seems that, in addition, for there to be a social practice, members of the group must display certain attitudes towards their J-ing. Of course, there are many types of attitudes (expectations, preferences, beliefs, and so on), but what attitudes must obtain need not concern us now. The point is that any social practice, in terms of its structure, seems to consist of a group of people regularly J-ing and displaying certain attitudes towards their J-ing.

A social practice can be described in terms of its *content* also. For instance, we refer to the social practice of greeting one's neighbour, of dressing formally for special events, of driving on the left, and so on. The content of a social practice seems to be a particular description of the regularity that obtains among the members of the relevant group. Put otherwise, the content of a social practice seems to be a particular description of the "J-ing" that appears in a characterization of its structure.

A further aspect of social practices is that we distinguish between *categories* of social practices. There are traditional practices, customary practices, conventional practices, ritual practices, cooperative practices, and so on. It seems natural to claim, I think, that two practices belong to the same category when they have the same basic particular structure. And when faced with two practices of the same category (e.g. the tradition in Oxford of wearing a gown in graduation ceremonies and the tradition of leaving five pounds to the Porter when leaving for good), we find it natural to say that they only differ in their content: both are traditions, i.e. social practices characterized by their having the same particular structure, but both have different contents (i.e. the relevant regularity is different in each case). Thus, one can determine to what category a particular practice belongs by determining its basic particular structure, and establish the main difference between this particular practice and other practices within the same category by considering their distinct contents.

These distinctions help to formulate our questions more precisely. The practice of norm-applying officials seems to belong to a category of practices with which we are familiar. Put otherwise, it seems to have the same basic particular structure as other practices with which we are acquainted. And it seems that it can be distinguished from practices with the same structure primarily by its special content. But what is its structure? And what is its content?

Hereinafter, for brevity's sake, I shall refer to the practice of norm-applying officials simply as "legal practice", and to norm-applying officials simply as "officials". This deviates from the standard use of "legal practice" (for, as claimed, legal practice is the practice of all members of a political community governed by law) and from the standard use of "officials" in the literature (for the term is normally used to refer either to norm-applying or to norm-creating officials). But I am using the terms in this sense as a short-hand only, for simplicity. So we can put our two questions thus: *What is the particular structure of legal practice* (so understood)*? And what is its content?*

3 The Inquiry

As anticipated, there is long standing debate about the nature of legal practice among contemporary legal theorists.

H.L.A. Hart's views were groundbreaking. In *CL* he states, very roughly, that legal practice is the social practice among officials of evaluating the conduct of members of a community by applying norms that satisfy certain criteria (e.g. they are norms contained in a special document). By "social practice" he means a regularity of behaviour among officials – a pattern of behaviour – plus a distinctive attitude toward such a pattern called "acceptance". This attitude is a disposition to take the pattern as a guide to conduct. It is apparent in officials' appeal to the pattern as a basis for justification for compliance and criticism of deviance.[2] Hart also claims that practices of the sort considered constitute social rules.[3] He calls the social rule that constitutes legal practice a "rule of recognition".[4] In the Postscript to the book, he states that his account should be called "conventionalist" because such a social rule is a social convention.[5] He offers a rather sketchy characterization of conventions: "rules are conventional social practices if the general conformity of a group to them is part of the reason which its individual members have for acceptance".[6]

So Hart answers our questions in a particular way. Legal practice has the same particular structure as *conventional practices*, practices that obtain when there is a convention. We are familiar with them. There are conventions as to whether one is to drive on the right or on the left, as to how one is to address one's interlocutor in informal conversations, and so on. Conventional practices are defined by a particular *structure*. On Hart's view, the structure is this: a group of people regularly J-s (where this amounts to claiming that members of the group regularly J) and there

---

[2] *CL* 55–58, 84–85.

[3] *CL* 255.

[4] *CL* 94.

[5] *CL* 256.

[6] *CL* 255.

are particular attitudes displayed by members towards their J-ing, namely they are disposed to J because they accept J-ing regularly (the pattern of behaviour) as a guide of conduct, and part of the reason why members accept it is that others J. On Hart's view, legal practice has the same structure. And it also has a particular *content* that distinguishes it from other conventional practices. It consists of evaluating the conduct of members of a community by applying norms that satisfy certain criteria.

Hart's doctrine has created a great controversy. There are, one the one hand, several theories that are continuous with it: they accept, roughly, his characterization of the content of legal practice, but they propose slightly different characterizations of its structure. Consider three views in this respect.

The first claims, by relying on some developments in game-theory, that legal practice has the same structure as a sub-category of conventional practices, namely *coordinative conventional practices*, practices that obtain when there is a coordinative convention. We are also familiar with these practices. The driving-on-the-left practice is a typical example. There are several versions of this approach,[7] but we can focus on its core idea. It claims that the structure of coordinative conventional practices consists of a group of people regularly J-ing (where this amounts to claiming that members of a group regularly J) plus an interlocking set of attitudes among members. Very roughly, members expect that the others J regularly, and prefer to J as long as others J, for general conformity is seen as a solution to a particular type of problem (a coordination problem). The solution is arbitrary in the general sense that everyone prefers that everyone else acts on a different regularity so long as everyone does. Thus, the driving-on-the-left practice is, it is claimed, a coordinative convention, for members of the group regularly drive on the left, expect that others do so, and prefer to do so as long as others do, for driving on the left is seen as a solution to the coordination problem of avoiding accidents (and the solution is arbitrary in the general sense that everyone prefers that everyone else drives on the right so long as everyone does). According to this view, legal practice has the same basic structure.

Note the differences with Hart's doctrine. This approach claims, just as Hart did, that the structure is in part that a group regularly J-s (where this amounts to claiming that its members J regularly). Although it does not mention dispositions to J, but preferences, the implication is that members are disposed to J, as Hart also claimed. Moreover, it accepts the idea that members prefer to J, and hence are disposed to J, in part, because other members regularly J, as Hart also suggested. But this is only part of the explanation. The explanation of why members regularly J gives a central role to the idea that they are trying to solve a particular kind of problem (a coordination problem), an idea that plays no explicit role in Hart's account. Furthermore, this view mentions specific attitudes (preferences and expectations) that do not play an explicit role in Hart's account either.

---

[7] Postema (1982, 176 ff); Coleman (2001b, 117) (although he later abandoned the view; see n 15 below). Marmor (2001, 212–217) and Lagerspetz (1989, 100–121) claim that legal practice is a conventional practice too, but they understand this in a way that differs both from Hart's and from the coordinative convention approach.

A second view is held by Joseph Raz. According to him the structure of legal practice is essentially this: *it is the practice that obtains when there is a social rule or rules among members of a group.*[8] We are familiar with social rules. There are social rules as to how one is to express gratitude to one's host, as to how one ought to behave in public, and so on. Social rules are rules, Raz claims, which are followed by members of a group.[9] A rule is so followed if members of the group act in accordance with it and believe that it is valid, that it ought to be followed.[10] According to Raz legal practice has the same basic structure as the practice that obtains when there is a social rule: a group J-s regularly (where this amounts to claiming that members J regularly) and certain attitudes obtain among members, i.e. they consider their J-ing as something required by a valid rule.[11]

Note the differences with Hart's view. On Hart's view, members are disposed to J because they accept J-ing regularly (the pattern of behaviour) as a guide of conduct, and part of the reason for their acceptance is that the other members J. For Raz, members are not disposed to J because they accept a *pattern* of behaviour as a guide of conduct. Rather, they J because they think that a valid *rule* so requires.[12] Besides, Raz does not claim that part of the reason why members J is that other members J. Finally, on Hart's view the fact that members are disposed to J because they accept J-ing regularly (the pattern of behaviour) as a guide of conduct and that part of the reason for their acceptance is that other members J means that there is a conventional social rule. Raz offers a different characterization of conventional social rules,[13] and he does not claim that the social rule that obtains when there is an instance of legal practice is necessarily a conventional social rule.[14]

Consider, finally, some relatively recent theories which, by relying on some developments in the theory of mind and action, claim that legal practice consists of a *collective intentional activity*. Collective intentional activities are also familiar to us. They range from the simplest (like singing a duet or playing football) to the more complex (like fighting a war). There are several versions of this view,[15] but Shapiro's is, I think, the most sophisticated one. He claims, roughly, that collective intentional activities have a particular structure: a group J-s (where this is not necessarily tantamount to claiming that its members J, but to claiming that they do their parts of a complex action – J-ing – which is ascribable to the group as a whole) and participants display certain attitudes towards their J-ing, the J-ing of the group, namely they intend to do their parts of that group-action. For instance, suppose that two persons are preparing a sauce by way of one of them pouring milk into a pan

[8] *PRN* 146–148.

[9] *PRN* 81.

[10] *PRN* 81, 148.

[11] *PRN* 81, 146–149.

[12] *PRN* 52–82, 146–148.

[13] *PRN* 81–82.

[14] *PRN* 147–148.

[15] LPPR 417–441; Kutz (2001, 442, 460–465); Coleman (2001a, 98).

and another stirring its content. Intuitively this is a collective intentional activity. The group is preparing a sauce (J-ing). But it is not the case that one of the members J-s (prepares the sauce) and the other J-s (prepares the sauce). Rather, each is doing her part of their J-ing (their preparing a sauce), an action that is ascribable to the group as a whole. For Shapiro, legal practice has the same basic structure as collective intentional activities: a group regularly J-s and participants intend to do their parts of the group-action of J-ing.

Note the differences with Hart's doctrine. For Hart (and for the coordinative-convention approach and for Raz's account) that "a group regularly J-s" means that its members J. On Shapiro's view this is not necessarily so. And for Hart that members display certain attitudes towards their J-ing means in part that they are disposed to J. By contrast, on Shapiro's view the attitudes displayed by members towards their J-ing is their intending to do their parts of J-ing, and the latter is not necessarily tantamount to their being disposed to J.

This is a very general picture of some of the main theories that attempt to propose an account of legal practice in a way continuous with Hart's. Consider, now, the other main side of the debate.

Ronald Dworkin has put forward a powerful objection against Hart's account which seems applicable to his followers as well. The objection points to a fact about legal practice which is very common. The fact is that participants often disagree about what the norms to be applied are. Moreover, when this happens, they appeal to the practice itself in order to ground their views. It seems that Hart (and his followers) cannot explain this aspect of legal practice, and hence that an alternative explanation is needed.[16]

In effect, they basically agree on what the content of legal practice is: it consists of evaluating the conduct of members of a community by applying norms that satisfy certain criteria. For brevity, let us refer to this as "E-ing". And, although they have different views about the structure of legal practice, it seems that Dworkin's objection applies to all of them. For it seems that, if legal practice were a social practice as characterized by any of these theories, the type of disagreement that the objection mentions could not take place. If participants disagreed about what the norms to be applied are it seems that we cannot say that they are E-ing, that the regularity of behaviour required by all these theorists obtains. Besides, it seems that we cannot say that they are disposed to E, to do the same thing, so long as others E, as Hart required; or that they expect that members E (that they do the same thing) and prefer to E (to do the same thing) as long as others E, as the coordinative-approach demands; or that they regard their E-ing as something required by the same rule, as Raz requires; or that they intend to do their parts of their E-ing, i.e. to do their parts of the same group-action of E-ing, as Shapiro demands. So these theories seem bound to accept that, when this type of disagreement among officials occurs, there is no legal practice. Moreover, since there would be no legal practice, they seem

---

[16] *TRS* 54–58; cf Dworkin (1986, 5, 13, 15–30, 46).

bound to accept that participants' appeal to the practice itself to ground their assertions about what the norms to be applied are is completely absurd, unintelligible. And since in many legal systems this type of disagreement exists, these theories seem flawed.

This characterization of the objection is very abstract, but it helps to outline one of the problems that any theory of legal practice faces.

So let us take stock. We have two questions: What is the structure of legal practice? And what is its content? They are important, for an answer to them is necessary to improve our understanding of the law. And they are challenging also, for what the answer might be is not straightforward. The fact that there is an intricate debate in this respect amongst some of the most prominent contemporary legal theorists suggests that much.

In this study I shall attempt to provide an answer to these two questions. The argument will fall into two parts.

The first will be critical. I shall examine the theories proposed by Hart and those of his followers that I have mentioned. There are of course other theories. But I shall consider only these because they are representative of some of the main strands and because, although I believe that they ultimately fail, they contain important insights, and examining their flaws paves the way towards a correct account. I shall claim that they fail on three main counts.

Firstly, given that they attempt to characterize legal practice by showing that it has the same structure as other practices with which we are familiar, they should propose an adequate characterization of these practices. I shall argue that they fail on this count. That is, Hart's account and the coordinative-convention account do not capture the main aspects of (coordinative) conventional practices. Raz's account does not capture the main aspects of the practice that takes place when there is a social rule. And Shapiro's account does not capture the main aspects of collective intentional activities.

Secondly, even if we understood (coordinative) conventional practices, the practice that takes place when there is, more generally, a social rule, and collective intentional activities, as each of the relevant theories proposes, I shall argue that these theories do not capture the basic structure of legal practice. That is, its structure cannot be explained adequately in terms of (coordinative) conventional practices so understood, or in terms of the practices that take place when there is a social rule so understood, or in terms of collective intentional activities so understood. The main reason is this. All these theorists admit, as they should, that legal practice has an institutional character. It is the practice of a group of individuals (officials) who form an institution, the Judiciary. But a first approximation to this institution suggests that it has certain features – in particular, whenever this institution exists, its members consider themselves, qua members, as under a duty – and, I shall argue, these features are not, and cannot, be captured adequately in terms of the practices that each theory favours.

Finally, I shall attempt to show that these theories, as they stand, do not capture those instances of legal practice where the type of disagreement mentioned above takes place.

The second part of the argument will be constructive. I shall argue that legal practice has the content that these theorists claim it has, but I shall defend an alternative view of its structure: legal practice has the same basic structure as some types of *institutional practices*, which in turn have the same structure as some kinds of collective intentional activities (activities which, I shall argue, cannot be understood as Shapiro proposes). This view aims at retaining the main insights of the theories proposed by Hart and his followers, but it incorporates elements which they have failed to consider. Conceiving of legal practice in this way, I shall claim, captures all its main aspects – in particular, the fact that members of this institution conceive of themselves as under a duty qua members – including the fact that, in some instances, the kind of disagreement that the objection points out takes place.

4 An Overview

In *Chapter 1* I set the stage for further discussion. I propose three tests to assess any theory of legal practice that claims that it should be understood as having the same basic structure, although a distinct content, as other practices with which we are familiar. The theory should: (1) propose an account of the favoured categories of practices, such that (2) if legal practice is understood as having the same basic structure, although a distinct content, as the favoured category of practices, the main aspects of legal practice are captured, and such that (3) the objection from disagreement is met.

In *Chapter 2* I evaluate Hart's account and, very briefly, the coordinative-convention approach. I argue that neither of them meets all the tests.

In *Chapter 3* I attempt to show that Raz's account does not meet all the tests either.

In *Chapter 4* I claim that Shapiro's account also fails to meet all the tests.

The discussion so far will suggest that a proper account of collective intentional activities would be helpful to understand some institutional practices in general and, in particular, legal practice.

In *Chapter 5* I discuss one model of collective intentional activities (Kutz's) that, I think, is well oriented. But it has to be modified. Once this is done, we arrive at an alternative model. It captures the main features of the simplest instances of this type of activities. Some are, nevertheless, less simple. They are such that participants conceive of themselves as under a duty qua members of the group. I label them "the activities of groups with a normative unity", and distinguish between two possible sub variants: those where the fact that members conceive of themselves as under a duty qua members depends on their thinking that the group-activity is particularly valuable in relation to individuals other than themselves ("the activities of groups with a normative unity of type (I)"), and those where members think that they are under such duty even if they do not think that the group-activity is actually valuable in that way ("the activities of groups with a normative unity of type (II)"). The alternative model does not capture them, but I suggest that it could be expanded to do so. The point is important, for there is reason to think that some institutional practices in general, and legal practice in particular, are instances of the activity of groups with a normative unity.

In *Chapter 6* I propose a model of the activities of groups with a normative unity of type (I). I argue that some instances of institutional practices in general, and of legal practice in particular, can be understood in terms of this model. But not all of them can. To understand the latter, I suggest, we need an account of the activities of groups with a normative unity of type (II).

In *Chapter 7* I discuss very briefly one prominent account of collective intentional activities (Gilbert's) that, if correct, would be an adequate account of the activities of groups with a normative unity of type (II). I argue that it fails, though certain important lessons can be learnt from it. In particular, the idea of participants having agreed seems, at first glance, suitable to capture the activities of this type of groups. But the idea of an agreement should be elaborated.

In *Chapter 8* I propose an account of agreements.

In *Chapter 9* I deploy a model of the activities of groups with a normative unity of type (II) that draws on the conclusions arrived at so far. I suggest that this model captures those instances of institutional practices in general, and of legal practice in particular, that are not captured by our model of the activities of groups with a normative unity of type (I).

In *Chapter 10* I claim that the two models capture any possible instance of legal practice. Put otherwise, the two models add up to an account of legal practice that meets all the tests.

Chapter 1
Three Tests

1.1 Overview of the Chapter

I shall present now three tests to assess the adequacy of the theories of legal practice we shall discuss (Sections 1.2–1.4).

1.2 The First Test

These theories attempt to show that legal practice has the same basic structure as other practices with which we are familiar. So it seems clear that, for this strategy to be successful, they should propose a satisfactory account of the relevant category of practices. Thus, Hart's account and the coordinative-convention approach should propose an account of (coordinative) conventional practices that captures their main features; Raz should propose an account that captures the main aspects of the practice that takes place when there is, more generally, a social rule; and Shapiro's account should propose an account of collective intentional activities that captures their main traits. This will be, then, our first test.

I shall elaborate this test in further chapters. For the moment suffice it to say that it is of marginal importance. After all, each account of legal practice might fail to capture the main features of the favoured category of practices and, yet, legal practice might have the structure that each of these accounts claim it has. Nevertheless, the test will help to unveil the flaws and virtues of each theory as an account of legal practice.

1.3 The Second Test

These theories should also show that, if legal practice is conceived of as having a certain structure and content, its main aspects are captured. This will be, then, our second test. To elaborate it we need to see what the main pre-analytic aspects of legal practice are. Some general features stand out.

R.E. Sánchez Brigido, *Groups, Rules and Legal Practice*,
Law and Philosophy Library 89, DOI 10.1007/978-90-481-8770-6_1,

First, legal practice is the practice of a group of individuals (officials). It is not the practice of one individual. That much is implied in our regarding it as a type of *social* practice. Perhaps there are instances of law where only one official is involved. Yet I am focusing, as all the theories I shall assess do, on instances of law which are more complex, and one aspect of their complexity is that a group of officials is involved. Second, the practice has an institutional character. It is the practice of a group of individuals (officials) who form an institution, the Judiciary. Third, we treat this group as a group which acts intentionally. We can say, very generally, that the group evaluates the conduct of members of a community by applying certain norms. Ascribing intentional acts to groups might look suspicious, and some may claim that this is only a metaphorical use of the notion of intentional action. Whatever the case, we do ascribe intentional actions to this group. In fact, we ascribe the activity to the group only if its members act in a certain way. If members did not act at all, we would not ascribe any intentional act to this group. Finally, it is plain that the actions of its members are, in turn, regulated by some rule(s). Otherwise we would not consider the group an institution. The general idea of an institution is conceptually connected with the idea of rules.

We are familiar with institutions of this type. Churches, armies, universities, schools, clubs, trade unions, professional bodies, NGOs, charities, all have, normally, the same characteristics. They can be partially characterized as groups of individuals to which we ascribe the intentional performance of certain activities (providing education in the case of Oxford University, defending certain territories in the case of the British Army, protecting endangered species in the case of the WWF, etc) only insofar as its members act; and the actions of the members are regulated by some rule(s).

In short, these institutions can be partially characterized as groups which act intentionally only if its members act, and the acts of its members are regulated by some rule(s). And legal practice (the practice of officials) is the practice of members of an institution of this type.

Before proceeding let me make two clarifications about the scope of the latter claim. The claim relies on a recognizable, familiar way in which we use the term "institution". There is no denial that we employ this term in other ways also, to refer to other type of phenomena. Consider the institution of contract, the institution of religion, the institution of marriage, and the institution of money. Here the term "institution" does not refer to a group of individuals partially characterized as above. The institutions of contract, religion, marriage or money are not groups to which we attribute the performance of intentional acts, not even in a metaphorical sense. Besides, these institutions do not have members in any relevant sense. So my claim that, if there is law, there is the practice of members of an institution[17] does not

[17] MacCormick also notices that we use the term "institution" to refer, in some cases, to certain type of groups (which he labels "social institutions") and, in other cases, to institutions such as the institution of contract, money, etc. He also acknowledges that, if there is law, there must be an institution of the first type. But he is primarily concerned with providing an analysis of institutions of the second type. MacCormick and Weinberger (1986, esp. 25, 55–56, 74).

deny that there might be other uses of the term "institution".[18] Nor does it deny that there are links between these different uses of the term. For instance, it seems clear that, whenever we refer to something as an institution, we necessarily make reference to the existence of some rule(s) in a certain group; this is precisely the case in the two types of institution I have mentioned. But the truth of the claim does not depend on elucidating these links. It only depends on acknowledging that there is a recognizable notion that refers to groups characterized as in the previous paragraph. Hereinafter, unless otherwise stated, whenever I use the term "institution" I will be referring to this type of groups.

The second clarification is this. Many legal systems contain, or might be interpreted as containing, their own characterization of what counts as an institution, and of the Judiciary in particular. For instance, many legal systems contain provisions as to how officials are elected, what their competence is, etc. But when I claim legal practice is the practice of members of an institution (the Judiciary) I am not relying on these technical characterizations. I am focusing, rather, on a type of group picked out by the recognizable, non-technical notion of an institution mentioned above, as it appears in any legal system (whether it has a technical characterization of the Judiciary or not).

I shall now focus on these institutions in more detail. I am concerned with elaborating the second test, i.e. with identifying the main aspects of legal practice (i.e. the practice of members of one particular institution, the Judiciary), those aspects that a theory of legal practice should capture. And I shall do so by taking an indirect route: I shall put aside the Judiciary for the moment and consider some of the general, necessary features of all other institutions of this type.

1.3.1 Institutions: Preliminary Remarks

As said, these institutions are in part groups which act only if their members act. But it is clear that the actions that are necessary for the group to act are not any actions whatsoever. They are the actions regulated by the relevant rule(s). If there is an institution of this type, there is a group which acts only if its members act in a particular way: only if they follow some rule(s). Moreover, these institutions are somehow continuous. They are in part groups which act for a significant period of

[18] The term is also used as a theoretical construct in sociology that refers, *inter alia*, to: (a) institutions such as the institution of money, contract, etc; thus, it is stated that institutions are "social practices that are regularly and continuously repeated, are sanctioned and maintained by social norms and have a major significance in the social structure" (Abercrombie 1988, 124); or (b) the two types of institution I mentioned and perhaps others types of institution as well; thus, it is claimed that "institutions consist of cognitive, normative, and regulative structures and activities that provide stability and meaning to social behaviour" (Scott 1977, 33); or (c) any type of phenomenon that is, broadly speaking, of sociological interest; thus communities, society, organizations, groups, social activities and social practices all form "the institutional world" and are referred to as "institutional forms" (Morton 1998, Chapters 1 and 2).

time, and this is the case only if its members follow some rule(s) through a relatively extended period of time. How long this period of time may be is a question of degree, so it would be senseless to provide a determinate answer. Yet it is plain that, if there were a group whose members have followed a rule on only one occasion, it would not qualify as an institution. Furthermore, for the group to qualify as an institution, it is not only necessary that its members follow the relevant rule(s) each time the occasion arises and do this during a significant period of time (as if it were only necessary that they realized on each occasion "alas, I should follow the rule now", and a series of discrete actions of this sort took place during a relatively long period of time). There must be among them a standing disposition to do this. So it seems we could conclude that, if there is an institution of this type, there is a group which acts intentionally for a significant period of time only if its members are disposed to follow, and do follow, some rule(s) for a significant period of time.

Notice, however, that this partial characterization is not careful enough. Perhaps in some cases *all* members of a group must be disposed to follow, and follow, some rule(s) during a significant period of time for the group to qualify as an institution. But there are institutions (and hence there are groups which act) where certain individuals count as members of the institution (and hence as members of the group which acts) even if they do not follow the relevant rule(s), or even if they are not disposed to follow such rule(s). For instance, a soldier counts as a member of the army even if he does not follow the relevant rule(s). Of course, he might be expelled. But this presupposes that he is a member. So, in these cases, an institution is in part a group which acts intentionally even if not all its members (are disposed to) follow the relevant rule(s). The question of how many members should (be disposed to) follow some rule(s) for a group to qualify as an institution is, I think, a question of degree. So it would be senseless to provide a determinate answer. But it is clear that, if none of the members were in such a position, the group would not be an institution. So we can say that, in some cases, if there is an institution of this type, there is a group which acts intentionally for a significant period of time only if *most* of its members (the "most" is intentionally vague) follow, and are disposed to follow, some rule(s).

In short, we should characterize the first general trait of institutions thus: if there is an institution of this type, there is a group which acts intentionally for a significant period of time only if (most of) its members follow, and are disposed to follow, some rule(s) for a significant period of time.

Secondly, the activity we ascribe to this type of group has special characteristics: it is an activity of which its members think, or would think if they considered the matter, as purporting to be valuable in relation to (some aspect(s) of) the life of the community or society as a whole. This idea is, of course, very imprecise, but this is because the notion with which we are concerned has imprecise boundaries. There is no point in being more precise.

In many cases, its members think (or would think upon reflection) of the activity as purporting to be valuable in relation, primarily, to general human interests of non-members of the institution, as it happens with armies, charities, and some NGOs. I shall label this type of institutions "other-regarding institutions". In other cases, members (would) consider the activity as purporting to be valuable in relation, primarily, to general human interests of its members only, as it happens with schools, trade unions, clubs, and many others. I shall label them "self-regarding institutions". But in all cases, even in self-regarding institutions, members (would) think of the activity as also purporting to be valuable in relation to (some aspect(s) of) the life of the community or society as a whole. This is what distinguishes these institutions, among other things, from other groups. Suppose John and Paul have agreed to create a development joint venture, and that they have done so with the only purpose of increasing their incomes. They have rules stating how investments are to be made, when, by whom, etc. Suppose further that these rules have been followed during a significant period of time, and that ascribing the performance of certain acts to the group is appropriate ("the joint venture has acquired this property", etc). Here there is a group which acts whose members follow some rule(s). But this group would not count as an institution. And this is so, I take it, because the activity is conceived as promoting the individual interests of John and Paul only, not as purporting to be valuable in relation to some aspect of the life of the community or society as a whole in any sense.

It seems we could conclude, then, that, if there is an institution, there is a group which acts intentionally for a significant period of time whose members (would) consider the activity of the group as purporting to be valuable in the way described. Yet the same caveat mentioned above applies here as well. For there are cases where not *all* members must (be disposed to) think of the activity in this way for the group to qualify as an institution. The question of how many members should (be disposed to) think of the activity in the way described for a group to qualify as an institution is, again, a question of degree. But it is clear that if none of the members were (disposed to) think of the activity in the way described, the group would not qualify as an institution.

So, in short, we should say that, if there is an institution, there is a group which acts intentionally during a significant period of time, and (most of) its members (would) think of the activity in the way described.

Finally, it seems clear that, whenever there is an institution, its members believe, or would believe if they thought about the matter, that they are under a duty, qua members of the institution, to perform the relevant acts. There is no institution if members thought of the relevant acts as something they are at complete liberty to do or not to do, and not as something they have a duty to do qua members of the institution. This is only an approximation, nevertheless. For, put in those terms, the idea seems to presuppose that there is no institution unless its members had the concept of an institution, and there is no particular reason to think that. There might be cases where members only believe that they have a duty qua members of a group described in terms of the two traits mentioned above (and hence not strictly speaking qua members of the institution). Of course, members normally have the concept, and that is why, normally, they believe that they have duties qua members of the institution. But this need not, I think, be the case. Besides, perhaps in some cases *all* members must (be disposed to) think that they have a duty qua members for the group to qualify as an institution. But there are institutions where not all satisfy that condition. The question of how many should satisfy this condition is also a question of degree. But it is plain that we would not refer to a group as an institution if none of its members regarded (or were disposed to regard) themselves as under a duty qua members. Consider the army and suppose that none of its members were disposed to think of themselves as under a duty to perform certain actions *qua* members. Suppose that they thought of these actions as completely optional. It is clear that it would not be recognizable as an institution.

So, in short, we should say that, if there is an institution, there is a group described in terms of the two features already mentioned, (most of) whose members (would) think that they have certain duties qua members of such group (and in many cases they think that they have certain duties qua members of the institution).

We can now list more precisely some of the pre-analytical, necessary aspects of these institutions. (Hereinafter, for brevity and unless otherwise stated, whenever I refer to attitudes such as "believe/think/consider/conceive that . . .", I shall be referring either to *actual* attitudes *or* to *counterfactual* attitudes; thus, for instance, instead of saying that members believe that they are under a duty *or* would believe that if they thought about the matter, I shall simply say that they so believe; but this must be understood as referring either to an actual belief or to a counterfactual belief.) If there is an institution of this type, then:

(i) there is a group which acts intentionally for a significant period of time only if (most of) its members follow, and are disposed to follow, some rule(s) for a significant period of time;
(ii) (most) members of the group think of the activity as purporting to be valuable in relation, primarily, to its members (self-regarding institutions); or in relation, primarily, to non-members (other-regarding institutions); but, in addition, in all cases the activity is considered by (most) members as purporting to be valuable in relation to (some aspect(s) of) the community or society as a whole;
(iii) and (most) members of the group just described (i.e. the group characterized by features (i) and (ii)) think that they have a duty qua members of such group (although in many cases they think that they have a duty qua members of the institution).

This partial characterization squares well, I think, with the paradigmatic cases mentioned above. Consider charities. A charity is in part a group which acts intentionally during a significant period of time. We can say, roughly, that it provides help to individuals (non-members) with certain needs. The group acts intentionally only if (most) of its members are disposed to follow, and do follow, some rule(s) for a relatively long period of time. If that were not so the group would not qualify as an institution. The main activity of this group is seen by (most of) its members as purporting to be valuable in relation to non-members, but also in relation to some aspects of the life of the community at large. Besides, unless (most) members of the group just described regarded themselves as under certain duties qua members of such group, the group would not count as an institution: if its members were to consider their activities optional, i.e. if they considered themselves at liberty not to perform the relevant acts, a charity would be completely unrecognizable. Oxfam, The Red Cross, Tearfund, and Christian Aid are groups which satisfy these conditions. If they did not, we would not consider them institutions.

Consider an institution such as a university. Its members are, primarily, teachers and students. We refer to the group as an institution only to the extent that it is continuous, i.e. to the extent that it is a group which performs an activity for a significant period of time. And the latter would not be the case unless most of its members followed, and were disposed to follow, the rules that regulate their actions for a relatively long period of time. The group performs an activity that, although seen by most as purporting to promote primarily the interests of its members (the general interest of teaching and learning), is also seen as purporting to be valuable in relation to the life of the society or community as a whole. Besides, most members regard themselves as under a duty qua members of the university. If they did not it would be distorted beyond recognition. The same can be said of clubs, trade unions, armies, professional associations, and NGOs, which are typical examples of institutions: they are groups which exhibit the three features mentioned in our partial characterization.

The characterization also rules out items which, clearly, are not institutions. A four-member gang is also a group of individuals to which we attribute the performance of intentional acts only if its members act. The actions of members are also normally regulated by rules. But at least one of the conditions is clearly not met: the group-activity is not seen as purporting to be valuable in relation to any aspect of the life of the community as a whole, and for this reason, among others, it is not considered an institution.

This clarifies, I believe, related uses of the notion. For instance, the mafia, which is normally seen as a gang writ large, is sometimes considered an institution. Yet here, I think, the notion only applies by extension.[19] One of the differences between the four-member gang and the *Cosa Nostra* is that the latter is more stable: its members have followed the relevant rule(s) during a very long period of time, to the point of being a group that, by contrast to the four-member gang, survives its original members. It is for this reason that the *Cosa Nostra* is sometimes considered an institution, that is, to emphasize that it is a well established and continuous group, which is a standard trait institutions. But the characteristic I am considering (the fact that most members need not think of the activity as purporting to be valuable in relation to some aspect(s) of the community or society as a whole) shows in what sense the notion only applies by extension.

Similar considerations explain why standard business corporations are sometimes (but only sometimes) considered institutions. For instance, IBM may be considered an institution. Yet here the notion also applies only by extension, to

---

[19] Unless you are using the notion in a different sense, such as a "cognitive, normative, and regulative structure and activity that provide stability and meaning to social behaviour" (see n 18 above).

emphasize the fact that it is well established and continuous. Not all business corporations have this trait, and hence not all are considered institutions. Besides, a business corporation may get involved in activities designed to promote the well being of some aspect of the life of the community as a whole. To the extent that this is the case it is in fact an institution. Or, to be more precise, one aspect of its activity is institutional in the sense mentioned above. But this feature (the fact that a business corporation may get involved in activities purporting to promote the well-being of the community) is not a necessary aspect of a business corporation in any sense. And this is another reason why business corporations are only sometimes considered institutions.

The same applies to similar uses of the notion. Sometimes we say "this man is an institution". For instance, we might claim that in relation to a philanthropist. But the import of the statement is to highlight that the philanthropist resembles an institution in some relevant respects (e.g. that he has followed a rule throughout his life according to which he should invest part of his resources to improve the standard of living in his community). Our philanthropist does not satisfy all the conditions, and in part for this reason the claim is only metaphorical in character.[20]

Let us consider now a case that, if some variations are introduced, seems to be a counterexample to our partial, pre-analytic characterization. Suppose that in S-ville, a primitive community, it is thought that young S-villeans should require the advice of the group of eldest men about how to conduct their affairs, and that they regularly do this. The eldest men have always followed, and have been disposed to follow, a rule according to which, when advice is requested, they ought to meet to discuss the matter and arrive at a conclusion by voting. They think that they are under a duty to do this because it promotes the interests of young S-villeans and, indirectly, the interests of the community as a whole. Were they not to think in this way, they would not consider themselves as under a duty. So they think that, qua members of this group, they have a duty to provide advice in the way described. They do not think that they have such a duty qua hunters, or qua warriors, etc. In principle it seems that there is an institution in S-ville, a group whose activity is that of providing advice in the way described. The fact that the main traits that I have considered are met supports that conclusion.

But consider now a modification of the scenario. Suppose that the eldest men did not consider themselves as under any duty. They regularly provide advice in the way described, but they consider their doing this as something that is completely

[20] You may object that the pre-analytic characterization mentioned above, when claiming that members think of the activity as purporting to be valuable in relation either to themselves or to non-members, and always to some aspect of the life of the community, ignores the case of activities that purport to be valuable *simpliciter*. But my claim does not ignore that. It does not deny that some activities may be pursued for their own sake, because they are thought to be, in and of themselves, valuable. It only emphasizes that members think that either themselves or non-members, and always the community, will be those who participate in the value that is being promoted (even if it is a value pursued for its own sake). There are no institutions whose members have no view as to who will participate in the value that is thought to be promoted. Or, at any rate, I cannot think of an example.

optional, as something they are at liberty to do or not to do. It just so happens that they have always done this. An imaginary objector might claim that there would still be an institution in S-ville despite one of the traits I have mentioned not being met. So, the objection goes, the fact that members recognize themselves as under a duty cannot be a necessary condition for there to be an institution of this type.

The objection derives whatever force it may have from the fact that, in S-ville, there is still an institution, but not in the sense we are envisioning. In the scenario just described the eldest men do not form an institution, although the practice of consulting them is of an institutional character. The institution of consulting them exists, in the same sense in which we say that in a certain community the institution of marriage, or the institution of contract, or the institution of a promise exists, but the eldest men themselves do not form an institution.

1.3.2 Institutions: Further Remarks

Let us focus now in more detail on some aspects of our partial characterization of institutions above. Three considerations will help to make it more precise.

(a) Consider feature (ii). It states, in part, that there is an institution only if (most) members of the group recognize themselves as being under a duty qua members. Statements of the form "qua an X I/you ought to do A in circumstances C" are employed. What do these statements mean?

The statement "*one ought to* do A in C" can be treated in many contexts, *latissimo sensu*, as equivalent to "there is a reason to do A". In a stricter sense, it can be treated as equivalent to "there is a reason, other things being equal, to do A in C which is not defeated by other reasons".[21] Yet in an even stricter sense it brings in the idea that one is under a *duty* to do A in C. This is the sense which the "ought" statements in question have. So consider statements of the form "*as an X* I/you ought to do A in C" where the "ought to" brings in the idea of duty. These statements are familiar to us, and we use them in a variety of contexts. I believe that they have a simple structure. They are of the form "as an individual described in terms of a particular property or properties only, I/you ought – I/you have a duty – to do A in C".[22]

Begin with contexts which are non-institutional contexts in our sense. For instance, if you promised to meet somebody at Carfax we can say "as a promisor you ought to go to Carfax". Or consider cases of office-holders in non-institutional

---

[21] Cf *PRN* 213.

[22] Acting qua statements where the "ought to do A in C" only brings in the idea that there is an undefeated reason (not a duty) to do A in C have the same form. For instance, "qua salesman you ought to be competitive when trading" normally means "as an individual interested in trading to obtain a profit, you ought to be competitive". Here the statement is not employed to claim that the salesman is under any duty but that, insofar as interested in trading for a profit, he has, other things being equal, an undefeated reason to be competitive.

contexts: "as a secretary of this company you ought to respond to these emails". Or consider individuals who, more generally, perform a certain role: "as a father you ought to give priority to your son's interests". In all these cases the statements are of the form: "as a person whose situation is described in terms of his or her satisfying a particular property or properties only – having promised to go to Carfax, being a secretary of this company, being a father – you ought to...".

These statements have several features. They imply that, had the individual not satisfied the relevant property or properties, he or she may have had no duty to do the relevant thing. For instance, in the case of the promise, the statement implies that, had you not promised, you may have had no duty to go to Carfax. Had our secretary not been one, she may have had no duty to respond to these e-mails. And had our father not been the father of this child, he may have had no duty to give priority to this child's interests.

Besides, it is implied that the situation of the agent is described in terms of his having a particular property or properties alone, putting other considerations aside. This presupposes that, if all relevant considerations are taken into account, the duty in question might be overridden. For instance, as a promisor you ought to go to Carfax but, if other considerations are taken into account (e.g. not meeting your friend is necessary to save somebody's life), the duty in question might be overridden. The same applies to our secretary, and to the father who should give priority to his son's interests.

In short, these statements consist in a partial normative assessment of one's situation. This leads us to a final feature. Given that the partial assessment of one's situation is a normative assessment, it is implied that there is some general normative consideration, which makes reference to the relevant property or properties, grounding the statement. In the case of our promisor, that normative consideration seems to be the rule that promisors ought to keep their promises (more generally, that promises ought to be kept). In the case of our secretary the matter is not that easy. One possible reading could be "as a person who has been hired to respond to these e-mails, you ought to respond to them". The general normative consideration would be the rule that contracts ought to be kept. In the case of our father, the consideration could simply be, we can assume, the existence of a norm of the form "parents should give priority to their son's interests".

Consider now these normative statements in the institutional contexts in which we are interested. They have the same structure. When a member claims that he has a duty qua member of the institution, he is claiming that, as a member (as a person described in terms of a particular property or properties only, i.e. his being a member), he ought to do certain things. It is presupposed that only insofar as he is a member he has a duty to do certain things. If he were not a member, he may not have such a duty. It is implied as well that, if all relevant considerations are taken into account, the duty in question might be overridden. And it is implied that there is some general normative consideration of the form described (a normative consideration according to which, if one satisfies the relevant properties – i.e. those which add up to one's being a member – then one has a duty to do certain things). Of course, being a member might consist of satisfying a complex set of properties. And it might be the case that not all these properties are seen as normatively significant in the way described. But at least one or some of them must be so considered.

This helps to bring feature (iii) above into sharper focus. What (most of) the relevant individuals believe is that: (1) they are members of a group characterized by features (i)–(ii) above (or, in the normal case, they believe that they are members of an institution); (2) they are under a duty to do certain things because they satisfy certain properties (those which add up to their being members) and because there is some general normative consideration according to which, if one satisfies one, some or all the properties that amount to being a member, then one is under a duty to do certain things; (3) such that, had the relevant property or properties not been applicable, they may have had no duty, and such that, had all relevant considerations been taken into account, the duty might be overridden.

(b) Consider now another aspect of feature (ii) of our partial characterization of institutions. I claimed that, if there is an institution, there is a particular type of group (most of) whose members believe that they are under a duty qua members. I have said something as to what the "qua member" component involves, but I have said practically nothing of the idea of a duty. What do members believe in when they believe that they are under a *duty*?

To answer this question one should examine the nature of duties, but this issue is out of the scope of this study. So I shall make some assumptions that will help to clarify the content of these beliefs.[23]

Firstly, duties are reasons, considerations that count in favour of an action. If one has a duty to do A, one has a reason to do A. But duties are special kinds of reasons in the following sense. They are a form of categorical requirement: that one is under a duty to do A brings in the idea that this form of conduct is not optional, that one is not at liberty not to do A whenever one finds that all things considered it would be desirable not to do A. Put otherwise, it is part of the idea of a duty to do A that one has a reason to do A irrespective of (at least some of) one's goals, desires and interests. For instance, if I have a duty to do A because I promised to do A, then I have a reason to do A regardless of whether I want to do A, or whether doing A favours my interests or goals.

Secondly, if one has a duty to do A, one cannot extinguish such duty by simply forming an intention, or deciding, or planning not to have that duty any more. Duties cannot be extinguished by this type of mental act. For instance, if I have a duty to do A because I promised to do A, I cannot extinguish it simply by deciding that I am no longer under such duty.

Thirdly, reasons have a dimension of strength or weight. Some are more weighty than others, and there can be reasons with very little weight or strength. Accordingly, duties can have more or less, or very little, weight or strength. Suppose that you have a tendency to forgetfulness, and compare my promise to remind you of the time at

[23] To make these assumptions I shall rely heavily on Raz's general conception of reasons and duties, as outlined in *PRN* and PO, putting technicalities and issues of detail aside.

which the football match starts with my promise to remind you of the time at which you are getting married. One of the duties is trivial, while the other has much more weight.

Fourthly, there might be conflict of reasons. To put it crudely, reasons conflict when they require incompatible actions. That is, there might be considerations in favour and against doing A on the same occasion that cannot be conformed to simultaneously. Accordingly, there might be conflict of duties. One might have agreed, for instance, to do A, and promised another person not to do A. Insofar as both agreements and promises create duties, the duties can conflict.

Fifthly, reasons can be cancelled. They can stop being grounds for actions. Accordingly, duties can be cancelled. My promise is a reason to deliver the thing promised, but if you release me the reason created by the promise is, in an intuitive sense, no longer a reason. It has been nullified.[24]

These assumptions also help to characterize feature (iii) above more precisely. When the relevant individual believes that she is under a duty qua member, she believes, *inter alia* (see above), that she is under a categorical requirement – a requirement that cannot be extinguished simply by forming an intention, or by deciding, or by planning not to be subject to it – that may have more or less weight, and that may conflict with other reasons (and accordingly with other institutional duties that she may have).

(c) Another feature of institutions I considered (see feature (i) above) is that they are, in part, groups which act intentionally only if (most) members follow some rule(s) requiring them to perform certain acts. What is involved in the idea of following a *rule* that requires one to do something?

To answer this question one should explore the nature of rules, and this issue is also out of the scope of this study. So I shall simply make a very abstract and general assumption in this respect: to follow a rule is not to act on an ordinary reason; it is to act on a special kind of reason.

Reasons for action are, as claimed, considerations in favour of an action. They might conflict. Some conflicts between reasons are solved (if that is possible) by comparing their relative weight. Let us label reasons of this sort "ordinary reasons". Undoubtedly rules are reasons for action, but they have some peculiar characteristics. Rules are reasons for action only if they are valid. For them to be reasons they must be justified by other reasons. But since a justified rule that requires doing A (a reason to do A that is supported by other reasons) is itself a reason, the rule cannot be an ordinary reason in favour of doing A. If that were so, there would be no point in having rules in the first place. Rules, we can say, reflect a judgement that, within the scope of the rule, certain ordinary reasons in favour of doing A defeat various, though not necessarily all, conflicting ordinary reasons against doing A. Metaphorically speaking they are expressions of compromises, of judgements about

[24] See *PRN* Chapter 1 (on reasons in general), 25–26 (on conflict), 27, 187, 202 (on cancellation), and PO 223 (on duties).

the outcome of conflicts of this sort.[25] So rules are not ordinary reasons. They are special reasons in the abstract sense mentioned. All this implies that acting on a rule that requires doing A is not to act on an ordinary reason in favour of doing A. It is to act on a special reason. And this is what members of our institutions are in part doing.

This helps to characterize feature (ii) more precisely. These institutions are in part groups which act intentionally during a significant period of time only if (most) members follow, and are disposed to follow, some rule(s) during a significant period of time, i.e. only if (most) members act, and are disposed to act, on a special kind of reason during a significant period of time.

In sum, I have elaborated some of the pre-analytic features that partially characterize these institutions. Some of these elaborations (those related to the ideas of duties and rules) are grounded on certain assumptions, and hence have not been argued for. Yet these assumptions help to clarify some aspects of these ideas that are relatively uncontroversial.

1.3.3 A Distinction

In an other-regarding institution (most of) its members consider the activity performed by the group as purporting to be valuable in relation to individuals other than themselves and in relation to (some aspect(s) of) the life of the community or society as a whole. But in some cases they may think that it does not *actually* further any value. They may be in that sense *alienated.*

Suppose that there is a jockey club. Its activity is to promote the practice of betting on horse races and, more generally, turf culture. Its members consider this activity as purporting to further, primarily, the interests of non-members (those who bet). Say, the interest of being entertained. And, in promoting turf culture, they also consider the activity as purporting to be valuable, indirectly, in relation to some aspects of the life of the community as a whole. But its members, let us suppose, do not think of the activity as in effect being particularly valuable in this way. They do not think of promoting the practice of betting or, more generally, turf culture, as immoral in character in any sense, but they do not think that it has any particular value either. They have become members for other reasons. Say, because being a member of the club increases their social status. Yet they regard themselves as under a duty qua members to perform the relevant tasks (e.g. attending the meetings, voting at the committees, etc), the tasks that will result in the group performing the relevant activity.

So there are other-regarding institutions that exist even if (most, or even all, of) its members do not recognize the group-activity as in effect promoting a value in the way described. They are alienated, but still they consider themselves as under a duty qua members.

[25] This is Raz's (1989, 1153, 1155–1156) general approach to rules: PO 221; *PRN* 187. For his detailed analysis: *PRN* Chapters 2, 3 and Postscript.

Other-regarding institutions are not always like this. Some of them are such that, for them to be institutions at all, (most of) its members must recognize the activity, not only as purporting to be valuable in the sense described, but also as in effect being valuable in that sense. This is the case of the eldest men of S-ville considered above (in the original version of the example). They think of themselves as under a duty to provide advice in the way described because they believe that this promotes the interests of young S-villeans and, indirectly, of the community as a whole. If each of them did not think that the activity actually promotes such interests, they would not consider themselves as under any duty.

We can conceive of a thought-experiment to establish when an other-regarding institution is of the first type or of the second type. When envisioning an other-regarding institution, suppose that (most of) its members think of the activity as being actually valuable in the sense described. Suppose now that each of the relevant members stops thinking, individually, of the activity in this way. If, because of his or her realization that the activity is not actually valuable in the way described, each would stop thinking of himself or herself as under a duty, then the institution is an institution of the second type. (In fact, we should say that the institution *was* an institution of the second type, for a necessary condition for there to be an institution is that its members think of themselves as under a duty.) If, by contrast, each of the relevant members would still consider themselves, despite each of them realizing that the activity is not actually valuable in the sense described, as still under a duty qua members, then the institution is an institution of the first type.

I shall label the first type of other-regarding institutions "other-regarding, *developed* institutions", and the second type "other-regarding, *non-developed* institutions". An other-regarding, non-developed institution is one that exists only if (most of) its members think that the activity is actually valuable in the sense described, and where their thinking of themselves as under a duty depends on their thinking of the activity in this way. An other-regarding, developed institution is one that exists – among other conditions, (most of) its members think of themselves as under a duty qua members – even if (most of) its members do not think of the activity in this way. I use the labels "developed" and "non-developed" because an other-regarding institution of the first type is such that it can survive the very obvious possibility of alienation. An institution of the second kind cannot.

1.3.4 Legal Practice

It is time to return to legal practice, which is the practice of members of one particular institution, the Judiciary. We have explored some pre-analytical features of institutions in general, and it is clear that the Judiciary has the same features. This helps us to describe the main traits of the practice of its members (of legal practice) more precisely.

If there is an instance of legal practice, there is a group which acts intentionally for a significant period of time: it evaluates the conduct of members of a community by applying certain norms. If this were not the case, there would be no instance of the Judiciary, and hence no instance of legal practice. The group acts in that way only if (most of) its members (officials) follow, and are disposed to follow, some rule(s) that regulate their actions for a significant period of time. Were officials to stop following the relevant rule(s), the Judiciary, and hence legal practice, would disappear. And if they simply followed the relevant rule(s) each time there is an occasion to do so, without there being a standing disposition to do this, the Judiciary (and hence legal practice) would be distorted beyond recognition. The activity of this group is considered by (most of) its members as purporting to be valuable, primarily, in relation to individuals other than themselves and, more generally, in relation to the life of the community or society as a whole. If that were not so the Judiciary would not be the institution with which we are familiar. The Judiciary is, in other words, an other-regarding institution. Besides, (most) officials believe that they have duties to apply the relevant norms qua officials (i.e. qua members of the Judiciary, the institution, or, more guardedly, qua members of a group characterized by the aforementioned properties). Were they not to conceive of themselves as under such a duty, the institution would also be distorted beyond recognition. So "acting qua" normative statements are typically used, and when they are used they have the same structure as in any context.

It is clear too that there might be instances of legal practice where the Judiciary is a non-developed institution, and instances where the Judiciary is a developed institution. But I would say that most actual instances of legal practice are of the second sort. That is, in most actual instances of legal practice (most) officials would regard themselves as under a duty qua officials even if they did not think of the group-activity as in effect particularly valuable in the sense described. In most actual instances of legal practice the Judiciary is an institution that can survive the possibility of alienation. Consider the thought-experiment. Assume that most members of the American Judiciary (officials) think of the activity of the group as being actually valuable in the sense described. Suppose now that each of the relevant officials is at home and that each, individually, stops thinking of the activity in this way. It seems clear that each would still consider himself or herself, despite not thinking any more of the group-activity as valuable in the sense described, as still under a duty qua member. They would perhaps think that they should resign. But resigning is an act that is thought of as extinguishing their duties qua officials. This presupposes that they still think of themselves as under a duty. They would not believe that their realization that the activity is not valuable in the way described is sufficient to extinguish their duties qua officials, qua members of the Judiciary.

1.3.5 Bringing the Second Test into Sharper Focus

I have considered some of the main aspects of legal practice, and this will help to make our second test more precise. A theory of legal practice that claims that it should be understood as having the same basic structure, although a distinct content, as other practices with which we are familiar, should:

(a) provide a characterization of its content;
(b) provide a characterization of its structure in terms of the favoured category of practices;
(c) such that conceiving of legal practice in those terms captures the main features on which we have focused, namely that it is the practice of members of one particular kind of institution (a set of individuals who form a group with the special traits mentioned above).

Conditions (a) and (b) will be understood as involving standard requirements: the characterization must be clear, internally consistent, not uninformatively circular, etc. In particular, the favoured category of practices (the practice in terms of which legal practice should, according to the theory, be understood) cannot be characterized using the notion of an institution in an un-analyzed way. We are trying to understand the practice of members of this institution in terms of other practices, and an attempt to perform this task by ultimately describing the favoured category of practices as the practice of members of an institution would not be illuminating.

Condition (c) will be understood in a particular way. Given that the theories we shall assess propose an account of legal practice in terms of necessary and sufficient conditions (or can be intelligibly read as so doing), I shall demand that the conditions be actually necessary for there to be an instance of legal practice. In other words, the conditions should not be superfluous. And I shall also require that the conditions be actually sufficient: the account should entail that, if there is an instance of legal practice as construed by it, then there is the practice of members of an other-regarding institution (a group whose intentional activity consists of evaluating the conduct of members of the community by applying certain norms, (most of) whose members follow, and are disposed to follow, some rule(s) that regulate their actions, etc) which can be developed or non-developed.

Thus, this condition is not met if it turns out that, according to the theory, there can be an instance of legal practice without there being a group (most of) whose members follow some rule(s), without acting on, we have assumed, a special kind of reason(s). The same happens if it turns out that, according to the theory, there can be an instance of legal practice but no group which acts intentionally. Or if it turns out that, according to the theory, there can be an instance of legal practice but the beliefs of (alienated) members to the effect that they are under a duty qua members to apply the relevant norms are completely absurd (i.e. that the beliefs that they are under, we have assumed, a categorical requirement, are completely senseless).[26]

This last point will be important, so let me elaborate it. The theory must not only entail that these beliefs are not absurd. It should also explain why this is so (in

[26] This presupposes that the beliefs are not absurd. The theories we shall assess, I think, presuppose that too. So this cuts no ice in our assessment of them.

particular, it should explain why these beliefs are not absurd in the case of alienated participants, who believe that they are under such a duty qua members even if they do not consider the resulting activity – the activity ascribable to the group – as particularly valuable in the sense described). That explanation, I shall require, should have a certain form. Given that officials' beliefs that they are under a duty to do certain things qua members are grounded on the belief that they satisfy certain properties (those which add up to their being officials – i.e. to their being members of the institution, the Judiciary, or, in more simple cases, those which add up to their being members of a particular type of group) and on the belief that there is some normative consideration(s) according to which, if one satisfies at least some of these properties, then one has a duty to do certain things, the theory should specify what these normative considerations are. They cannot be just any considerations. They should be plausible normative considerations, considerations capable in principle of giving rise to a duty. Otherwise the beliefs would be senseless.[27]

1.4 The Third Test

Our third test requires that the objection from disagreement be met. The objection was stated for the first time by Dworkin against Hart's doctrine as it appears in *CL*. Dworkin contends that Hart states that duties exist when social rules exist providing for such duties, and that social rules exist, for Hart, when certain conditions (which Dworkin labels "practice-conditions") are satisfied. Dworkin illustrates such conditions through an example. If there is a group of churchgoers and (a) each man removes his hat before entering church, (b) when a man is asked why he does so, he refers to "the rule" that requires him to do so, and (c) when someone fails to remove his hat before entering church, he is criticized by the others, then Hart's practice-conditions are met. The community has a social rule to the effect that men must not wear hats in church. Participants' assertions about the existence of a duty should be understood as two-fold: participants assert that the practice-conditions are met and, in addition, they indicate their disposition to conform to that practice.[28]

---

[27] The theories we shall assess would, I think, also accept this. For instance, they would reject an account of legal practice that claims that its structure is that of there being a mere habit among officials of doing A, on the ground that, if officials believed that they have a duty to do A qua participants in such practice (i.e. qua individuals who satisfy the property of doing A habitually), these beliefs would be senseless; and the theories would claim that these beliefs would be senseless because there is no plausible normative consideration according to which, if there is the habit of doing A, one should do A. Of course, it is difficult to say precisely when a normative consideration is plausible or implausible. But there is no need to deal with that issue here, for there are undoubtedly clear cases where the distinction applies (such as the one I have just mentioned), and the argument of the book will rely on cases of that sort.

[28] *TRS* 49–50.

Dworkin shows that this theory's scope is limited. First, it is an explanation of what is meant by a claim to duty "only in one sort of case, namely, when the community is by-and-large agreed that some such duty does exist".[29] Second, it is only applicable to cases of "conventional morality", namely when members are agreed in asserting the same normative rule, and they count the fact of that agreement as an essential part of their grounds for asserting that rule.[30] The objection is that the theory is inadequate:

> It is not adequate because it cannot explain the fact that even when people count a social practice as a necessary part of the grounds for asserting some duty, they may still disagree about the scope of that duty. Suppose, for example, that the members of the community which 'has the rule' that men must not wear hats in church are in fact divided on the question of whether 'that' rule applies to the case of male babies wearing bonnets. Each side believes that its view of the duties of the babies or their parents is the sounder, but neither view can be pictured as based on a social rule, because there is no social rule on the issue at all.[31]

Dworkin's objection is that a similar kind of disagreement appears in law.[32] Participants often disagree about what the norms to be applied are (about what their duties in this respect are), and they appeal to the practice itself in order to defend their views. Moreover, Dworkin implies that participants may never reach an agreement about what the rules to be applied are (about what their duties in this respect are); they may debate about this endlessly.[33]

Notice how the argument affects Hart's doctrine of legal practice. Roughly, Hart claims that legal practice should be understood in terms of there being a social rule (a rule of recognition) among officials which requires them to evaluate the conduct of ordinary citizens by applying norms that satisfy certain criteria. Such a social rule, Hart claims, is *constituted* by a regularity of behaviour (officials must apply the norms in question) and certain attitudes (they must be disposed to do so). But if there is the type of disagreement that the objection points out, i.e. disagreement about what the norms to be applied are, the regularity and dispositions that Hart mentions would be absent, and hence there would be no social rule (no rule of recognition). And since there would be no social rule, Hart seems bound to admit that there would be no legal practice. Furthermore, participants could not intelligibly appeal to the practice itself (to the rule of recognition) as grounding their assertions as to what their duties are (what norms they should apply), for there would be no practice (no rule of recognition).

Let me consider now two well-known responses against the objection. One of them is put forward by Jules Coleman, the other by Joseph Raz.

[29] *TRS* 53.

[30] *TRS* 53.

[31] *TRS* 54.

[32] *TRS* 58.

[33] In Dworkin (1986) the objection became more sophisticated, but we need not focus on these refinements here.

Coleman claims that, when there is a social rule, there is a difference between what the rule *is* (its content) and what the rule *requires* (the cases that fall under it, or its application). Officials may agree about what the rule is, but disagree amongst themselves about what the rule requires. They could not disagree, he contends, in every case or even in most cases, for such a widespread disagreement would make unintelligible the idea that they are following the same rule. But they can disagree in some cases. For instance, he claims, if there is a rule of recognition in which morality is one of the conditions of legality, officials can disagree in some (though not in all or most) significant cases about which norms satisfy moral demands (what the rule of recognition requires or its application) and still agree that morality is a condition of legality (they can still agree about the content of the rule of recognition).[34] In short, in Coleman's view disagreement can be accommodated. The presence of disagreement about what the rule requires (about its application) does not imply that there is no rule.

I am uncertain as to whether this response is correct but, for argument's sake only, I shall suppose that this view is tenable: if officials disagree only in *some*, but not in *all or most,* significant cases about which norms satisfy the criteria, there would still be a rule of recognition (this being a situation that falls under the label "disagreement about what the rule requires, or about its application, not about its content"). I shall make that supposition because, I believe, the objection can be reconstructed in a way that avoids this type of reply, and noticing this shows something important about legal practice. To that end I shall describe a hypothetical scenario.

I shall call this scenario "D". In D there is a rule which is generally followed that requires officials to judge conduct by applying norms that satisfy criteria C1 and C2. But it so happens that the sets of norms that satisfy each criterion do not have any elements (any norms) in common. In fact in D, for a property to qualify as a criterion of legality, it must pick out norms that form a set that has no elements in common with those sets of norms that satisfy other criteria. The intersection between the sets must be vacuous. For instance, criterion C1 stands for this property: "the norms enacted by a special organ"; and criterion C2 stands for this property: "the norms that qualify as customs in the community at large". Each picks out, let us suppose, two sets of norms which do not contain any norms in common. Their intersection is vacuous.

Suppose that officials agree about all the norms that satisfy C2, but disagree about some of the norms that satisfy C1. For instance, officials agree that norms N1 and N2 satisfy C1 (for they agree that N1 and N2 have been enacted by the special organ), but disagreement appears as to whether N3 has been enacted by the special organ. The reply claims that there would still be a rule requiring them to apply norms that satisfy C1 and C2. It so happens that there is "disagreement about what the rule requires (about the application of the rule)", but this does not mean that there is no rule. I admitted, *arguendo*, that this could be claimed. The situation where there is "disagreement about what the rule requires" can be perhaps better described in this

---

[34] Coleman (2001b, 130–131; 2001a, 116–117).

way: officials have different but overlapping conceptions of the criterion C1 (call these conceptions C1* and C1**). These conceptions pick out sets of norms that partly overlap. C1* picks out a set formed by N1, N2 and N3, and C1** one that contains N1 and N2 only. So officials claim that they should apply the norms that satisfy C1 and C2, but they have different conceptions of C1, i.e. C1* and C**. Here there is only disagreement, the reply goes, about which norms satisfy the criteria, about what the rule of recognition requires, but everyone agrees that the relevant criteria are C1 and C2. So we can still claim that there is a rule of recognition that requires applying norms that satisfy C1 and C2.

But suppose now that some disputes are not adjudicable by appealing to the norms that satisfy criteria C1 and C2. Some officials (say, half of them) begin to adjudicate these cases by applying a set of principles which they deem bear a particular relation with the norms that satisfy criteria C1 and C2. For instance, they think of these principles as partly justifying the relevant norms. They think that it is their duty qua officials to apply these principles. In fact, they claim that this is what they were always required to do; it so happens that there has been no opportunity, so far, to solve disputes by appealing to these standards. The others claim that this is not so. They claim that the cases should be adjudicated by another, different set of principles. For instance, in their view, these cases should be adjudicated *ex aequo et bono.* They also claim that this is, and has always been, their duty qua officials. Suppose that the set of standards that each side favours has no elements in common. Since, *ex hypothesi*, the criteria in this system must be properties that pick out sets of norms that do not overlap, let us call the properties that pick out each set of standards the putative criteria C3 and C4. So some officials think that they should evaluate conduct by applying norms that satisfy C1, C2 *and C3*, while others think that they should evaluate conduct by applying norms that satisfy C1, C2 *and C4*. Each side defends its own position in a similar way: by appealing in part to the practice itself to claim that they should apply, and that it has always been their duty to apply, norms that satisfy C3 (or C4) too. Each side believes that its view is sounder, and the debate proves endless.

It seems clear that the reply cannot claim that there is a social rule requiring officials to apply norms that satisfy C1, C2 *and C3*, or one requiring them to apply norms that satisfy C1, C2 *and C4.* Here the reply seems bound to accept that there is, not disagreement about what the rule *requires* (about its application), but about this aspect of *the rule itself* (about part of its content). Yet half of the participants think that it is their duty, and has always been, to employ norms that either satisfy C3 or C4 too, and they ground their assertions to that effect by appealing in part to the practice itself.

So our third test requires that the theory provide a characterization of legal practice that explains why in D, a conceivable instance of legal practice where the criteria are conceived as picking out sets of norms which do not overlap, officials disagree about what some of the criteria are; when they disagree, they count their social practice as grounding their assertions about what the criteria that should be applied are; each believes that his or her view is sounder, and disagreement proves endless.

Granted, the scenario in D is artificial. Its artificial character lies in the way in which the criteria of legality are construed. But the scenario is not as unrealistic as it may seem. For instance, in Argentina it is indisputable that norms enacted by Parliament are law, and that officials are required to apply those norms. This is, in the artificial language employed so far, a criterion of legality (call it C1). Yet in this legal system there is an intense, and relatively recent debate, as to whether certain decisions by the Supreme Court (the holding of certain cases) should be followed by lower tribunals (or, to be more precise, whether lower tribunals should follow these decisions when unable to find new and compelling arguments to the contrary).[35] So there is a dispute as to whether certain decisions by the Supreme Court are a criterion of legality (call it C2). And the debate is of importance, in part, because (or to the extent that) C1 and C2 have no norms in common. In other words, it is interesting because (or to the extent that) its intersection is vacuous. I would not claim, of course, that this is the best reconstruction of the situation. My only point is that it resembles D, the scenario described above, in many respects. So D is not as artificial as it may seem at first glance.

Consider now Raz's response. Although it is proposed against a much more sophisticated version of Dworkin's objection, its main conclusions are relevant here. Besides, despite the complexity, the main idea can be expressed in a relatively simple way. So a short rendering will suffice.

Many concepts are concepts possession of which, claims Raz, consists in the possession of rules setting criteria for their correct use. Possessing the concept of "table", for instance, is possessing the rule that sets out the criteria for using it correctly. Thus, we can assume, something is a table only if it is an item of furniture with a flat top normally used to place things on. One way of explaining such concepts (which Raz labels "criterial explanations") is, then, to state the rule setting out the conditions for the correct use of the concept, the explanation being true if it is a correct statement of the rule actually used by those who use it.[36]

Now the doctrine that Raz wishes to criticize claims that, assuming that we can give a criterial explanation of some concepts, we cannot disagree about what the criteria are. In other words, the doctrine claims that, if two individuals disagree about the criteria (e.g. whether having a flat top is a condition of an item of furniture being a table), they are talking past each other necessarily, and hence the disagreement is not genuine. Raz thinks that such doctrine is incorrect. For, he claims, a criterial view of concepts does not presuppose (as the doctrine criticized seems to assume) that the criteria are fully specified in a set of personal rules that happen to be shared. That individualistic view is incorrect. Each person takes his use of the concept to be governed by the common criteria for their use. People who think that they understand a concept think that they have at least some knowledge of what the common criteria are. They may be wrong. They may be partially or completely mistaken

---

[35] For the best description of the state of the dispute, see Rivera and Legarre (2006, 1333–1352; 2009, La Ley 1–6).

[36] TVNL 258–265.

about the common criteria. Of course, what the criteria are does depend on what people think they are. Those that are generally believed to be the correct criteria are the correct criteria.[37]

Now let us come back to D. It is quite clear that the scenario in D parallels the scenario just described, where there is disagreement about a concept. In both scenarios there are rules. Besides, in D the community is split as to what the correct criteria of legality (stated in the relevant rule) are, and in the example of the concept of "table" two individuals are also split as to what one of the conditions for applying the concept of "table", stated in the relevant rule, are. But there is an importance difference between both scenarios. For in the scenario where there is disagreement over the concept of "table", it is not the case that the whole community is split as to what the correct criteria are. If that were so, the two individuals could not disagree significantly. This is not what happens in D. Here the whole community is split as to what the correct criteria are. So Raz's reply cannot rescue Hart's theory from the objection.[38]

There is, nevertheless, an important lesson to be learnt from Raz's response. He claims that two individuals cannot disagree about the conditions for applying a concept if each is following his own, personal rule stating what the conditions are. To disagree, they should take the use concept to be governed by the common standard for their use (if even if they are not fully aware, or cannot make explicit, what the standard is). This is, I think, correct. Raz states, correctly, a pre-condition of disagreement. So, to the extent that the situation in D is not absurd, officials could not disagree in the way described if each were following his own, personal rule stating what the criteria of legality are. To disagree, they should take the question as to what the criteria of legality are as a question to be answered by a common standard (if even if they are not fully aware, or cannot make explicit, its content). So, unless a theory of legal practice shows that in D each official is not following his own, personal rule, and that each thinks that his view is answerable to a common

[37] TVNL 261–265.

[38] Raz then goes on to propose a more detailed refutation of the objection, in terms of the complexity and non transparency of criterial explanations and in terms of the relatively interdependence of concepts. The first argument suggests that we have to deny the view that because the explanation of concepts is judged by their faithfulness to the shared rules governing their use, such explanations are so transparent that they leave little room for doubt about their correctness (TVNLP 266). And the second argument suggests that there can be disagreements about concepts like "just war", assuming that they can be criterially explained and assuming that proportionality of the harm inflicted is one of the criteria for something being a "just war", for people might have the same concept and yet be at a loss as to how to compare the severity of various harms, because the latter is not criterially explicable (TVNLP 269–270). But these two arguments presuppose the rejection of individualism (he claims that this – the non-individualistic view of criterial explanations – "in and of itself does not explain the possibility of theoretically interesting disputes about such criteria; to do that we have to add other elements to the rejection of individualism" (TVNLP 265)). In other words, here there is no disagreement as to what the criteria are. Accordingly, the two additional arguments are not useful to avoid the objection.

standard (even if not fully aware of its content or not being able to make it explicit), the theory is flawed.

1.5 Conclusion

I have presented three tests to assess the adequacy of any theory of legal practice that claims that it should be understood as having the same basic structure, although a distinct content, as other practices with which we are familiar. Basically, any such theory should: (1) propose an account of the favoured categories of practices that captures its main aspects, such that (2) if legal practice is understood as having the same basic structure, although a distinct content, as the favoured category of practices, the main aspects of legal practice are captured, and such that (3) the objection from disagreement is met.

I have elaborated the second test. Essentially, it demands that the theory capture the fact that legal practice is the practice of members of an institution (the Judiciary), a group which has some general and peculiar characteristics. In particular, the theory should explain why members conceive of themselves as under a duty qua members.

I have also elaborated the third test. Essentially, it demands that the theory explain why a particular type of disagreement obtains in a hypothetical scenario, D, and it excludes any explanation that appeals to the idea that officials are following his own, personal rule.

In the following chapters I shall elaborate the first test before presenting each family of theories, and then assess each account by using all the three tests.

Chapter 2
Accounts Based on the Idea of a Social Rule (I): Hart's Account and the Coordinative-Convention Approach

2.1 Overview of the Chapter

Hart and the coordinative-convention approach claim that legal practice has the same structure as the practice that obtains when there is a (coordinative) convention. Raz claims that it has the same structure as the practice that obtains when there is, more generally, a social rule (not necessarily a conventional social rule). Given that a convention is a particular type of social rule, these theories have something in common: they all conceive of legal practice's structure as the practice that obtains when there is a (particular type of) social rule. Of course, they are also different, for each proposes a different characterization of (the relevant type of) social rules.

In this and the next Chapter I shall assess this family of theories. I have elaborated the second and third tests, but I still need to elaborate the first one in relation to them. It demands, generally, that the theory provide an account of the favoured category of practices that captures its main aspects. So I shall explore the main aspects of the practices that obtain when there is a social rule and, more particularly, a convention (Section 2). I shall then focus on Hart's account and on the core idea of the coordinative-convention approach, and argue that neither of them meets our three tests (Sections 3–5).

2.2 Elaborating the First Test: Social Rules and Conventions

These theories focus on social rules such as that of driving on the left, or baring one's head in church, rules which are not strictly speaking authoritatively created, but which normally emerge somewhat progressively. I shall consider their main pre-analytical aspects. Given that a convention is a particular type of social rule, let me begin with social rules in general.

Social rules always appear in groups. That much is implied in the idea that these rules are *social* rules. It is also clear that social rules are *rules*, and hence that they are, I have assumed, special kinds of reasons. Besides, there would be no social rule if most members of the group did not follow the rule. How many members should so behave, and for how long, is a question of degree. But if no members of the

R.E. Sánchez Brigido, *Groups, Rules and Legal Practice*, Law and Philosophy Library 89, DOI 10.1007/978-90-481-8770-6_2,

group followed the rule, there would be no social rule. For instance, the driving-on-the-left convention would not exist if nobody drove on the left.[39] Or consider the eastern custom of removing one's shoes when entering houses. There would not be such a rule if nobody in the group removed their shoes in those circumstances. This suggests a partial characterization of social rules: if there is a social rule, then there is a rule which is generally followed by most members of a group.

Another feature of social rules is that most members (would be disposed to) invoke the fact that there is a social rule as justifying action. Assertions of the form "I/you ought to do A because there is a social rule that requires doing A in circumstances C" are typical. For instance, if there is a convention of driving on the left, most participants (would be disposed to) claim: "I/you ought to drive on the left because there is a convention to that effect". Or suppose that there is a custom of giving a small present to one's host. Assertions of the form "I/you ought to take a present because we have a custom that so requires" are typical. It is because social rules are seen by members as justifying action that, when a member deviates, most participants (would be disposed to) invoke the existence of a social rule as grounding criticism of deviance, a criticism that might take many forms, from mildly rebuking the deviant member to physical aggression.

The latter aspect of social rules is, as claimed, typical. Yet despite its familiarity there is something paradoxical about it. Let us take a closer look.

Consider what it is involved in participants' claims of the type "I/you ought to do A in C because there is a *social rule* that requires doing A in C". Undoubtedly not all rules are social rules, but social rules share with rules *simpliciter* a similar feature. Rules *simpliciter* are also invoked to justify or criticize action. Assertions of the form "I/you ought to do A in C because there is a rule that so requires" are typical. We can safely claim that the statement "there is a rule that so requires" means, in the context of justifying or criticizing action, that the rule is justified and that it applies. If that were not so it would be pointless to invoke the rule. In the case of *social rules* something similar occurs. The statement "there is a social rule that so requires" means, in this context, that the social rule is justified and that it applies. If that were not so it would be senseless to invoke the social rule. Given this, and the fact that, when there is a social rule, there is a rule which is generally followed by most members of a group, we can partially construe these claims thus: "I/you ought to do A in C because there is a (justified and applicable) rule which is generally followed

[39] Some deny this. Margaret Gilbert, for instance, claims that there might be a convention of giving Festschrifts to scholars who reach 60 but, since few scholars reach that age, the rule is not actually followed; or that there might be a convention of sending hand-written thank-you notes to one's host but, since nobody is used to hand-writing any more, nobody sends the notes any more, albeit thinking that they should (*OSF* 344–346; along similar lines, Sartorious 1987, 51). I think that these are not examples of conventions (or, more generally, of social rules), for regular conformity to the rule is absent. That is why the situation of the thank-you note case is most plausibly captured by statements like "we *had* a convention of sending thank-you notes" or "our convention is fading away". The Festschrift case is not an example of a convention either, unless it is meant that members have entered into an agreement to give Festschrifts. But this, as Gilbert recognizes, is a different sense of "convention".

by most members of the group that so requires". Notice the difference between rules *simpliciter* and social rules. In the first case, a *rule* is invoked as justifying the "ought" conclusion. In the second case, a rule *which is generally followed by most members of the group* is invoked as justifying the "ought" conclusion. And this is somewhat paradoxical. With rules *simpliciter* no problem seems to appear, for there is nothing awkward involved in the claims. After all, if there is a justified rule that requires doing A in C, and one is in C (and this is what the utterer claims), then one ought to do A. But in the case of *social* rules there is something odd. Why would the fact that the rule is generally followed be in any way relevant to justify conformity or criticize deviance?

Let me introduce a technical notion, which I shall characterize broadly, that helps to see more clearly the apparent paradox. Suppose that John and Mark go to the bus station. When asked why, John replies that (a) a friend who is arriving would be pleased to meet him, and that (b) he wants to please his friend. Mark replies that (a') he has promised his friend to go there, and that (b') there is a rule that promises ought to be kept. There is a sense in which each of the facts that John and Mark mention, taken in isolation, are invoked as *parts* of their reasons to go there, and a sense in which, when both facts are taken together, each has invoked *one* reason to go there. Each has invoked what I shall call a "complete reason".

We can say, very roughly, that a person x *invokes the fact that p as a complete reason for her (x) or another person (y) to do A* if, and only if, she believes that, for any individual z who understands the statement that p, if z believes that p, then z should believe[40] that there is a reason for the person in question (x or y) to do A, regardless of what other beliefs z has.[41] The characterization should be read as implying that, if p can be subdivided in parts, x believes that there are no components of p which are irrelevant from a justificatory point of view.

Consider Mark's case, which is important for our purposes because it involves the idea of rules. It is the fact that there is a *rule* which requires doing A in C which is invoked by him as a complete (special, not ordinary) reason to do A. As noted, "the fact that there is a rule" here means that the rule is justified and that it applies. So he believes that, for any person z who understands the statement that p (that there is a rule that requires doing A in C, which here means that it is justified and that it applies), if she believes that p, she should believe that there is a (special) reason for him to do A. And he does not consider any of the component parts of p (the fact that the rule is justified, and that it applies) to be irrelevant. It seems clear that there is nothing awkward in invoking rules *simpliciter* as complete (special) reasons.

Social rules are also invoked by members of the group as complete (special) reasons. Participants make claims of the form "I/you ought to do A in C because there is a social rule that so requires". So most participants believe that, for any person z who understands the statement that p (that there is a *social rule* that requires

---

[40]Assuming she has a minimal grasp of basic principles of practical reasoning.

[41]Cf *PRN* 22–25.

doing A in C, which here means that the social rule is justified, and that it applies), if z believes that p, she should believe that there is a (special) reason for a member of the group to do A. And they do not consider any of the components parts of p (that there is a justified social rule, and that it applies) to be irrelevant. But by contrast with rules *simpliciter*, here there is something odd. A member of this group, x, would believe at least that, for any person z who understands the statement that p (that there is a rule that requires doing A in C – which here means that the rule is justified and that it applies – *which is generally followed by most members*), if z believes that p, then z should believe that the person in question, x or y, has a special reason to do A, regardless of what other beliefs z has. In contrast with what happens with rules *simpliciter*, this belief seems awkward: why would the fact that the rule is generally followed by most members of the group be relevant? After all, it seems that the first two facts are sufficient. Thus, unless we suppose that invoking social rules as complete reasons is in effect unintelligible (and there is no particular reason to suppose that), this aspect of social rules stands in need of explanation.

A final aspect of social rules is that, as I have already intimated, there are many types of social rule, such as conventions, customs and traditions. Each has its own normative connotations. Conventions for instance are somewhat arbitrary. The typical example of the driving-on-the-left convention suggests that they are arbitrary in the sense that participants (would) think of them as stipulating one way, among others equally suitable (e.g. driving on the right), to solve a problem of coordination. Customs have a different normative connotation which is very difficult to pin down, but it is clear that the idea of a custom is not necessarily linked to the ideas of arbitrariness or of solving a problem. Consider the eastern custom of taking off one's shoes when entering houses. Participants, I submit, do not think, nor are disposed to think, of this social rule as arbitrary, nor as solving any particular kind of coordination problem. Something similar can be said of traditions. The tradition in Oxford of wearing a gown in graduation ceremonies is not thought of, I submit, as arbitrary, nor as solving any problem of coordination. But it is not, I believe, a mere custom either. Customs are not related to the past in the same way in which traditions are. Each has its own normative connotations.

These are, in short, the main pre-analytical features of social rules. A theory that claims that legal practice is essentially the practice that obtains when there is a (particular type of) social rule is *prima facie* appealing, for there is some parallel between some features of legal practice and of the practice that obtains when there is a social rule: in both cases there is at least a rule which is followed by (most) members of a group.

Be that as it may, a theory of legal practice of this sort should provide an account that captures the main aspects of (the relevant type of) social rules. So this is our first test for assessing this kind of theory. The theory should:

(a) propose an account of (the relevant type of) social rules;
(b) that captures the main aspects of (the relevant type of) social rules mentioned above.

I shall understand condition (a) as involving standard requirements, such as consistency, non-uninformative circularity, etc. I shall not require that, in order to meet it, the theory propose an account of rules. This issue is, as said, out of the scope of this study. In fact, I shall assume that, if the theory uses the notion of a rule in its account of social rules, it is referring to rules understood as I have assumed they should, namely as special kinds of reasons.

I shall understand condition (b) in the following way. Since these theories provide, or can be intelligibly read as providing, a characterization of (the relevant type of) social rules in terms of necessary and sufficient conditions, I shall require that the conditions be necessary, that is, that the account not be subject to counterexamples, and that they be sufficient, that is, that the theory entail that, if there is a social rule, then there is an item with the pre-analytical features mentioned above. Thus, the conditions are not sufficient if it turns out that, according to the theory, there is a (particular type of) social rule but there is no rule practised by most members of a group. Or if it turns out that the theory does not explain how it is possible that social rules are invoked, intelligibly, as complete reasons.

We have elaborated then our first test in relation to a family of theories, and we can now assess them. Hart's doctrine should be, undoubtedly, our first target. For it was Hart who introduced the notion of a social rule as the key notion for our understanding of law, and of legal practice in particular. The reasons why he thought so are well known. Roughly, he thought that only by appealing to the notion of a social rule could one explain why, when there is law, certain kinds of conduct are no longer optional (they are obligatory in some sense). The fact that there are *rules* would explain it. And he also thought that the fact that there are *social* rules would explain law's specificity, the fact that it is different from other systems of norms such as morality. But Hart's reasons for employing the notion need not concern us. It is his doctrine which interests us, and the question of whether it contains a good theory of social rules, whether it contains a good explanation of the fact that the Judiciary is an institution, and whether it can accommodate disagreement. In other words, we need to see whether it satisfies our three tests.

2.3 Hart's Account

Hart famously claimed in *CL* that a necessary condition for the existence of a legal system is the presence among norm-applying and norm-creating officials of three social rules: first, a social rule specifying the criteria that the norms must satisfy to be part of the system ("a rule of recognition"); second, a social rule specifying how to introduce new norms to the system ("a rule of change"); finally, a social rule specifying who is empowered to apply the norms of the system ("a rule of adjudication").[42] The other necessary condition of the existence of a legal system is that the

[42] *CL* 114–117.

norms of the system be generally obeyed by ordinary citizens. Both conditions are also jointly sufficient, according to Hart, for the existence of a legal system.[43]

It is the first condition which interests us, for it is in Hart's characterization of the relevant social rules that we shall find Hart's doctrine of the structure and content of legal practice as understood here, i.e. as the practice of norm-applying officials.

Consider the idea of a rule of recognition. Hart claims that this rule will specify some features possession of which by a suggested norm is taken as a conclusive affirmative indication that it is a norm of the system.[44] For instance, a very simple rule of recognition might stipulate that the relevant norms are those which satisfy this criterion: their being enacted by a specific body (call that criterion "C1"). Since Hart claims that the rule of recognition requires norm-applying officials to evaluate the conduct of members of the community by applying norms that satisfy certain criteria,[45] the standard interpretation of Hart's doctrine states that the rule of recognition should be seen as having this form: "norm-applying officials *ought* to evaluate conduct by applying norms that satisfy criteria C1...Cn".[46]

Consider now the idea of a rule of change, i.e. a rule that specifies how new norms are introduced to the system. For Hart, the rule of recognition must make reference to it in some way. He claims:

> Plainly, there will be a very close connection between the rules of change and the rules of recognition: for where the former exists the latter will necessarily incorporate a reference to legislation as an identifying feature of rules.[47]

Consider now rules of adjudication, which empower certain individuals to make authoritative determinations of the question whether a norm of the system has been broken when evaluating conduct.[48] These individuals are the norm-applying officials of the system. Accordingly, the existence of a rule of recognition (which requires *norm-applying officials* to evaluate conduct by applying norms that satisfy certain criteria) already presupposes that there is a rule of adjudication, for it is this rule which identifies who the norm-applying officials are.

So there are three social rules involved in Hart's conception of legal systems, but the rule of recognition is the key element. For, as it has been shown, by making reference to the rule of recognition reference is already made to a rule of change

---

[43] *CL* 114–117. But see n 54 below.

[44] *CL* 94–95.

[45] *CL* 114–116.

[46] *PRN* 146; *CLS* 198–199; *AL* 92–93; Hacker (1977, 23); MacCormick (1981, 105, 109); Coleman (2001a, 85). There are other possibilities. For instance, Hart's contentions at *CL* 94/95 suggest that a rule of recognition has this form: "the norms of the system are those which satisfy criteria C1...Cn". Yet at other points Hart implies that a rule of recognition confers powers on norm-applying officials to evaluate conduct of members of the community by applying norms that satisfy certain criteria (*CL* 97). This suggests that a rule of recognition has this form: "Norm-applying officials have the power to evaluate conduct by applying norms that satisfy criteria C1...Cn". I shall assume, nevertheless, that the standard interpretation is correct.

[47] *CL* 96.

[48] *CL* 96–97.

and to a rule of adjudication (both necessary, in Hart's view, for there to be a legal system, and hence for there to be an instance of legal practice as understood in this study). From this we can extract his view of legal practice as understood here, i.e. the practice of norm-applying officials. One can capture his doctrine in this very succinct form: *there is an instance of legal practice if, and only if, there is a rule of recognition among norm-applying officials that requires them to evaluate conduct of members of the community by applying norms that satisfy certain criteria.*

We have to consider, nevertheless, this characterization more closely, for the rule of recognition is a social rule, and we have not inspected yet how Hart conceives of social rules. He suggests that the following conditions are necessary and sufficient for there to be a *social rule* that requires doing A in C in a group:

1) there is a pattern of behaviour: most members of the group regularly do A in C;[49]
2) most members display a critical reflective attitude to this pattern called "acceptance": they are disposed to treat this pattern of behaviour as a standard of conduct for the group as a whole;[50]
3) this critical attitude manifests itself in the presence of demands for compliance when there is threatened or actual deviation from the standard; both the demands and the criticism are regarded as legitimate or justified, and hence are not met with counter-criticism;[51]
4) it also manifests itself in the use of expressions such as "I/you ought to do A in C".[52]

Of the conditions just mentioned, (1) and (2) are the central elements, for (3) and (4) are just elaborations of (2). They clarify how acceptance (the critical reflective attitude) manifests itself. As Hart claims, social rules are *constituted* by both a pattern of conduct regularly followed by most members of the group (condition 1) and a distinctive normative attitude to such pattern called acceptance (condition 2).[53]

This is, in short, Hart's characterization of social rules. The rule of recognition is a social rule and, as claimed, there is an instance of legal practice (the practice of norm-applying officials) if, and only if, there is such a social rule among them. So there is an instance of legal practice if, and only if, there is a group of individuals (norm-applying officials) who (i) regularly behave in a certain way and (ii) display the attitude of acceptance, i.e. they are disposed to treat this pattern of behaviour as

[49] *CL* 55, 255.
[50] *CL* 56–57, 255.
[51] *CL* 55–57.
[52] *CL* 57.
[53] *CL* 255.

a standard of conduct for the group as a whole.[54] This is, basically, Hart's characterization of the *structure* of legal practice in the book. And, given that the rule of recognition requires norm-applying officials to evaluate the conduct of members of the community by applying norms that satisfy certain criteria, and that for this rule to exist there must be general conformity among norm-applying officials, it follows that, for Hart, the *content* of legal practice is that of evaluating conduct by applying norms that satisfy certain criteria.[55]

This is, in short, Hart's doctrine as presented in *CL*. Many years after the book appeared, nevertheless, he introduced some modifications in an unfinished Postscript. Owing to his acknowledgement of some criticisms, Hart claims here that his account of social rules, as deployed in the book, is best seen as an account of one type of social rule only, namely *conventional social rules*. He states that "rules are conventional social practices if the general conformity of a group to them is part of the reason which its individual members have for acceptance".[56]

Given his claims to the effect that his account of social rules is best seen as an account of conventions, one would think that he is stating that social conventions should be characterized in terms of the key conditions (1)–(2) above. It is clear, nonetheless, that a minor modification needs to be introduced.

---

[54]Hart sometimes suggests that the existence of a rule of recognition is manifest in the general practice of officials *and/or ordinary citizens,* who also display the attitude of acceptance (*CL* 61, 101). I have characterized Hart's doctrine as requiring acceptance by officials only because those suggestions seem introductory remarks revised later (*CL* 114–117). Besides, it makes more sense. For a legal system to exist, ordinary citizens need not display any attitude of acceptance. This is, I submit, the standard interpretation of his doctrine.

[55]Some advocates of the standard view claim that the rule of recognition is understood by Hart, not simply as a social rule as characterized above, but as a *duty-imposing* social rule, a notion that, as these theorists acknowledge, Hart construes in a slightly different way (*AL* 92–93; *CLS* 147–148, 199; Hacker 1977, 17, 23; MacCormick 1981, 55, 56, 105, 109). For Hart, a social rule that requires doing A in C is *duty-imposing* if, and only if, (a) conditions (1) and (2) above are met; (b) conditions (3)–(4) obtain in a particular way: the demands of conformity must be insistent, and the social pressure must be great; (c) the standard of behaviour in question is thought by participants to be important for the maintenance of social life or some highly prized feature of it; (d) the conduct required may conflict with what participants wish to do (*CL* 86–87). I am uncertain as to whether this view is acceptable as a reconstruction of Hart's position (cf Hacker's own doubts in Hacker (1977, 25)). But I shall consider it as a possibility. If the rule of recognition is a duty-imposing social rule, the account of legal practice we attributed to Hart should be revised. It should state that there is an instance of legal practice, the practice of norm-applying officials, if, and only if, there is a *duty-imposing* rule of recognition (a particular duty-imposing social rule) among them. That is, if and only if there is a group of individuals (norm-applying officials) who (i') regularly behave in a certain way and (ii') display the attitude of acceptance, i.e. they are disposed to treat this pattern of behaviour as a standard of conduct for the group *insistently and forcefully; besides, they consider the pattern important for the maintenance of social life, or some highly prized feature of it; and there might also be conflict with what they wish to do*. So this would be, on this view, Hart's characterization of the *structure* of legal practice. Hart's conception of the *content* of legal practice would remain the same: it consists of evaluating conduct by applying norms that satisfy certain criteria.

[56]*CL* 255.

Condition (1) should remain identical, for Hart in the Postscript recognizes that, if there is a convention, there is general conformity. But condition (2) should be rephrased. As seen, Hart claims in the Postscript that conventions are standards which most members of a group *accept*. So they must be disposed to treat the pattern of behaviour as a standard of conduct for all. Nevertheless, since Hart claims now that part of the reason for acceptance is that most others conform, this idea should be included. So the original condition (2) should be replaced by a similar condition (2'): "participants are disposed to treat this pattern of behaviour as a standard of conduct for all *in part because most others conform*".

So, in the book, the rule of recognition is, according to Hart, a *social rule*. In the Postscript there is a significant change of view. Hart claims now that a rule of recognition is a *conventional social rule*.[57] There is an instance of legal practice, the practice of norm-applying officials, if, and only if, there is such a conventional social rule among officials. That is, if and only if there is a group of individuals (norm-applying officials) who (i'') regularly behave in a certain way and (ii'') display the attitude of acceptance, i.e. they are disposed to treat this pattern of behaviour as a standard of conduct for the group as a whole, *in part because others conform*. This is, basically, Hart's characterization of the *structure* of the practice in the Postscript. His views about the *content* of legal practice remain the same.[58]

2.4 Assessing Hart's Conception

For some commentators, Hart's contentions in the Postscript should not be taken seriously because they were still being elaborated.[59] Others claim that they do represent Hart's final position, although perhaps not a very sophisticated one.[60] In the introduction to this study I presented Hart's account as a conventionalist one, for the latter seems to be the most popular view. But we should leave the question open. So I shall assess his account of legal practice as outlined in the book, and as outlined in the Postscript, separately.

2.4.1 Meeting the First Test

Let us begin with Hart's account, outlined in the book, of social rules. He characterizes them in terms of conditions (1)–(4) above, of which conditions (1) – there is a

[57] *CL* 256.

[58] Perhaps one should consider another possibility, parallel to the one suggested by some advocates of the standard view, namely that Hart would conceive of the rule of recognition as a *duty-imposing conventional* social rule. But Hart said nothing in this respect. And although one could conjecture how a Hartian account of duty-imposing conventional social rules would look like, I shall not do so here.

[59] Dworkin (2004).

[60] Among others, Coleman (2001b, 100–101); Marmor (2001, 194–197).

regularity of behaviour – and (2) – most members are disposed to treat this regularity as a standard of behaviour for the group as a whole – are the key elements. Does this account capture the main aspects of social rules? Does it satisfy our first test?

A well-known argument,[61] which I think is correct, claims that it does not. Hart conceives of social rules in terms of regularities of behaviour and attitudes among members of a group towards such a regularity, i.e. they are disposed to treat the pattern as a standard of conduct for all members. Although the latter is not altogether clear, the most natural way of interpreting the idea is that participants are disposed to behave regularly in a particular way because they think of doing so as a form of behaviour supported by reasons. But notice that nothing in this account suggests that these reasons are special kind of reasons. On the contrary, they might be ordinary reasons (with more or less weight). Accordingly, our test is not met. This test demands that the theory entail that, if there is a social rule, then most members of a group act on a *rule* (*a special kind of reason*). Hart's account does not entail that. For him, if there is a social rule, most members of a group might be acting regularly on an *ordinary reason*. Hart's account fails to distinguish between social rules and widely accepted reasons.

Consider an example to show it. Suppose that most members of a group regularly sleep on a tatami, and that most are disposed to do this because they think that it is a form of behaviour supported by reasons (say, they think that it provides a good night sleep). On Hart's account this would be a social rule. But this is counterintuitive. This is so, in part, because here most members are only acting regularly on a widely accepted reason, not on a rule. To think that there is a reason to do A regularly, that doing A regularly is a good thing to do, is not to think that there is a rule that requires doing A. Rules, we claimed, are special kinds of reasons. They reflect a judgement that, within the scope of the rule, certain ordinary reasons in favour of doing A defeat various, not necessarily all, conflicting ordinary reasons against doing A. Metaphorically speaking they are expressions of compromises, of judgements about the outcome of conflicts of this sort. So acting on a rule that requires doing A, or following a rule that requires doing A, is not merely acting on an ordinary reason in favour of doing A regularly.

The account is counterintuitive for another reason, which is spelled out by a second objection: it does not capture the fact that social rules are invoked as complete (special) reasons. On Hart's account invoking them as complete (special) reasons would be absurd. Suppose, as is typical, that a member of the group, x, addresses another member of the group, y, and claims "you ought to do A because there is a social rule that so requires". On Hart's account he would be invoking the fact that most members do A and that most are disposed to do A (because each thinks that there is at least a reason in favour of doing A), as a reason for y to do A. Suppose that y is one of the members of the group who is relevantly disposed. By definition of the idea of "invoking the fact that p as a complete reason", this individual x would believe that, for any person z who understands the statement that p (that most do A regularly and that most are disposed to do A regularly because each thinks that there

---

[61] *PRN* 55–56; Warnock (1976, 45–46); Marmor (2001, 196).

is a reason in favour of so doing), if z believes that p she believes that there is a reason for y to do A. And this belief would be absurd. The fact that most members do A regularly, and/or that they are disposed to do A regularly because they think that there is a reason to do so, is not, in and of itself, a reason for y to do A. Moreover, here only ordinary reasons are in play. And social rules are not invoked as ordinary complete reasons, but as special complete reasons. (Notice that, if y were not one of the relevantly disposed members, the objection would apply even more forcefully.)

Consider the tatami example again. A member of this group could not invoke the fact that most sleep on a tatami regularly and that most are disposed so to sleep because they think that this provides a good night rest as a complete special reason for another member of the group, y, to sleep regularly on a tatami. This would be senseless. The facts that most sleep on a tatami regularly, and/or that they are disposed so to sleep because they think that this provides a good night rest, could not be a reason for y to sleep in that way. Y has a reason to sleep regularly on a tatami only if this provides a good night rest. The other facts are irrelevant. Moreover, the reasons in play which participants think apply are only ordinary reasons.[62]

So Hart's conditions are not sufficient for there to be a social rule. If they were, there would be no distinction between a social rule and a widely accepted reason, and one crucial aspect of social rules (that they are invoked as complete special reasons) would not be captured.

Let us consider now Hart's account, outlined in the Postscript, of *conventional social rules*. Recall that there is such a rule in a group if, and only if, (1) members regularly do A, and (2') they are disposed to treat the pattern as a standard of conduct for all, *in part because most conform*. This account is subject to similar objections.

First, the most natural way of interpreting condition (2') is, again, that most participants are disposed to do A because they think that doing A regularly is supported by reasons which they think apply only if there is general conformity. For instance, suppose that most students spend most of the day locked in their rooms studying, but at 7 pm they go to the common room for a break. Most go there so long as most others do, for each wants to distract himself, at least by seeing other people. In other words, Hart's conditions are met. Most go regularly to the common room at 7 pm (condition 1), and most are disposed to do so because they think that this form of conduct is supported by a reason (the need to distract oneself) that they think applies only if most do this regularly (condition 2'). This would be, accordingly, a conventional social rule. Yet this is counterintuitive. It is so, in part, because the students

[62] What about Hart's account of *duty-imposing* social rules? The first objection would still apply, for Hartian duty-imposing social rules are, essentially, just regularities of behaviour and dispositions to do something regularly. The fact that doing so is thought important by members for the maintenance of social life, or that there might be conflict with what participants wish to do, adds nothing. Rules are still absent from this analysis of duty-imposing social rules. The second objection would apply too: the fact that most members do something regularly, that most are disposed to do so, that most think that this is important for the maintenance of social life, and that there might be conflict with what most wish to do, cannot be invoked by x, without absurdity, as a complete reason for y to do the same thing.

are only acting on a widely accepted reason in favour of doing something regularly. They simply think that doing this is a good thing to do. They are not acting on a rule, which is a special kind of reason.

Another part of the reason that explains the intuition is spelled out by the second objection: the account does not capture the fact that conventions are invoked as complete (special) reasons. One of our students, x, could not address another, y, and claim "you ought to go to the common room at 7 pm because there is a convention that so requires" (suppose, again, that y is one of the relevantly disposed members). For on this account he would be invoking the fact that most students go to the common room regularly and the fact that most are disposed to do so because each thinks that there is a reason for doing that (the need to distract oneself) which each considers applicable only if most go, as a reason for y to do A. And this would be senseless. Y has a reason to go there if he wants to distract himself in the way described and if others go. The other facts are irrelevant. (Notice that, if y were not one of the relevantly disposed members, the objection would apply even more forcefully.)[63]

So Hart's account of conventional social rules must be rejected also. His conditions are not actually sufficient. If they were, there would be no distinction between a social convention and a widely accepted reason, and one important aspect of conventions (that they are invoked as complete special reasons) would not be captured.

2.4.2 Meeting the Second Test

We can set aside these objections. After all, Hart could be wrong about social rules and conventions but legal practice could have a structure which is only explicable in terms of Hartian social rules or conventions. Does conceiving of legal practice in terms of the practice that obtains when there is a particular Hartian social rule or convention – a rule of recognition – capture its main aspects, i.e. the fact that it is the practice of members of an institution, the Judiciary? Does Hart's account meet our second test?

Consider the requirement that the theory must entail that, if there is an instance of legal practice as construed by it, the beliefs of (alienated) officials to the effect that they are under a duty qua officials to evaluate conduct by applying the relevant norms are not absurd. We saw that, when they believe this, each believes in part that he is an individual who satisfies a property or properties (those which add up to his being an official) and that there is a normative consideration or considerations according to which, if one satisfies at least some of these properties, one is under a duty.

---

[63] I shall not explore what would happen if Hart had provided an account of *duty-imposing* conventional rules. For under any plausible reconstruction built out of the same elements, the same objections would apply.

Given that members believe that they are under a duty *qua officials*, in order to see whether this requirement is met (i.e. whether Hart's account captures these self-understandings) one needs to see how Hart characterizes officials. But Hart does not provide a direct response, and one has no option but to think of possible ways of doing so within his theory.

One could appeal to the idea of a rule of adjudication, for Hart claims that officials are those individuals who are empowered by this rule to apply the relevant norms. But this is problematic. There are, in principle, no restrictions whatsoever on what the content of such a rule could be. It could have this form: "the eldest men in the community have power to apply norms that satisfy criteria C1...Cn". On a system with such a rule of adjudication,[64] officials could not conceive of themselves as under a duty qua officials. For officials' self-understandings should be construed somewhat along these lines: "as an individual who satisfies this property – I am one of the eldest men – I have a duty to apply norms that satisfy criteria C1...Cn". And this is senseless. Compare it with standard beliefs of this sort in non-institutional contexts, e.g. "as a promisor I have a duty to fulfil the promise", "as a father I have a duty to take care of my son's interests", etc. There is no plausible normative consideration according to which, if one satisfies the relevant property alone (i.e. being eldest), one is under such a duty. (Notice that there is no reason why, e.g. in rudimentary legal systems, the rule of adjudication could not mention particular individuals: "John, Mark, Steven etc have power to ...". Here the case for the objection is even stronger.)

One could perhaps appeal to the idea of a rule of recognition to see how Hart characterizes officials. But it is the actions and attitudes of *officials* which, for Hart, *constitute* a rule of recognition. So one cannot extract from the notion of a rule of recognition Hart's characterization of officials. One seems to be in stale-mate position.

Some commentators have focused on this problem. They claim that this group of individuals performs two distinct roles in the account. At a preliminary stage, where we need not identify them as officials, they do something regularly – they evaluate conduct by applying norms that satisfy certain criteria – and display certain attitudes. When the practice is well established, and when additional conditions are met (e.g. when other institutions such as the legislature appear) the practice in question can be adequately described as a "rule of recognition", and the relevant individuals as "officials".[65] Let us assume that this is right. The officials would be simply those individuals whose practice is constitutive, at some stage, of the rule of recognition.

When the rule of recognition is conceived as a Hartian social rule, this entails that officials are those individuals who satisfy this property: they evaluate conduct by applying norms that satisfy certain criteria regularly – for brevity, let us refer to

---

[64] I am ignoring that, as Raz claims (*AL* 92), Hart has not proposed an account of power-conferring social rules.

[65] Coleman (2001a, 101); Kutz (2001, 462).

this as "their E-ing" – and are disposed to E regularly because they think that E-ing is supported by reasons. Hart emphatically claims that officials may (be disposed to) do what they regularly do for *many different kinds of reasons*: out of personal ambition, self-interest, lethargy, desire of identification of others, or whatever.[66] Suppose, as it is possible, that there is a legal system where most officials E regularly out of personal ambition only. Put otherwise, they are alienated, i.e. they do not think of the activity of the group (E-ing) as particularly valuable in relation to individuals other than themselves or in relation to the community as a whole. On this scenario, officials' self-understandings (that they are under a duty *qua officials*) should be described somewhat along these lines: "as an official – *as an individual who satisfies this property: I regularly E because it furthers my personal ambitions* – I have a duty to E regularly".

This would, undoubtedly, be absurd. Compare it, again, with standard beliefs of this sort in non-institutional contexts. There is no plausible normative consideration according to which, when one does something out of personal ambition (or in fact, out of purely self-interested reasons of this sort), one is under a duty to do that. One might have an undefeated reason for doing that regularly, but not a duty. Perhaps there is a general normative consideration according to which, other things being equal, if doing something enables one to promote one's personal ambition, one is required to do it. If this general normative consideration is valid then, when applicable, it could be seen as giving rise to a requirement. But this should be conceived of as a *teleological requirement*, a requirement that applies only if it promotes some of one's own interests, desires or goals. By contrast, that one is under a duty brings in the idea that one is under a *categorical requirement*, a requirement that applies irrespective of (some of) one's goals, interests and desires. So our officials could not conceive of themselves as under any duty to apply the relevant norms.

It is clear that similar considerations apply if we conceive of the rule of recognition as a Hartian conventional social rule, so I shall not elaborate the idea.[67]

Perhaps Hart would characterize officials otherwise. But he has not clarified how. So the theory, as it stands, does not capture this aspect of legal practice.

---

[66] *CL* 257.

[67] The picture would perhaps look different if the rule of recognition were conceived of, as some commentators insist, as necessarily a Hartian *duty-imposing* social rule (recall that here the relevant individuals think of the pattern as important for the maintenance of social life, or some highly prized feature of it). Perhaps something can be said in favour of this account as capturing participants' self-understandings to the effect that they are under a duty. Nevertheless, it is clear that at least some instances of the Judiciary, namely those which are developed, would not be captured. In developed instances of legal practice most officials could be alienated. That is, it is possible that they do not think that the activity of the group is in effect valuable in relation to individuals other than themselves or for the society as whole, and accordingly that they do not think of it as actually important to the maintenance of social life (yet they would still conceive of themselves as under a duty to perform their tasks). So these instances would not be captured. We do not know what would occur if one conceived of the rule of recognition as a Hartian *duty-imposing conventional* rule, for Hart did not characterize the latter. But, under any plausible reading built on similar elements, it is clear that the criticisms apply.

There is a further drawback to Hart's account. The second test also requires that the theory entail that, if there is an instance of legal practice as construed by it, there is a group of individuals who follow a rule. It seems clear that this requirement is not met. As argued in the previous section, if there is a Hartian social rule or a Hartian convention, members of the group could be simply acting regularly on an ordinary reason, *not necessarily on a rule*. Accordingly, if there is a Hartian (conventional) rule of recognition, there could simply be officials E-ing regularly on ordinary reasons only, not on a rule. It follows that legal practice, as conceived of by Hart, is not the practice of members of an institution necessarily. For there to be an institution of any kind, we noticed, its members must be following some rule(s).

To sum up, there are two decisive difficulties with the account.[68] First, it does not capture officials' self-understandings to the effect that they are under a duty qua officials when they are alienated. Second, it entails that there can be an instance of legal practice without there actually being a group whose members act on rule. So Hart's account does not entail that the Judiciary is an institution. Hart's conditions for there to be an instance of legal practice are, therefore, not sufficient.

2.4.3 Meeting the Third Test

Our third test requires that a theory of legal practice provide a characterization of it that explains why in D, a conceivable instance of legal practice where the criteria are conceived of as properties that pick out sets of norms which do not overlap, officials disagree about what some of the criteria are (they all agree that they should apply norms that satisfy criteria C1 and C2, but disagree about whether they should also apply norms that satisfy criterion C3 or C4); and when they disagree they count their practice as grounding their assertions as to what the criteria that should be applied are. Besides, in D officials cannot disagree in the way described if each official were following his own, personal rule stating what the criteria of legality are. The theory should exclude this possibility, and show that participants take the question as to what the criteria of legality are as a question to be answered by a common standard (if even if they are not fully aware, or cannot make explicit, its content).

On Hart's account, there is an instance of legal practice if, and only if, there is a rule of recognition among officials, a rule that requires them to apply norms that satisfy criteria C1...Cn. That there is such a rule means, in any version of the account (whether one interprets the rule as a Hartian social rule or as a Hartian convention), that there is a pattern of behaviour among most – they evaluate conduct by applying C1...Cn – and certain attitudes toward that pattern: they are disposed to treat that pattern as a standard of conduct. The rule is constituted, on this account, by these two elements.

---

[68] As the argument of the book progresses, it will become clear that there are many other difficulties with Hart's account.

It is clear then that in D there is no Hartian rule of recognition requiring officials to apply norms that satisfy C3 or C4. For in D the conditions required by the account for that to be the case are not met. The regularity does not obtain (in D neither C3 nor C4 are generally employed, so there is no pattern of behaviour in this respect), and it is not the case that most officials are disposed to apply norms that satisfy C3 (or C4) either (so the convergent dispositions are absent). Consequently, on Hart's account participants could not disagree as to whether C3 or C4 are the criteria that should be employed and intelligibly appeal to their practice to ground their claims to the effect that they should apply norms that satisfy C3 (or C4), for on Hart's account there is no rule of recognition (and hence no practice) to that effect. Notice, besides, that nothing prevents us for understanding the practice that obtains when there is a Hartian rule of recognition as the practice that obtains when there are several individuals each following his or her personal rule (for his or her reasons). In other words, the account does not exclude the possibility of understanding the rule of recognition as a set of personal rules that happen to be shared. Nothing in Hart's account makes intelligible the idea that participants take the question of what the criteria are as a question answerable by appealing to a common standard. In short, on Hart's account there is no explanation of the disagreement that appears in D. It is in fact impossible.

2.5 The Coordinative-Convention Approach

Some accounts, by relying on some developments in game-theory, have elaborated further Hart's suggestion to the effect that legal practice is conventional in character. There are several versions of this approach,[69] but I shall focus on its core idea only, ignoring technicalities,[70] for I believe that, however one construes the technical aspects, the general approach is substantially flawed for essentially the same reasons as Hart's.

This approach focuses, first, on the idea of a coordinative convention as construed by David Lewis. His model of conventions is based on the concept of a coordination problem. A classical example of such a situation is this. Two people are talking on the telephone and the connection goes dead. Each wants to restore it, and neither cares who calls back or waits. The only way in which the connection can be restored is by one calling back and the other waiting. Each has to decide whether to wait or call back, but has no ground to decide one way or the other. A coordination problem is thus, roughly, a situation where there are two or more agents and two or more possible combinations of their actions such that each agent prefers that, if all but one person do their parts in that action-combination, the remaining person does likewise. Thus, if the telephone situation is solved the first time by the original caller

[69]Postema (1982, 176 ff); Coleman (2001b).

[70]Shapiro (2002, 391–392), Marmor (2001, 200–201) and Kutz (2001, 454) present this approach in a way similar to the one I suggest in the text.

calling back and the other waiting, it will probably be the case that this strategy be followed if the problem appears next time. If it does and a pattern emerges, then a social convention appears.[71] So, according to Lewis, a *convention* is a regularity R in the behaviour of members of a group that are in specific situation S (they face a recurrent coordination problem) such that:

1) everyone conforms to R;
2) everyone expects everyone else to conform to R;
3) everyone prefers to conform to R on condition that everyone does, since S is a coordination problem and uniform conformity to R is a combination of their actions such that no one would have been better off had any one agent alone acted otherwise, either himself or someone else.[72]

Thus, in the telephone-call situation, everyone conforms to the regularity "original caller calls back, the other waits", expects everyone to conform, prefers everyone to conform if everyone does and, since agents are facing a coordination problem, everyone prefers that the other regularity be followed ("original caller waits, the other calls back") as long as everyone conforms to it. (It is possible that each agent cares about who calls. For instance, if the one who calls is to be charged, but still prefers above all to restore the connection.)[73]

The second step in the strategy is to claim that Hart's rule of recognition can be construed as a coordinative convention so understood. The argument goes, very coarsely, like this. If there is to be law, then some group of individuals must evaluate conduct according to norms that satisfy certain criteria. Surely there will be a broad range of possible sets of criteria, and the question of which set of criteria to settle on can be conceived as a coordination problem that appears recurrently. (It is also possible, of course, that each may, *ex ante*, prefer a particular set. Although each person's first preference is that all settle on his favoured set, each prefers (second) that all settle on the *same* set – regardless of which one it is – over the (third-ranked) alternative of settling on his own first-choice while others settling on their own, which is tantamount to having no legal system at all).[74] Most likely, the problem is solved by the emergence of the relevant regularity, i.e. a regularity that satisfies the conditions mentioned above. So the Hartian rule of recognition can be conceived of, it is suggested, as a coordinative convention.

From this we can extract a view about legal practice. According to this approach, there is an instance of legal practice if, and only if, there is a rule of recognition (so conceived) among norm-applying officials. Notice that the view about the *content* of

---

[71] Cf Lewis (1969, 36–42).

[72] I am only paraphrasing Lewis' first definition of conventions (not his refined definition) to show what the core idea is. Cf Lewis (1969, 14, 42, 78).

[73] Lewis' model is also designed to capture that situation. Cf Lewis (1969, 10).

[74] Coleman (2001b, 114–121); see also his (2001a, 92); Postema (1982, 176 ff).

legal practice is identical to Hart's: it consists of evaluating the conduct of members of a community by employing norms that satisfy certain criteria. The view about the *structure* of the practice is also similar to Hart's. Every official evaluates conduct by employing norms that satisfy certain criteria, expects every official to do so, and prefers to do so on condition that every other official does, since S is a coordination problem and uniform conformity to R is, roughly, a solution to it.

Would this account satisfy our tests? Consider the first one, which requires that the model capture the main features of conventions. A convention is, on this account, essentially a regularity of behaviour among members a group such that each expects everyone else to conform and prefers to conform so long as everyone does, for each wants to solve a coordination problem. The account is more elaborated, but is not different from Hart's account of conventions in the relevant respects: nothing in this account suggests that members are acting on a rule. On this account, each is simply acting regularly (and displaying other attitudes) on an ordinary reason (his wish to solve a coordination problem). So our first test is not met. The theory does not entail that, if there is a convention, then there is a group whose members are acting on a *rule* (a special kind of reason). The coordinative-convention account only entails that, if there is a convention, then members of a group act regularly *on an ordinary reason*.

Consider the second test, which broadly demands that the theory capture the main aspects of legal practice, namely that it is the practice of members of an institution, the Judiciary. One of our requirements is that the theory must entail that officials' beliefs to the effect that they are under a duty qua members, or qua officials, are not absurd. To see whether this requirement is met we have to ask how this account characterizes officials. Insofar as this account is an extension of Hart's, we can arrive at similar conclusions. If we consider the idea of a rule of adjudication as a possible answer to the question, we would end up with the same difficulties as Hart's account. And if we appeal to the idea of a rule of recognition itself to answer the question, we would not obtain, just as we did not when considering Hart's approach, an answer, unless we suppose that officials are simply those individuals whose practice constitutes the rule of recognition (understood now as a coordinative convention) at some stage. If we suppose that, the characterization of officials would be this: it is a set of individuals who face a coordination problem, each of whom regularly E-s (each evaluates the conduct by applying norms that satisfy certain criteria), expects everyone else to E, and prefers everyone else to E so long as everyone does (for E-ing regularly is a solution to the problem that everyone wishes to solve). So officials' self-understandings (that they are under a duty *qua officials*) should be described somewhat along these lines: "as an official – *as an individual who, together with others, satisfies this property: I face a recurrent coordination problem, I regularly E, I expect the others to E, and I prefer to E so long as others do (because E-ing is a solution to the problem*), I have a duty to E". The type of considerations I mentioned when examining Hart's account are also applicable here. For the preferences in question might be any type of preferences (participants might wish to solve the problem of which norms to apply simply because doing so will enable each to foster, e.g., their personal ambition), and beliefs in duties, in these cases, would be absurd.

Advocates of this approach mention an argument, nonetheless, to avoid this type of objection. It is claimed that, in conforming, participants will have induced others to expect, to their detriment, that they will conform. And under a suitable moral principle, these expectations create duties.

I shall not discuss such a normative principle. One can concede that some version of it is plausible and that this could account for participants' self-understandings (if the idea is elaborated). The problem is that it would not do so in all cases. It is not a necessary feature of legal practice that officials must have given rise to expectations in the relevant way, nor that they think that they have a duty for this reason. Non-developed instances of the Judiciary are a case in point. Here participants' thinking that they have a duty depends on their thinking of the activity of the group as valuable in relation to individuals other than themselves, and indirectly in relation to the community as a whole. It does not depend on their having generated expectations, in the right way, on other officials (nor on having generated the relevant expectations on other individuals). In short, the conditions mentioned by the approach are not sufficient.

Consider now the requirement according to which the theory must entail that, if there is an instance of legal practice, there must be a group of individuals who follow a rule. This requirement is not met either. As argued above, the theory entails that members of the group (officials) are only acting regularly on an ordinary reason, not on a rule. It follows that legal practice, as conceived of by this approach, is not the practice of members of an institution. For there to be an institution of any kind, we noticed, its members must be following some rule(s).

There is an additional objection against this account which is well known and, I think, correct.[75] Roughly, it claims this. The notion of a coordination problem is built into the account and, with it, the idea that the solution (the regularity that everyone conforms to) is arbitrary. The solution is arbitrary in the sense that everyone prefers that everyone act on a different regularity so long as everyone acts likewise. For instance, in the telephone case, everyone prefers that the other regularity be followed ("original caller waits, the other calls back") as long as everyone conforms to it. To claim that the rule of recognition is a coordinative convention so understood commits one to claim that every official prefers that everyone apply norms that satisfy a different set of criteria so long as every other official does. And this is not conceptually necessary. One can easily conceive of instances of legal practice where officials do not think in this way, where they would not settle on a different regularity (they would not prefer that everyone else apply norms that satisfy a different set of criteria – different, that is, from the set that is already being employed) so long as everyone does so.

Finally, our third test is not met, for there cannot be the type of disagreement that the objection points out. The same argument we considered when assessing Hart's account in this respect applies, *mutatis mutandis*, to this approach.

---

[75] Marmor (2001, 201–202); LPPR 392–393.

2.6 Conclusion

Hart's (conventionalist) account and a more elaborated approach that develops his suggestions further, the coordinative-approach, do not meet our tests. We shall consider now another account of legal practice based on the idea of a social rule. Since it proposes a different conception of social rules, it may be adequate as a model of legal practice. It is deployed by Raz.

Chapter 3
Accounts Based on the Idea of a Social Rule (II): Raz's Account

3.1 Overview of the Chapter

I shall first present Raz's account of legal practice (Section 2) and then assess it according to our tests (Sections 3.2–3.6).

3.2 Raz on Legal Practice

Raz's model is based on a particular conception of law as a normative system and of social rules. So I shall begin by presenting his view succinctly, and as it appears in one of his main works, *PRN*.

In the most abstract sense, normative systems are groups of norms. Raz claims that we group norms together according to different criteria, such as the fact that they apply to certain subjects, or that they regulate one type of activity. But some groups of norms are special in this sense: the fact that the norms form a group involves the idea that the existence of some of the norms has normative impact on the operation of the others. More precisely, some groups of norms are internally related: the existence of one norm is part of a sufficient condition for the existence of the other, or the content of one can be fully explained only by reference to the other. This is characteristic of some normative systems such as, Raz claims, the law. For instance, immigration officers may have powers given by a law to issue stay permits, and another law may impose on immigrants the duty to ask for stay permits. This latter norm is internally related to the power-conferring norm: it presupposes its existence and its content cannot be fully explained unless one makes reference to it.[76] So some normative systems contain sets of interlocking, that is, internally related, norms, and the law is one of them. Yet there are many normative systems of this type which are very different from the law, such as, in Raz's view, games.[77] Legal systems must have, then, some other characteristics that give them their distinctive aspect.

---

[76] *PRN* 107, 111–113.

[77] *PRN* 113–123.

R.E. Sánchez Brigido, *Groups, Rules and Legal Practice*, Law and Philosophy Library 89, DOI 10.1007/978-90-481-8770-6_3,

One such feature is, Raz claims, that legal systems are *institutionalized* normative systems. This means that they at least contain norm-applying institutions.[78] This distinguishes them from others, such as games, for games may not contain norm-applying institutions. The presence of these institutions, Raz argues, is relevant for our understanding of several aspects of some normative systems such as the law.

Firstly, by focusing on norm-applying institutions we can understand in what sense legal systems are the systems *of* a particular community. When there is a legal system, we refer to it as "the legal system of community C" or "the legal system in force in C", implying that the legal system is practised. The criterion used to establish whether it is practised is not necessarily that the addressees of the norms of the system practise them. We are familiar, Raz claims, with legal systems which are practised and where this condition is not met, such as systems where the bulk of the population conforms to the norms but is unaware of the content of many laws, or conforms for reasons other than the fact that they are legal norms. General conformity is necessary for there to be a legal system which is practised. Yet it is not sufficient, for it is possible for a community to conform to a system of norms which is not in force in it. For instance, Raz argues, we can imagine a model legal system proposed by some scholars that, because its norms partly overlap with the system which in effect is in force, is in fact generally conformed. So we must require an additional condition. This condition is, Raz suggests, that the officials (institutions) of the system accept the norms of the system and guide their behaviour accordingly.[79] So legal systems are institutionalized systems. They have a criterion for being practised which is not identical with all their norms being practised but requires that the institutions set up by the norms of the system practise them.

Secondly, focusing on norm-applying institutions helps us to understand in what sense certain norms are the norms *of* the system. For every normative system we require a criterion for determining which norms belong to the system. In the case of institutionalized systems, the norms are identified by their relation to the institutions which characterize those systems. Normative systems with this kind of criteria for being practised consist of norms, Raz claims, which have internal relations to the norms setting up and regulating the institutions.[80]

In short, in Raz's view legal systems are normative systems which contain sets of interlocking, internally related norms. But they also contain norms which set up norm-applying institutions. They are institutionalized normative systems.

Raz then goes on to propose a more concrete characterization of norm-applying institutions (he also refers to them as officials, or as primary organs).[81] He distinguishes norm-applying institutions from norm-enforcing institutions (i.e. institutions that are concerned with the physical implementation of norms) and from ordinary citizens (who may express their opinions about the normative situation

---

[78] *PRN* 123.

[79] *PRN* 123–126.

[80] *PRN* 126–127.

[81] Eg *PRN* 132–136; also *AL* 105–110.

of people, but intuitively they cannot be identified with norm-applying organs). Norm-applying organs are concerned with the authoritative determination (that is, a determination that is binding even if wrong) of normative situations in accordance with pre-existing norms. That primary organs are required to judge the conduct of individuals by applying pre-existing norms is essentially connected, Raz argues, with the fact that institutionalized systems attempt to guide individuals. These are the norms that the norm-applying organs are bound to apply, and that is why they provide guidance. Besides, that the norm-applying institutions are so bound means that they are not at liberty to disregard these norms whenever they find their application undesirable, all things considered.[82]

Some final remarks complete Raz's characterization of institutionalized systems. He compares his doctrine with Hart's doctrine of the rule of recognition, which he endorses in the following version. First, in every legal system, Raz claims, there is, at least, one rule (a rule of recognition) requiring officials to apply norms identified by criteria of validity included in it. It requires officials, the norm-applying institutions, to treat these norms as valid when using their powers to issue authoritative applicative determinations. There might be, nevertheless, several rules of recognition. The doctrine that there must be one such rule is normally endorsed to account for the system's unity but, Raz argues, this need not be so. A system's unity depends on the fact that it contains only norms which certain primary organs are bound to apply. Second, every rule of recognition must be practised by the officials of the system to which it belongs if the system is in force. A rule of recognition is a social rule, Raz claims, and hence it is practised by the officials when the system is in force, for it is part of the test for a system being practised that primary organs apply its rules, which entails that if it is in force then its primary organs practise and follow its rules of recognition. Third, the latter does not entail that officials hold the rules of recognition to be morally justified. That a rule is followed by a person requires only that he holds it to be valid, i.e. that he believes that the addressees of the norm are justified in following it, but the rule might be considered justified for a variety of considerations, not necessarily moral considerations.[83] One might follow a rule (and hence consider it justified) for prudential reasons, i.e. reasons of self-interest (such as personal ambition or fear).

In sum, an institutionalized system consists, basically, of the norms its primary organs are bound, by norms they practise, to apply. An institutionalized system includes, first, all the rules addressed to them (rules of recognition) and, secondly, all the norms addressed to ordinary individuals which the primary organs are required to apply by rules addressed to them. This second class of norms consists of the norms identified by the rules of recognition of the system. The latter are social rules.[84]

---

[82] *PRN* 132–139.

[83] *PRN* 146–148.

[84] *PRN* 147–149.

This is not yet, however, a complete characterization of legal systems. There might be, Raz claims, many other institutionalized systems with the same features which are not legal systems (e.g. the rules of clubs, or schools). What distinguishes legal systems from other institutionalized systems is, very roughly, that legal systems: (i) are comprehensive in the sense that they claim authority to regulate any type of behaviour; (ii) claim to be supreme, i.e. they claim authority to regulate the setting up and application of other institutionalized systems by its subject-community; (iii) are open systems, that is, they contain norms the purpose of which is to give binding force within the system to norms which do not belong to it (e.g. they might recognize the binding force of contracts, agreements, and rules of associations which are not normally regarded as part of the legal systems which recognize them).[85]

This is, in short, Raz's view on the law as a normative system. We need to consider now Raz's account of social rules, for this idea plays a central role in his account, and only by inspecting it can we arrive to a characterization of Raz's view of legal practice.

According to Raz, social rules are rules which are followed by most members of a particular society or community.[86] His account of *rules*[87] need not concern us. Suffice it to say that, for Raz, a rule is a special kind of reason that satisfies the general characterization of rules I put forward in Chapter 1. Besides, on Raz's view, a rule that requires doing A is followed by an agent if, and only if, its norm-subject (a) acts in accordance with it, i.e. he does A, and (b) he considers this form of behaviour as justified because of the rule, which in turn presupposes that he believes that the rule is valid, that it is a special kind of reason for doing A.[88] Since a *social* rule is a rule which most members of a community follow, then, when there is a social rule, most members of a community act in accordance with the rule (there is general conformity) and so act because they believe that the rule is valid, that it ought to be followed.

We can now see how Raz conceives of legal practice (as understood in this study, i.e. the practice of officials). The most general characterization we can attribute to him is that it is the practice of certain type of norm-applying institutions, i.e. primary organs or officials. But we can be more precise.

Raz suggests that "it is part of the test for a system being practised that its primary organs apply its rules, which entails that if it is in force then its primary organs practise and follow its rules of recognition".[89] We can construe this idea as implying

---

[85] *PRN* 149–154.

[86] *PRN* 81.

[87] *PRN* 58–84.

[88] *PRN* 81, 148.

[89] *PRN* 147. At some points Raz claims that a legal system exists only if officials "endorse and follow the rules of the system" (*PRN* 126) This deserves two comments. Firstly, the idea of "endorsement", or as he sometimes puts it, "acceptance", means, as far as I can see, that the individuals consider the rules valid (*PRN* 42–45, 72, 76, 81, 148). So the idea of endorsement is already captured in the idea that officials follow the rules. As mentioned above, Raz claims that if somebody follows a rule, he considers it valid. So if somebody follows a rule he endorses it.

that legal practice exists only if officials follow the rules of recognition. And given that Raz does not speak of any other condition as necessary (and indeed, no other condition seems to be necessary in his theory), we can also attribute to him the view that legal practice exists *if* officials follow the rules of recognition. So we can claim that, for Raz, legal practice exists if, and only if, most officials follow the rule(s) of recognition, i.e. if and only if there is a particular type of social rule or rules among them. In fact, we can disaggregate this idea. For the rule(s) of recognition require, according to Raz, that officials evaluate conduct by applying the norms that satisfy the criteria contained in them, and these norms form a special kind of system (a system of internally related norms which is comprehensive, open and supreme). So we can attribute to Raz this view: *there is an instance of legal practice if, and only if, most officials follow some rule(s) which require that they evaluate conduct by applying norms that satisfy certain criteria, norms which form a system (they are internally related) which is open, comprehensive, and supreme.*

From this we can extract Raz's view as to the content and structure of legal practice. Given that Raz claims that when a rule is practised there is conformity to it, the content of legal practice must be the regularity that takes place when the rule or rules of recognition are practised. It follows that, on Raz's view, the *content* of legal practice is that of evaluating the conduct of members of a community by applying norms that satisfy certain criteria.

There are also certain attitudes displayed by officials towards the regularity just described. These attitudes are in Raz's view, I submit, that they see their doing this as required by the relevant rule(s), which in turn involves a belief that the rule or rules are justified or valid. This is the *structure* of legal practice. As claimed, this does not necessarily involve the idea that the rule or rules are justified for moral considerations; they may consider the rule(s) justified for other reasons, such as the need to secure a comfortable life, personal ambition, etc. This is, in short, Raz's model of legal practice.

3.3 Assessing Raz's Model: Meeting the First Test

The model claims that legal practice has the same structure as the practice that obtains when there is a social rule. Does Raz's account of social rules capture their main aspects? More precisely, does it satisfy our first test?

Clearly, Raz's account contains a necessary condition, for if there is a Razian social rule then most members of a group are acting on a special kind of reason, and this is indeed one of the pre-analytical aspects of social rules. But the conditions put

---

Secondly, the statement seems to imply that, for a legal system to exist, officials must endorse not only the rules of recognition but also the rules identified by it. This reading should, nevertheless, be discarded. The statment is only an introductory remark revised later, where Raz explicitly claims that a rule of recognition does not requiere officials to regard the rules identified by it as their norm-subjects should. It only requires them to treat these rules *as if* they were valid (*PRN* 148). Besides, the idea is implausible. A legal system may exist even if officials do not endorse or follow the rules identified by the rule of recognition.

forward by Raz do not seem to be sufficient. Recall that, for that to be the case, the account should explain how it is possible that social rules be invoked, intelligibly, as complete reasons. It seems that Raz's theory fails on that count.

If member x invoked the fact that there is a Razian social rule that requires doing A as a complete reason for another member, y, to do A, he would be invoking the fact that p (the existence of a rule that requires doing A, which in this context means that the rule is valid and that it applies, *and the fact that most members follow it*) as a reason for y to do A. Thus, by definition of "invoking the fact that p as a complete reason", he would believe that any individual z who understands the statement that p, if z believes that p (that there is a rule that requires doing A, which here means that it is justified and that it applies, and that most members follow it) z should believe that y has a reason to do A, regardless of what other beliefs z has. And this belief would be absurd. The fact that most members of the group follow this rule is not a reason for y to follow it. In fact, the first consideration (that there is a rule, which here means that it is justified and that it applies) suffices; the second one, i.e. that most follow it, is irrelevant. So Raz's account of the practice that obtains when there is a social rule does not explain how it is possible that social rules be invoked, intelligibly, as complete reasons.[90]

3.4 Meeting the Second Test

We have seen Raz's theory social rules is unsatisfactory. This is not a conclusive objection, nevertheless, against his theory of legal practice. For perhaps legal practice needs to be understood as having the same basic structure as the practice that obtains when there is a Razian social rule or rules. Does Raz's account capture the

[90]Consider, nevertheless, Raz's account of conventions. According to Raz, a convention is a rule which most members of a community endorse and follow and where the fact that it is so practised is considered a necessary condition for its validity (*PRN* 57, 81–82). Put otherwise, conventional rules are rules which most members of a community follow only if most others follow it (for the latter is considered a necessary condition for the rule to be valid). If this characterization of conventional rules were read as a characterization of social rules in general, the objection would be, I suggest, avoided. For, basically, the fact that others follow the rule is not irrelevant. Notice, besides, that this idea would avoid the shortcomings of most of the accounts of social rules (and conventions) available in the literature. These accounts fail either because they conceive of them as obtaining even if there are no regularities of behaviour (*OSF* 222, 344–346; Sartorious 1987, 51); or because they conceive of them basically as regularities of behaviour, not as rules of a certain sort (cfr *CL* 55; Lewis 1969, 78; Postema 1982, 22; Burge 1975, 249, 253–254; Gauthier 1979, 3, 6; Endicott 2001, 199, 214–216); or because they cannot capture the fact that they are invoked as complete reasons and, arguably, they fail on this count because they do not recognize that general conformity to the rule is seen by most participants as a necessary condition for the rule to be valid. The latter is, I think, the flaw of Tuomela's (1995, 23–24) account of social rules. An account that avoids these difficulties is, I believe, Lagerspetz's (1989, 22–26, 106–107), but it faces other difficulties I cannot consider here.

main aspects of legal practice on which we have focused? More precisely, does it meet our second test?

Our second test demands, *inter alia*, that the favoured category of practices (the practice in terms of which legal practice should, according to the theory, be understood) should not be characterized using the notion of an institution in an un-analyzed way. We are trying to understand the practice of members (officials) of an institution (the Judiciary) in terms of other practices, and an attempt to do so by ultimately describing the favoured category of practices as the practice of members of an institution would not be illuminating. Raz's account fails, I think, in this respect.

His account of legal practice's structure claims, essentially, that it is the practice that obtains when there is a particular Razian social rule or rules (rule(s) of recognition) among officials or, as he also labels them, primary organs. In his view, officials are *norm-applying institutions*. It is clear that Raz is using the term "institution" in a sense different from the one employed in this study. Although the use is a bit strained (for instance, we do not refer normally to a single official, as Raz does, as an institution, nor do we refer to a single official, as Raz does, as an organ or as a "centralized body with authority"),[91] this does not represent any particular problem, save for the fact that Raz does not provide an analysis of what he means by "institutions". He has provided a characterization of *norm-applying* "institutions", but he has not clarified what an "*institution*" is in his sense, nor has he clarified in what sense the Judiciary (which I have claimed is undoubtedly an institution whose members are officials, i.e. Razian "institutions") is an institution (in the sense in which this notion is understood in this study, i.e. a particular type of group).

It is remarkable that Raz avoids clarifying how he understands "institutions". He explicitly claims, when referring to his characterization of norm-applying "institutions", that "the nature of institutions in general is presupposed and is not explained in it".[92] And, to my knowledge, he has not clarified the matter in any of his works.

So legal practice is the practice that obtains when there is a Razian social rule among "norm-applying institutions" (officials), but we do not know what a Razian "institution" is. Consequently, the model does not meet the part of our second test that forbids that an account of legal practice employ the notion of an institution in an un-analyzed way.

We could examine, nevertheless, the following possibility. It is unclear what the defining features of the institution in which we are interested, the Judiciary, are according to Raz, for he does not propose an account of this institution strictly speaking. But it is clear that, in his view, if there is an instance of legal practice, there is a set of individuals all of whom, or most of whom, follow some rule(s) which require that they evaluate conduct by applying norms identified by criteria contained in it, norms that form a system (they are internally related) which is open, comprehensive and supreme. It is worth exploring whether these conditions could be regarded as an adequate characterization of legal practice, that is, as necessary

---

[91] *PRN* 132–136; *AL* 105–110.

[92] *PRN* 136.

and sufficient conditions for there to be an instance of the practice of members of the Judiciary. If this view were correct, officials would simply be the individuals who form the group just described, and the group just described would be the Judiciary. So we would have a clear-cut account of legal practice that does not appeal to the idea of an institution in an un-analyzed way. I shall label this view "the Razian simplified view".

I believe that the conditions mentioned by the Razian simplified view are necessary for there to be an instance of legal practice.

Recall that legal practice is the practice of members of an institution, the Judiciary. This institution exists, I claimed, only if there is a group of individuals (most of) whose members follow some rule(s). On this account this is precisely the case: there is an instance of legal practice only if there is a group of individuals (most of) whose members follow some rule(s).

The questions of whether it is a necessary condition that the relevant rule(s) require members of the group to evaluate conduct by applying norms that satisfy certain criteria, and whether these norms form a system (they are internally related) which is open, comprehensive, and supreme, are of course complex questions. An answer to them depends on a theory of legal systems, and this issue is out of the scope of the study. Nevertheless, I find the idea most persuasive. I cannot find any other suitable way of describing the relevant rule(s). And it seems that this condition must be met if legal practice is to be distinguished from the practice of members of other institutions (such as clubs, schools, and others) whose activities may also be also such that a system of internally related norms exists.

In sum, the conditions put forward by the simplified Razian view seem necessary for there to be any instance of legal practice.[93]

Let us consider now whether the conditions are also sufficient. Recall that, in all instances of legal practice, (most) members think that they are under a duty, qua members, to evaluate conduct by applying the relevant norms, and that we distinguished between instances of legal practice where (most) members' thinking of themselves as under a duty depends on their thinking of the activity, not only as purporting to be valuable, but as being actually valuable in relation to individuals other than themselves and to the community as a whole (non-developed instances), and instances where members think that they are under a duty even if they do not conceive of the activity as being actually valuable in that way (developed instances; here participants might be alienated).

Consider developed instances first. On the simplified Razian view one possible instance of legal practice where officials are in effect alienated would obtain if the following conditions are met: there is a group whose members follow a rule (which requires that they evaluate conduct by applying norms that satisfy certain criteria, norms which form a system that is open, comprehensive, and supreme) purely out of self-interested considerations of this sort: personal ambition, the need to secure

---

[93] Since Hart's and the coordinative-convention approaches do not incorporate as necessary the conditions I have just mentioned, this is another reason for thinking that they are inadequate.

a comfortable life, social status, etc. Recall that this is a possibility that Raz is willing to admit. Given that these conditions would be, according to the simplified Razian view, sufficient for there to be an instance of legal practice (a developed instance), we can now ask whether it would capture officials' self-understandings to the effect that they are under a duty qua officials to apply the relevant norms. I think it would not.

In this scenario the statement "qua an official I have a duty to judge conduct by applying these norms" should be construed somewhat like this: "as an individual who follows this rule (which requires that conduct be evaluated by applying norms that satisfy certain criteria, norms which form a system that is open, comprehensive, and supreme) because it enables me to achieve conformity with purely self-interest reasons of this sort, I have a duty to judge conduct by applying these norms". This would be senseless. The idea that, when one follows a rule that requires doing A out of reasons of this sort, then one is under a duty to do A, is unintelligible. One might have an undefeated reason for doing A, but not a duty. Perhaps there is a general normative consideration according to which, other things being equal, if following a rule that requires doing A promotes this type of personal interests, desires or goals, one is required to do A. And if this general normative consideration is valid it could be seen, when applicable, as giving rise to a requirement. But this would be a *teleological requirement*, a requirement that applies only if it promotes this type of personal interests, desires or goals. By contrast, that one is under a duty brings in the idea that one is under a *categorical requirement*, a requirement that applies irrespective of (some of) one's goals, interests and desires. So our alienated officials could not conceive of themselves as under any duty to apply the relevant norms. Consequently, the simplified Razian view does not contain sufficient conditions, at least in relation to developed instances of legal practice. Certain central self-understandings among members would be absurd.

Yet it seems that there is another reason for doubting the adequacy of the simplified Razian view. According to this view, for there to be a developed instance of legal practice (and hence for there to be a developed instance of the Judiciary), it suffices, ultimately, that there be a set of individuals who are following a particular type of rule. Put more crudely, a set of individuals each of whom is following his or her rule, even if this were so only by sheer coincidence, would be an instance of legal practice according to Raz. And it seems that we would not treat a set of individuals who, by mere coincidence, are merely following a rule (however complex), as a group to which we ascribe the intentional performance of acts. The individuals are acting intentionally, but it seems that there is no distinctive sense in which the group itself is acting. Something seems to be missing. Accordingly, this set of individuals cannot be conceived as an institution, for institutions in general (and the Judiciary in particular) are groups to which we distinctively ascribe the performance of intentional acts. Let us bracket this concern for the moment. I shall return to it later (in Chapter 9).

Are the conditions of the simplified Razian view sufficient to capture at least non-developed instances of legal practice, instances where members are not alienated? For instance, to capture instances where members follow the rule of recognition, not out of prudential considerations of the sort mentioned, but because they think that following this rule is in effect valuable, primarily, in relation to individuals other than themselves, and to the life of the community as a whole? A reason in favour of a negative answer has already been suggested. We would not treat a set of individuals who, by mere coincidence, are merely following a rule, however complex (even if each follows the rule for this type of reason), as a group which acts intentionally.[94]

So let us take stock. Raz's model of legal practice is not adequate, for to characterize legal practice he employs the notion of an institution in an un-analyzed way. Under one plausible reading that avoids this difficulty, i.e. the simplified Razian view, the account would contain necessary conditions for there to be an instance of legal practice, but not sufficient conditions, at least, I have argued here, in relation to developed instances.

3.5 Meeting the Third Test

A theory of legal practice should provide a characterization of legal practice that explains why in D, a conceivable instance of legal practice where the criteria are conceived of as properties that pick out sets of norms which do not overlap, officials disagree about what some of the criteria of legality are (they all agree that they should apply norms that satisfy criteria C1 and C2, but disagree about whether they should also apply norms that satisfy criterion C3 or C4); when they disagree, they count their social practice as grounding their assertions as to what the criteria that should be applied are. Each believes that her view is sounder, and disagreement proves endless. Besides, in D officials cannot disagree in the way described if each official were following his own, personal rule stating what the criteria of legality are. The theory should exclude this possibility, and show that participants take the question as to what the criteria of legality are as a question to be answered by a common standard (if even if they are not fully aware, or cannot make explicit, its content).

According to Raz's account, and also according to the simplified Razian view, there is an instance of legal practice only if there is at least one social rule (a rule of recognition) that requires members to apply norms that satisfy criteria C1...Cn. There is such a social rule, in turn, only if most members apply norms that satisfy those criteria and consider this as something required by a rule. So the accounts could not claim that, in D, there is a social rule requiring members to evaluate conduct by applying criterion C3 (or C4), for a necessary condition for there to be a social rule requiring that is, under any of these accounts, that most participants regularly employ C3 (or C4), and that most think of this as required by a rule. And this

[94] These suggestions also cast doubt on Hart's and the coordinative-convention approaches. For both claim that it is sufficient for there to be an instance of legal practice (be it developed or non-developed) that there be a set of individuals merely following a particular kind of rule (and in any case, as shown in Chapter 2, these approaches do not provide an adequate account of the idea of following a rule).

is not the case. So there is no social rule that requires them to apply C3 (or C4), and hence no practice to that effect. Accordingly, participants could not disagree as to whether C3 or C4 are the criteria that should be employed and intelligibly appeal to their practice to ground their claims to that effect, for on these accounts there is no social rule (and hence no practice) to that effect. Notice, besides, that the theories do not have resources to exclude the possibility of understanding the practice as the practice that obtains when there are several individuals who, by coincidence, each following his or her personal rule (for his or her reasons). In other words, the accounts do not exclude the possibility of understanding the rule of recognition as a set of personal rules that happen to be shared. Accordingly, participants could not take the question of what the criteria are as a question answerable by appealing to a *common* standard. So on these accounts there is no explanation of this disagreement. It is in fact impossible.

3.6 Conclusion

Raz's account of legal practice is defective on several counts. It does not meet our first test, for his account of social rules is not an account of the social rules with which we are familiar.

Raz's account of legal practice, which is based on the idea that there is a Razian social rule, does not meet our second test either. For to characterize legal practice it employs the idea of an institution in an un-analyzed way. One plausible reading of Raz's account that avoids the aforementioned objection, the "simplified Razian view", would contain necessary conditions for there to be any possible instance of legal practice, but not sufficient conditions, at least, I have argued, in relation to developed instances.

Finally, Raz's account does not meet our third test. The same applies to the simplified Razian view.

We have considered a family of theories that claim that legal practice has the same basic structure as the practices that obtain when there is a (particular type of) social rule (i.e. Hart's account, the coordinative-convention approach, and Raz's account). I have tried to show that they are unsuccessful. We shall explore now a different kind of theory.

Chapter 4
Collective Intentional Activities: Shapiro's Model

4.1 Overview of the Chapter

There are several accounts that claim that legal practice is a collective intentional activity.[95] Among them, Shapiro's account is, I think, the most sophisticated one. In this Chapter I shall be concerned with assessing it according to our tests. I have elaborated the second and third tests, but it is still necessary to elaborate the first test in relation to this type of theory. It demands, generally, that the theory provide an account of the favoured category of practices that captures its main aspects. So I shall explore the main pre-analytic aspects of collective intentional activities (Section 4.2). Having done this, I shall assess Shapiro's approach and claim that it does not meet our tests (Section 4.3).

4.2 Collective Intentional Activities

We ascribe the performance of intentional actions to groups. We claim, for instance, that the orchestra is performing a symphony, that the team has won the tournament, that the gang is robbing the bank, and so on. One could ask when our ascriptions of intentional acts to groups are true. Put more generally, one could ask what a collective intentional action is.

One cannot claim that, since individual intentional action is the action of an agent who acts in accordance with his intention, collective intentional action is the action of a group understood as an agent with its own mind who acts in accordance with its intention. For this is highly counterintuitive. When we ascribe the performance of intentional acts to the orchestra, for instance, we do not think of it as having a mind of its own, not even in a metaphorical sense. On the other hand, one cannot claim that a collective intentional action is simply tantamount to there being several individuals acting in parallel, each performing intentionally certain actions which they conceive of as completely unrelated. Compare these situations: two persons

[95] LPPR; Kutz (2001, 460–465); Coleman (2001a, 98).

R.E. Sánchez Brigido, *Groups, Rules and Legal Practice*,
Law and Philosophy Library 89, DOI 10.1007/978-90-481-8770-6_4,

running in a park and two persons doing exactly the same movements as part of a ballet performance.[96] In the ballet performance a distinctive phenomenon is taking place, i.e. the group is performing a ballet, and that cannot be described adequately in terms of there being two individuals acting in parallel. A collective intentional activity, we can say, takes place when members of a group are acting *together, or jointly*.

The idea of acting together, or jointly, seems to be a plausible first approximation. As said, it is not the action of a group understood as an agent with a mind of its own, and it does not consist of several individuals acting in parallel. Although the idea is difficult to pin down, there are clear instances. Our examples of the orchestra, the team, and the gang suggest that; members of a group are here acting jointly, or together. So, we can conclude for the moment, an intentional collective action is an action that takes place when members of a group are acting jointly, or together. The problem is, precisely, what acting jointly amounts to.

Another feature of collective intentional activities is that there can be many types of groups involved. In some cases, the groups involved might be sets of individuals who act jointly and whose members regard[97] themselves as linked by normative relations in a special way. In other cases, the groups involved might be sets of individuals acting jointly who do not so regard themselves. Consider some examples in order to characterize the distinction more precisely.

Suppose that two strangers, Mark and Jane, are rescuing, together, an individual from drowning by each pulling a rope to which the individual is desperately holding. The situation is such that both think of themselves as being under a duty to perform the relevant actions, the actions that are conducive to the joint end. In fact, they think that "acting qua" normative statements of the form "as a member of this group I ought to (I have a duty to) ..." are applicable to them. For, notice, it is their contributions to the joint effort which is considered due. It is for this reason that, if one of them fails to perform the actions conducive to the joint-end (e.g. he or she gets distracted and stops pulling consistently), they would consider criticism justified. In short, they believe that there is something about being a member of this type of group such that, when coupled with a normative consideration, entails that they are under a duty to perform the relevant actions. They form, I shall say, "a group which acts with a normative unity".

Consider how an explanation of these self-understandings could go. Groups, in the most abstract sense, are sets of individuals defined extensionally (e.g. Mark and Jane) or intensionally (e.g. the strangers). We could say that "being a member of a group which acts with a normative unity" amounts to belonging to a set of individuals who satisfy certain properties, one of them being that they conceive of the joint action as valuable because it promotes the interests of individuals other than themselves. This, plus their believing in a plausible normative consideration according to

[96]Searle's example (1990, 401, 403).

[97]Recall that whenever I refer to attitudes such as believing/thinking/conceiving/regarding etc, I mean actual or counterfactual attitudes.

which one must do one's part of a joint action which is valuable in that sense, seems to explain the strangers' self-understandings.

Yet this type of explanation does not seem to apply to all cases of groups which act with a normative unity. Suppose that Jack and Sue are on a walk together, a joint activity. Now this might well occur: if Jack draws ahead inadvertently, Sue might call out Jack and say, somewhat critically, "you will have to slow down; I can't keep your pace". She is rebuking Jack, albeit mildly. And Jack might think that Sue's reaction is justified.[98] Jack might be walking together with Sue out of purely prudential considerations, say, to stretch out after a heavy dinner. Yet Jack thinks of himself as being under a requirement to perform the actions conducive to the joint-end (that they walk together) regardless of whether the prudential considerations are still applicable. For instance, if while drawing ahead he suddenly realized that he is not interested in walking together any more because this is demanding much more effort than he thought sufficient to stretch out, he would still understand that Sue is entitled to rebuke him. Naturally, he might explain to Sue that he has lost interest in the joint project, and this might well put the whole initiative to an end. But the point is that he thinks that he should tell her that he wants to call the project off, and that until he does so he is still subject to the requirement. (Notice that this would be so even if Jack knew that Sue has become aware that he is not interested in the joint project any more). So he thinks that the requirement applies irrespective of (at least some of) his interests and goals until the project is called off. This implies that Jack sees himself as being under a duty, albeit one of very little weight, to wait for Sue to catch up. Put otherwise, he sees himself as under a categorical requirement, a requirement that applies irrespective of (some of) his interests, desires or goals. And this strongly suggests that they think that "acting qua" normative statements of the form "as a member of this group I ought to (I have a duty to) do certain things" are applicable too. So they must think that there is something about being a member of this type of group such that, when coupled with a normative consideration, entails that they are under a duty to perform the relevant actions. In other words, they also form a group which acts with a normative unity.

Yet here the explanation mentioned above does not work. We cannot say that "being a member of a group which acts with a normative unity" amounts, as it seems to do in the case of the strangers, to belonging to a set of people defined by certain properties, one of them being that they conceive of the joint action as valuable in relation to individuals other than themselves. For although this might be the case, it need not. Neither of them might think of walking together in those terms. Jack is walking together with Sue, as we saw, out of purely prudential considerations. He conceives of the joint action as valuable because it promotes his own interests. Sue might be in the same position. And we cannot characterize the idea of "being a member of the group which acts with a normative unity" as belonging to a set of people defined by certain properties, one of them being that each conceives of the joint action as valuable for purely prudential considerations of this sort. For they

---

[98]The example is Gilbert's, but my treatment of it is somewhat different. Cf. *LT* 178–184.

do not think that their satisfying such properties, when coupled with a normative consideration that mentions them, entails that they have a duty. Jack's case shows that much. More importantly, it seems that there is no plausible normative consideration according to which one has a duty to do one's part of a joint action because it enables one to comply with purely prudential reasons of this sort. So an alternative explanation is needed.

In short, the two examples are examples of groups which act with a normative unity, i.e. set of individuals who are acting together and whose members think that they have a duty qua members to perform the actions conducive to the joint-end. But there is a difference between them. In the first case, their thinking that they have a duty qua members depends on their thinking that the joint activity is valuable in relation to individuals other than themselves. In the second case, they think that they have a duty qua members even if they do not think that the group-activity is valuable in that way. I shall label the first type of group "groups which act with a normative unity of type (I)", and the second type "groups which act with a normative unity of type (II)".

Naturally, in some groups which act not all of its members think that they have a duty qua members. Only some members do. But these groups still display, we can say, *some degree* of normative unity. So the issue of whether a group which acts displays a normative unity is a question of degree. The extent to which a group which acts has a normative unity is, we can say, a function of the number of members who believe that they are under a duty qua members. The larger the number of members who believe that they are under a duty qua members, the greater the normative unity of the group. To capture this idea I shall adopt the following stipulation. I shall say that a group which acts displays a normative unity if, and only if, *all* its members think that they have a duty qua members. And that a group which acts is a group which displays *a certain degree of normative unity* if, and only if, *most* of its members (the "most" is intentionally vague) think that they have a duty qua members.

In other cases no normative unity is present. Suppose that Steve and Matthew are having a picnic and it begins to rain heavily. Steve picks up the plates and runs for shelter, supposing that Matthew will pick up the rest. Matthew does so. It seems clear that they have saved the picnic jointly. Yet Matthew, let us assume, does not consider himself entitled to rebuke Steve if he had not picked up the rest. He simply expected that Steve *would* do this, not that he *should* do it. It was not a normative expectation. This suggests that neither of the members of this small-scale group consider themselves as under any duty to perform the actions conducive to the joint end. This is, I shall say, "a group which acts with no normative unity".

In short, collective intentional activities have several pre-analytic features: they are the intentional activities of groups, of sets of individuals who act jointly, or together, and the groups might be groups which act with a normative unity (or with some normative unity) of type (I) or (II), or with no normative unity.

Let me make one clarification before proceeding. I have referred several times to the idea that a group acts intentionally. Given that, undoubtedly, a group acts intentionally only if its members perform certain intentional actions (those which amount to their acting jointly), I should say something about the notion of intentional action. But since the nature of intentions, and intentional action, are out of the scope of this study,[99] I shall simply make some assumptions in this respect.

I shall assume that, in the weakest possible sense, an action is intentional if it was not performed inadvertently, or accidentally. In the strongest possible sense, I shall assume that an action is intentional when the agent acts in accordance with and because of his or her intention (when he or she executes, or carries out, his or her intention).[100] Suppose that you describe my actions as "my running the marathon". If I intended to run the marathon, and acted in accordance with, and because of, my intention, then my running the marathon is intentional in the strong sense. Suppose that you see, on the other hand, that while running the marathon I wear down my trainers. If I believed that, while running the marathon, I would wear down my sneakers, but did not intend to wear them down, then my action of wearing them down is also intentional, but in the weak sense.

Following Michael Bratman, an influential philosopher of mind and action, I shall also assume that intentions are mental states proper (distinct from desires, or combinations of desires and beliefs) such that, if one intends to do A, one is committed (and hence disposed) to doing A. When one intends to do A, the matter is in some sense settled. There is a disposition not to reconsider, without restriction, whether one is to do A or not.[101]

Let us return to the main thread. We can now elaborate our first test to assess theories that claim that legal practice is a collective intentional activity. A theory of this sort should provide an account that captures the main features of collective intentional activities. Put otherwise, it should:

(a) propose an account of collective intentional action;
(b) such that it captures the main pre-analytic features I mentioned above.

Condition (a) will be understood as bringing in standard requirements. The account should be clear, simple, not uninformatively circular, etc.

Condition (b) will be understood in the following way. Since this type of theory proposes a construal of collective intentional action in terms of necessary and sufficient conditions, and since there are two main types of collective intentional activities (the activities of groups with no normative unity, and the activities of

---

[99]Thus, I shall not focus on a huge variety of problems that lurk behind the notions of intention and action such as: the difference between intending, willing, endeavouring and trying; the distinction between intentional action, acting with an intention, and intending; the problem of deviant causal chains and side-effects; the difference between "present-directed intentions" and "future-directed intentions"; the problem of whether intentions are reasons or causes; the distinction between conditional intentions and standing intentions; the difference among action, results, events and omissions.

[100]So an action in this sense might be intentional under one description but not under others.

[101]Bratman (1987, 4–18 ff). Since intending to A is being disposed to A in the way described, to establish when somebody intends to A a counterfactual test is normally needed.

groups with a normative unity), the conditions favoured by the account must be actually necessary and sufficient for there to be a group which acts with no normative unity and for there to be a group which acts with a normative unity. I shall demand that, for the conditions to be sufficient in relation to the latter, a particular requirement should be met: the account must entail that the beliefs of participants to the effect that they are under a duty are not absurd. Moreover, it must explain why this is so. I shall demand that an explanation of this involves the following. Given that members' beliefs that they are under a duty qua members of the group are grounded on the belief that there is something about being a member such that, when coupled with some normative consideration(s), then one has a duty to do certain things, the theory should specify what this normative consideration or considerations are. They cannot be just any considerations. They should be plausible normative considerations, considerations capable of giving rise to a duty.

We have, then, our first test elaborated. And this test, together with the other two, will enable us to assess this type of theory. We can now focus on Shapiro's account of legal practice.

4.3 Shapiro's Account

Shapiro's focuses, first, on a model of collective intentional activities developed by Bratman which he labels JIA (for "joint intentional activity").[102] He thinks that Bratman's model, which applies to groups with only two members who are not linked by authoritative relations, can be extended to capture cases where there are more than two members who are linked by authoritative relations. Accordingly, Shapiro proposes a model of medium or large-scale collective intentional activities where members are linked by authoritative relations. Second, he claims that legal practice should be understood in terms of this type of activities. Let us begin with his approach to JIAs.

4.3.1 Shapiro on Collective Intentional Activities

Since Shapiro builds his proposal based on Bratman's, it is convenient to inspect his account first.

In cases of JIAs of two agents, the situation can be explained according to Bratman in terms of what you and I *intend*. Bratman's basic characterization of the notion of intention has been mentioned above already. Intentions are mental states proper, distinct from desires (or combinations of desires and beliefs), that involve a characteristic commitment. If I intend to A, then I am committed to A-ing.

Consider what two agents intend when they are involved in a JIA. Compare these situations: you and I are travelling alongside each other in a train, and two people

---

[102] *FI* 93–161.

are performing exactly the same actions but with this previous exchange of words: A: "Are you going to Chicago?"; B: "Yes"; A: "Shall I go with you?"; B: "Sure". The difference can be captured by what each of us intends. (Note that the exchange of words plays no special role, for a similar example can be construed without that exchange having taken place.) You and I travelling together to Chicago can be described according to Bratman, in part, as I intending "our travelling together" (or that we go to Chicago) and you intending "our travelling together" (or that we go to Chicago).

Bratman emphasizes that an account of JIAs cannot be presented in terms of intentions to do something cooperatively.[103] Otherwise it would be circular. The analysis of JIAs should appeal, he claims, to intentions in favour of joint activities characterized in cooperatively neutral ways. According to Bratman, cooperatively neutral actions are such that performing an act of that type may be cooperative, but it need not be. For instance, in the case of travelling together, I intend and you intend "our travelling together", where "our travelling together" leaves it open whether the activity so described has cooperative connotations (it is compatible with travelling alongside). In fact, in order to avoid circularity, an account of JIAs cannot be presented in terms of intentions to do something jointly intentionally.[104] According to Bratman, we must only consider contents that involve a concept of action that leaves it open whether the action is jointly intentional. In sum, the first ingredient of the definition of JIA is that "I intend that we J" and "you intend that we J", where "J" is the activity described in neutral terms.

The latter is necessary but still not sufficient for there to be a JIA. Bratman considers the case of intending to paint the house together in which I prefer red and you blue. Assume that neither of us is willing to compromise. Even if we end up painting the house with a combination of colours, our activity would not be cooperative.[105] Bratman claims that our plans (our general intentions) to paint the house agree but our subplans (our more specific intentions) disagree. There are two kinds of disagreements as regard subplans. Subplans might disagree and there is no way in which we could J fulfilling both subplans (as in the example of I preferring red and you blue), or subplans might disagree but there might be a possibility of executing both of them successfully (I want to buy paint at the corner store, and you do not care about that; you want to buy expensive paint, and I do not care; the subplans disagree, but they can be successfully executed by buying expensive paint at the corner store). In this case subplans "mesh".[106] Bratman suggests that each agent does not just intend that the group perform the (cooperatively neutral) joint action: "rather, each agent intends as well that the group perform this joint action in accordance with subplans (of the intentions in favour of the joint action) that mesh".[107] This condition

[103] *FI* 96–97, 114, 147.
[104] *FI* 147.
[105] *FI* 98.
[106] *FI* 99.
[107] *FI* 99.

includes for Bratman the intention to maintain the mesh. Suppose that our subplans mesh on colour, but we are not committed to maintaining that mesh. If I unexpectedly change my mind as regards colour and we are acting together with some level of cooperation, I should not replace the paint can when you are distracted. I should be disposed to act on this modified subplan, or to persuade you to the contrary, or to bargain with you. Otherwise the activity would cease to be cooperative.[108]

Such an intention would not be sufficient, however. Suppose that you and I intend to travel to Chicago together. You intend that I drive, and I intend that we go there by kidnapping you. The conditions mentioned so far would be met (you and I intend to go to Chicago together in accordance with our meshing subplans), but the case would not be cooperative. In intending to coerce you, Bratman claims, I "bypass your intentional agency".[109] Bratman suggests that, for there to be some level of cooperation, I must intend that we J in part *because* of your intention that we J and its subplans. Put otherwise, it is part of my intention that your intention and its subplans be effective. I intend that the performance of the joint activity be in part explained by your intention that we perform it. In this way we treat each other as intentional agents as regards J. Besides, since the content of my intention is that your intention, and its subplans, be effective, Bratman claims that it is a short step to including as well the efficacy of *my own* intention. In a JIA he contends, I will see each of the agents, including me, as participating, intentional agents. Thus, I should also include the content of my own intention and subplans in this content.[110]

According to Bratman, then, the following condition must be met for there to be a JIA: each agent intends that the group performs the joint action in accordance with, and because of, meshing subplans of each participating agent's intentions that the group so act.

This condition is not yet sufficient however. Bratman adds that all this must be common knowledge among participants. This structure of knowledge should be present: you and I know that each has these intentions; I know that, you know that; I know that you know that; and so on, *ad infinitum*.[111] This set of intentions plus common knowledge is called by Bratman a "shared intention".[112] We must have a shared intention, though perhaps for different reasons (I might want to talk to somebody while travelling, you might want somebody to wake you up when arriving).

Such a complex intention is, Bratman states, still insufficient. He contends that our intentions that we J by way of meshing subplans, if there is some level of cooperation, will lead each of us to construct our own subplans "with an eye to meshing with the other's subplans". This is mutual responsiveness of intention. He claims

---

[108] *FI* 99.

[109] *FI* 100.

[110] *FI* 100, 118–119.

[111] *FI* 102. Bratman claims that he is treating the idea of common knowledge as an un-analyzed notion (*FI* 102, 117). That is, I submit, he is treating it as a notion which might give rise to theoretical problems that he means to set aside. Whenever I refer to common knowledge I shall also treat the notion in that way.

[112] *FI* 121–122.

that we must also be mutually responsive as regards action: I pay attention carefully to what you do, and this helps me doing what I do; and vice versa.[113]

Bratman believes that the conditions mentioned so far are necessary and sufficient. So Bratman's definition of JIA could be put thus:

(JIA) For a cooperatively neutral J, our J-ing is JIA if, and only if,

(1) We J;
(2) (2)(a)(i) I intend that we J;
(2)(a)(ii) I intend that we J in accordance with and because of meshing subplans of (2)(a)(i) and (2)(b)(i);
(2)(b)(i) You intend that we J;
(2)(b)(ii) You intend that we J in accordance with and because of meshing subplans of (2)(a)(i) and (2)(b)(i);
(3) It is common knowledge between us that (2);
(4) (2) and (3) lead to (1) by way of mutual responsiveness (in the pursuit of J-ing) in intention and action.

This is, then, Bratman's model. As noted, Shapiro extends and modifies it in order to capture cases where two or more agents are involved. That is, medium or large-scale collective activities. He also labels these activities "JIAs". Next, he expands the latter model by adding some clauses in order to capture cases where most participants are linked by authoritative relations among them, which he labels "JIAAs". Any instance of a JIAA is a JIA: the JIAA model is only the JIA model plus some additional clauses; the JIAA model entails the JIA model, but not the other way round.

Consider, then, Shapiro's account of JIAs. The first modification is not very relevant. He appeals to the idea of a group J-ing. Bratman, we noticed, also used the notion, but it does not appear in his formal definition. Second, Shapiro requires the appropriate attitudes of *most* participants (instead of all participants). He argues that it is inevitable that, in large groups, some participants will be apathetic, lazy, etc.[114] Third, Shapiro argues that, in large social arrangements, it would be extremely unlikely that each participant will know the content of everyone else's intentions. So he replaces the common knowledge requirement for the requisite of public accessibility, namely that the content of the relevant intentions is publicly accessible in some way to each participant.[115] Finally, Shapiro appeals to the notion of "intending to contribute", instead of using the Bratmanian idea of "intending that we J". Shapiro claims that Bratman-like accounts are not readily applicable to large-scale cooperation arrangements. His explanation is this:

> ... it is often the case that participants will intend to contribute to the group effort but not care at all about whether their group is successful. Suppose I am hired by Microsoft to

---

[113] *FI* 106.

[114] LPPR 412.

[115] LPPR 412.

> work on a new version of its operating system. Because I get paid only if I contribute to the programming effort, I intend to contribute. However, I may not care at all if the software group is successful, given that I am paid regardless of whether the group is successful. To use Kutz's terminology, as an alienated worker, I have a 'participatory' intention to contribute to the collective project but I don't have the 'group' intention that such a project be successful.[116]

So Shapiro replaces the Bratmanian requirement that agents intend that the group J with the notion of agents' intending to contribute. This is a technical notion which, as he claims, he borrows from Kutz. An intention to contribute, or a participatory intention, is an intention to do one's part of a collective act.[117] Kutz adds, as Shapiro claims, that agents who act with a participatory intention need not care about the collective act being achieved. They must see their acts as contributing to the collective achievement, but this does not imply that they are actually aiming at it, as in Shapiro's example of Microsoft's employee.

Those are the only modifications that Shapiro introduced. So Shapiro's definition of JIAs is this:

For a cooperative neutral activity J and a group G, the J-ing of G is JIA if and only if:

(1) G J's;
(2) (2)(a)(i) Most participants intend to contribute to G's J-ing;
 (2)(a)(ii) Most participants intend to contribute to G's J-ing in accordance with and because of meshing subplans of those participants that similarly intend to contribute;
(3) (2) is publicly accessible to most participants;
(4) The attitudes in (2) lead most participants to contribute to J by way of mutual responsiveness in intention and action.[118]

4.3.2 Some Difficulties with Shapiro's Model: Meeting the First Test

Let us consider whether Shapiro's model captures the main aspects of medium or large scale collective intentional actions, where three or more individuals not linked by authoritative relations are involved.

Consider clause (4), which requires mutual responsiveness in intention and action. These notions were borrowed from Bratman's model. But Bratman does not elaborate the notion of mutual responsiveness *in action*. He simply claims that it involves the idea that I pay attention carefully to what you do, and that this helps me doing what I do; and vice-versa. However, he admits that mutual responsiveness

---

[116] LPPR 412.
[117] *C* 81–82.
[118] LPPR 412–413.

in action might be absent; in these cases, we have what he labels "pre-packaged cooperation".[119] For instance, suppose that three individuals plan to paint the house together and discuss in advance our roles: A will paint the front, B will paint the back, and C will paint the rest of the house. It seems that each participant need not pay attention carefully to what the others do for them to paint the house together, nor that each individual needs help from the other to perform her task. And I see no reason to deny that, if we each acted according to her role, this would be a collective intentional activity, though one that appears in a "pre-packaged" variant.

In fact, it seems that mutual responsiveness *in intention* need not be present. Bratman does not elaborate this notion either. He simply claims that it involves the idea that the attitudes mentioned in clause (2) of his model will lead each of us to construct our own subplans "with an eye to meshing with the other's subplans". But suppose that we are in the scenario mentioned in the previous paragraph, with the only difference that the individuals do not discuss their plans in advance. Put otherwise, suppose that, as it is possible, that their subplans mesh due to a happy coincidence. A intends that the house be painted jointly by A painting the back, B the front, and C the rest of the house. B and C intend likewise. Here the subplans have not been "constructed with an eye to meshing with the other's subplans". But the case would still be, I think, a case of collective action. So mutual responsiveness in intention seems unnecessary. Clause (4) of Shapiro's model is then superfluous.[120]

Consider now clause (3), which incorporates the idea of "public accessibility". Shapiro does not elaborate this notion. He only claims that it involves the idea that the intentions of most participants are accessible, in some way, to most of the others. If I understand this clause correctly, it requires that participants could know, if they so wished, what most participants intend. Public accessibility is nevertheless, I think, also superfluous. Consider this case. Three members of a company intend to contribute to the collective act of overthrowing the director hoping that the others do their parts. But each thinks that, if he disclosed his intentions, the others will be tempted to report it to get a promotion, for overthrowing the director is a second-best outcome compared with the first-rank preference of being promoted. So none of them would disclose his intentions to the others. Each believes that the others have these intentions, but does not know that for sure. So there is no public accessibility. And I see no reason why, if these individuals acted in accordance with, and because of, their intentions such that the director is overthrown, they would have not overthrown the director together or jointly.[121]

This leaves us with clause (2), which requires that participants intend to contribute by way of subplans. Put aside for the moment the notion of intention to

---

[119] *FI* 106–107.

[120] These conclusions apply to Bratman's model too, for clause (4) of his model is almost identical to Shapiro's.

[121] These criticisms apply, *a fortiori,* to Bratman's account, for clause (3) of his model requires common knowledge, which is a more stringent requirement. In fact, Bratman acknowledges in a footnote (*FI* 143) that an appeal to common knowledge might be too strong.

contribute, and consider the other aspect of the clause, namely the idea that participants are committed to meshing the subplans by, for example, negotiating. This requirement seems unnecessary too. For instance, A intends to paint the house together with B and C by way of A painting the front, B the back, and C the rest of the house. It is possible that, when painting, they discover that their subplans do not mesh. But it is also possible that this does not happen. I see no reason why, if their subplans do not disagree, and if each of them acts in accordance with, and because of, her intentions, even if they are not committed to negotiation if a lack of mesh appears, they would not end up painting the house together. So this part of clause (2) of Shapiro's model is unnecessary too.[122]

So far, then, it seems that most of Shapiro's clauses are unnecessary. The model, accordingly, does not meet condition (b) of our test.

Focus now on the notion of "intentions to contribute", the other aspect of clause (2). They are intentions to contribute to "*the group J-ing*", or intentions that "*we J*". One might ask what "we J" or "the group Js" really means. The question is important, *inter alia,* because the model is precisely designed to explain what it is a collective intentional activity, an activity performed by a group. The model cannot use the very notion which is supposed to elucidate. Otherwise it would be uninformatively circular. This is precisely what condition (a) of our test disallows. Unfortunately, Shapiro does not clarify the matter. We are faced then, I think, with two options: either he is using the bratmanian notion of "a group J-ing" or the Kutzian notion of a "group J-ing".

If he is using Bratman's ideas of "a group J-ing" or "that we J" the problem seems to remain, for Bratman does not explicitly elucidate them. Perhaps we could establish what he means by inspecting related notions. For instance, he claims that "my intention that we J" should not be described as my intention to play my part in our J-ing, where our J-ing, while not something I strictly speaking intend, is something I want.[123] This may be right, but it does not help us to understand what "our J-ing" means. It is only a negative requirement, and besides it employs the very idea to be explained.[124] Bratman also claims that "I intend *that we J*" is equivalent to intending that the group, of which I am a part, perform a certain *joint activity*.[125] This is not very illuminating either. Another way of describing the content of these

[122]The same applies, of course, to clause (2) of Bratman's model.

[123]*FI* 115.

[124]Bratman states that he wishes not to argue why he rejects such a reading. Perhaps he disavows this reading because, if "our J-ing" were something I want and not something I intend, then the roles played by shared intentions would not be fulfilled. When I intend to do A, we noticed, I am committed to A-ing. When I want A to occur, this commitment need not take place (1987, 15–16). I may want A to occur and let the world do the job. Similarly for shared intentions. If our J-ing were the object of our shared intention, each should be committed to doing what is necessary for the group to J. By contrast, if our J-ing were something each of us wanted only, these commitments would not take place necessarily. So perhaps this is why Bratman rejects the reading. Be that as it may, the point is that we have, so far, no positive characterization of what "we J" amounts to.

[125]*FI* 96, 99, 145, 159.

intentions that Bratman disallows is, as noted, a characterization that includes the very idea of acting cooperatively. The joint-act types must be described, he claims, in cooperatively neutral ways in order to avoid circularity. This helps little as an answer to our question, for claiming that the joint-act (i.e. the content of the agents' intentions) must be described in a cooperatively neutral way does not clarify what a joint-act is. Bratman states also that, when I intend that *we J*, I see your playing your role in our J-ing as in some way affected by me.[126] This is unhelpful too, for it does not clarify what "our J-ing" is. Finally, it is clear that we should not attribute to Bratman the view that "I intend that we J" is tantamount to my intending that you J and that I J. For many cases would not be captured by the model. For instance, the example of two individuals painting the house together by way of one of them scraping and the other painting. Here the agents do not intend that each paint the house. As far as I can see, then, we lack a clear characterization of what a joint activity, or "our J-ing", or a group-activity, is according to Bratman.

The same conclusion seems to apply if Shapiro is employing the Kutzian notion of an intention to contribute, for Kutz approaches the matter in terms of intentions to contribute to a *collective or group-act*, which is precisely the idea we are after. This is, however, only a provisional consideration. We need to inspect Kutz's model in detail to confirm it.

For the moment, then, we can conclude provisionally that Shapiro's model of medium or large scale collective activities does not satisfy condition (a) of our test.

Accordingly, Shapiro's account of medium or large scale intentional collective activity where participants do not perceive themselves as under any duty qua members is unsatisfactory. Its conditions are not necessary, and we have reasons to think that it is uninformatively circular.

Let us consider now the activities of groups with a normative unity. Shapiro says nothing about them. Nevertheless, given his reliance on Bratman's account, I suppose that he would be inclined to resort to his response. Bratman recognizes, in effect, that many groups which act are of this sort, and he makes several suggestions to explain why the relevant self-understandings – participants believing that they are under a duty qua members – usually obtain. For instance, he claims that, in arriving at shared intentions, we frequently (but not necessarily) make promises or reach agreements which generate corresponding obligations.[127] Another possibility that he suggests, absent the presence of promises or agreements, is that, when agents share an intention, acts of purposive creation of expectations normally ensue. When you and I are walking together it is likely that I will have led you to expect that I will participate if you do, and that you have led me to form an analogous expectation. Under a suitable moral principle these acts of purposive creation of expectations may ground the existence of obligations (on my part and your part to perform

[126] *FI* 116.
[127] *FI* 126.

the relevant actions) and this would explain why participants believe that special obligations accrue.[128]

I think that these suggestions by Bratman are well oriented, although they have to be elaborated. But since the to-be-developed model still includes the clauses which we have assessed (and, recall, the clauses are unnecessary and, on the other hand, we do not know what an intention that "we J" amounts to exactly), the would-be model would still be flawed.

In short, Shapiro's model does not meet all the aspects of our first test. We need to see, nevertheless, whether his model, even if the difficulties were avoided, would be useful to characterize legal practice.

4.3.3 Shapiro's Conception of Legal Practice

As claimed, Shapiro builds not only a model of JIA, but also a model of JIAAs. The latter are JIAs where members are linked by authoritative relations. A JIAA is a JIA with additional clauses. He then claims that legal practice, the practice of officials,[129] is a JIAA necessarily.

I believe that this last contention is incorrect however he construes JIAAs. If legal practice is a JIAA necessarily, then participants must be linked by authoritative relations necessarily. Authoritative relations are normally present among officials. The Supreme Court, for instance, has authority over other tribunals. But these relations need not be present. We can perfectly conceive of instances of legal practice where officials are not linked among them by relations of authority. In fact, Shapiro himself implicitly concedes this, as we shall see. So it is clear that, however Shapiro construes JIAAs, legal practice is not necessarily a JIAA.

We need to establish, nevertheless, whether legal practice is a JIA. In other words, we need to see whether this model meets our second test.

In order to see whether legal practice is a JIA, a type of practice that fits in the model deployed above necessarily, we need to know, as Shapiro puts it, "what the 'J' of law is".[130]

Shapiro contends that the J of law is the creation or maintenance of a system of rules with certain features that distinguishes it from other systems of rules (morality, etiquette, etc.). He takes Hart's characterisation of a legal system as a system that possesses a characteristic unity: "every rule in the system must pass the same tests for admission, the so-called 'criteria of legal validity'".[131]

Shapiro then claims that, to create or maintain a unified system of rules, officials must at least look to the same tests of validity and apply those rules that pass such tests. But that is not enough:

---

[128] *FI* 130–141.

[129] LPPR 418–419.

[130] LPPR 419.

[131] LPPR 419.

> ... the mere appeal to the same set of rules does not yet suffice to create *one* system of rules -it may create *many* systems of rules. If French legal officials suddenly decided to follow the United States Constitution, but did not defer to United States courts in constitutional interpretation, the French will still posses their own legal system. Like identical twins, the French and American systems would have the same genetic makeup, and might appear exactly the same, but would be two separate entities. In order for legal officials to be part of the same legal system, and for them to create and maintain one system of rules, it is not enough that they look to the same set of rules. They must also be committed to resolving disputes that might arise concerning the membership of this set or the proper application of any of its elements.[132]

Shapiro concludes that, in order to do their part in creating or maintaining a unified system of rules, most officials must: (a) look to the same tests of validity and apply the rules that pass those tests; (b) commit themselves to resolving their disputes about which rules pass such tests and how to apply such rules. Shapiro adds that, although disputes are normally solved through authoritative settlement, systems in which officials solve their disputes simply by negotiating are conceptually possible.[133]

So the J of law consists in creating or maintaining a unified system. Since Shapiro talks of the foregoing conditions as necessary and sufficient for creating or maintaining a unified system, we can claim that the J of law, creating or maintaining a legal system, *consists* for him of (a) looking to the same tests and (b) being committed to solving disputes (through negotiation or authoritative settlement) about which rules pass the tests and how to apply such rules.

The picture, nevertheless, is still incomplete. Long after presenting and defending his model of legal practice as a JIA(A), Shapiro, reinterpreting Hart's doctrine, claims:

> Like participants in all JIAs, legal officials manage to cooperate by formulating, adopting, and consulting plans. In particular, legal participants would select their authority structure by first formulating, adopting, and consulting 'rules of recognition'. These plans would specify those characteristics possession of which by a rule would render it authoritative.[134]

In addition, officials would also formulate, adopt and consult "rules of adjudication", a "plan that picks out those members who have the jurisdiction to determine whether the rules have been followed and under which circumstances their decisions are binding".[135]

It is difficult to see how this element (the fact that participants manage to cooperate by formulating, adopting and consulting certain plans) is to be related with

---

[132]LPPR 420.

[133]LPPR 420–421. This is the point at which, as anticipated, Shapiro concedes that it is not necessary, for there to be an instance of legal practice, that there be authoritative relations among participants.

[134]LPPR 434.

[135]LPPR 434–435. Shapiro claims as well that officials would also adopt "rules of change". I put this element aside because it is irrelevant for understanding Shapiro's view about legal practice as understood here, i.e. as the practice of norm-applying officials.

the specific clauses of the model. To adopt a plan is, in Shapiro's view, a mental act. He proposes examples such as adopting a plan of doing sit-ups, visiting friends, etc.[136] We can ask: is this new element just an elaboration of some clauses of the model? Put otherwise, is this element already implied by one of the clauses (and if so, which), or by all of them? Or is it an extra element that should be added to the model as an additional clause? Shapiro does not provide a response, and this is, I believe, a moot point. Anyhow, let us keep these two possible interpretations open.

We can attribute to Shapiro a very general view about the structure and content of legal practice. What would the *content* be? In Shapiro's view, if there is an instance of legal practice, then there is a group of officials which creates or maintains a unified system. This amounts, in his view, to claiming that officials look to the same tests or criteria and solve disputes about which rules pass the tests and how to apply such rules. So it seems that, in his view, the content of the practice is this: looking to the same tests and solving disputes about which rules pass the tests and about how to apply such rules.

What would the *structure* be? What attitudes are displayed by officials towards their J-ing? Essentially, officials intend to contribute to the group's J-ing. And they so intend in a particular way: in accordance with and because of meshing sub-plans (or more specific intentions), which are publicly accessible, of those officials who similarly intend to contribute, and being mutually responsive; besides, (all this implies that) they have adopted certain plans.

4.3.4 Assessing Shapiro's Model: Meeting the Second Test

Let us begin with conditions (a) and (b) of our test. I demanded that, for these conditions to be met, standard requirements such as consistency, simplicity, clarity, non uninformative circularity, should be met. Let us see whether Shapiro's account meets these requirements.

The joint activity should be an *activity* that is the object of officials' attitudes. Now, as seen, part of the description of the J of law (the activity) is, according to Shapiro, that officials commit themselves to doing something. To commit oneself to doing something is not an activity, but an attitude. Notice what we obtain when the J of law is defined as he proposes: officials intend to contribute to looking to the same tests and to commit themselves to solving disputes. Intending to contribute to commit oneself to something makes, I think, little sense.

I suppose that Shapiro would agree to remove the word "commitment" from his definition of the J of law. Now the J of law would consist in looking to the same tests and resolving disputes through negotiation. Although this seems to make sense, it is clear that Shapiro should not define the J of law in this way either if he wants to be consistent. Negotiating, if understood in its standard sense, is something we do

---

[136]LPPR 437.

together. It is similar to solving a problem together.[137] When two agents negotiate they are trying to achieve a joint outcome (say, an arrangement of their partially conflicting interests). In other words, they are acting cooperatively. Thus, if the J of law consists in part of negotiating, we would have a circular characterisation of the J of law, because the content of the intentions consists of performing a cooperative activity, and according to the model the J of law has to be described in cooperatively neutral ways.

Perhaps there is a way in which negotiating can be described in neutral ways, leaving it open whether it involves cooperation. Suppose that we spot an official who notices another applying one rule as satisfying a test, we see that there is some discussion, and that the first ends up applying the same rule. This would perhaps be a description that leaves it open whether there was some cooperation or not. So suppose that the activity (J) is described along similar lines. The J of law would consist in looking to the same criteria and negotiating, where this is described in cooperatively neutral ways. That would be a neutral description of J. But ultimately including the idea of negotiation in this sense does no particular work in the description. In the end, the main idea is that officials look to the same tests. So if the activity (J) were described only in terms of officials looking to the same tests the model would be simpler.

In sum, the model, as it stands, does not contain an adequate description of "the J of law" considering standard requirements, such as simplicity and clarity, and Shapiro's own requirements (that J should be defined in cooperatively neutral ways). It has to be modified, perhaps along the lines I have suggested.

Let us put this objection aside and see whether Shapiro's model meets condition (c) of our test. Recall that this aspect of our test demands that the account provide necessary and sufficient conditions for there to be an instance of legal practice. Must officials have the kind of attitudes that Shapiro requires?

Consider clause (2), which requires that officials mesh their subplans, an idea that brings in, necessarily, the requirement that they are committed to meshing them if disagreement as to what the norms that satisfy the criteria are appears. Subplans are more specific intentions to contribute, and meshing subplans requires resolving disputes over them. For instance, as one example by Shapiro suggests,[138] suppose that most officials intend to contribute to the group-activity of applying norms that satisfy criteria C1 and C2; it could be the case that some of them intend to contribute by applying norm N1 as satisfying C1, others by applying norm N2 as satisfying C1. According to Shapiro, they must be disposed to solve this dispute by meshing subplans (and indeed they must solve it if the activity is a JIA).

We can imagine cases, nevertheless, where this is not so. Suppose that officials belong to a theocratic community and intend to contribute to the group-activity of applying norms that satisfy criteria as defined in a certain text which they consider sacred. Suppose that they all agree as to what the norms that satisfy these criteria

---

137 Cf *FI* 96.

138 LPPR 427.

are. This is perfectly possible, though perhaps not likely. Disagreement is typical in legal practice, but not a necessary aspect of it. So our officials do not disagree as to their subplans. And since there is no disagreement, they are not committed to solving it. Furthermore, they might not be disposed to solve it if it appeared. Each might well think that, even if most others come to form one different subplan (e.g. they think that a certain norm satisfies a criterion, but he thinks that they are wrong), there is no reason why he should mesh his subplan with theirs. After all, they are wrong. In his view, the sacred text says otherwise. So it is not the case that officials would be committed to meshing their subplans. Clause (2) is therefore superfluous.

Notice that Shapiro's argument (the case of French judges applying the American Constitution) to the effect that officials must necessarily solve disputes (or defer to the same authorities) to be part of the same system is unconvincing. In such a case, French judges may regard their system as different from the American because the activity takes place between different groups (American and French judges). To be part of a group it is not necessary to negotiate about the ways in which the joint activity is performed (or to defer to the same authorities).

Consider clause (4), which requires mutual responsiveness in intention and action. Mutual responsiveness *in intention* requires that subplans be constructed by officials with an eye to meshing them with the others' subplans. Mutual responsiveness *in action* requires that each pays attention carefully to what the others do, and that this helps each to do what they are doing. If our previous example is correct, this need not be the case. There is no sense in which the subplans of officials of the theocratic community were constructed with an eye to meshing them with the others' subplans. And they need not pay careful attention to what others do, nor does this help them in any way to do what they are doing.

So most of Shapiro's conditions are unnecessary for there to be an instance of legal practice. The only conditions of the model that survive are these: participants intend to contribute to a collective activity (that of creating or maintaining a unified system); and these intentions are publicly accessible. I think that something along these lines is necessary for there to be an instance of legal practice.

Consider, now, whether Shapiro's conditions are sufficient. One of the main aspects of legal practice, i.e. the practice of members of a particular institution (the Judiciary), is that (most) members (officials) consider themselves, qua officials (i.e. qua members of the Judiciary, the institution, or, in more simple cases, qua members of a particular type of group) as under a duty to apply certain norms. We saw that, when they believe this, each believes in part: that he is an individual who satisfies a property or properties (those which add up to his being an official) and that there is a normative consideration or considerations according to which, if one satisfies at least some of these properties, one is under a duty.

Our test requires that, for the conditions to be considered sufficient, the account must entail, at least, that beliefs of the form "qua official I ought to..." are not absurd. To see whether Shapiro's conditions are sufficient in this respect, we need to see how he characterizes officials. Who are officials according to Shapiro?

Unfortunately he never characterizes officials. So one has to think of possible ways of answering the question within his theory. Notice that one cannot appeal to the idea of a rule of recognition in the search for an answer, for a rule of recognition is, for Shapiro, a plan that *officials* have adopted. So we cannot extract from Shapiro's idea of a rule of recognition a characterization of officials.

A natural way of approaching the question within Shapiro's theory that avoids this problem could be this. Suppose that officials were the individuals who satisfy these properties: (a) they intend to contribute to a group-activity (creating or maintaining a unified system) by way of meshing subplans (or more specific intentions); (b) they are mutually responsive (in intention and action); (c) their intentions are publicly accessible; (d) (all this implies that) they have adopted plans (in particular, they have adopted a plan or plans – rule(s) of recognition – which specify those characteristics possession of which by a rule would render it authoritative); (e) they create or maintain the system. If this characterization were correct, it should capture officials' self-understandings, both when there is a developed instance of legal practice and when there is a non-developed one.

Suppose now that there is a developed instance of legal practice, and that most participants are in effect alienated: they do not conceive of the group-activity as actually being particularly valuable in relation to individuals other than themselves or in relation to the community as a whole. They only act out of purely prudential reasons of this sort: personal ambition, their wish to acquire status, etc. An alienated official would be, on this account, one of the individuals of the set who intends to contribute, and contributes, to the group-activity, out of prudential reasons of this sort, by way of meshing subplans, who is mutually responsive, whose intentions are publicly accessible, such that (all this implies that) it is true of him that he has adopted, together with others, the relevant plan(s).

On this reading, his thinking of himself as an official would be tantamount to conceiving of his situation somewhat along these lines:

> I am an individual who, to foster my personal ambition, intends, together with others, to contribute, and contributes, to this group-activity, I am mutually responsive, my intentions are publicly accessible, and (all this implies that) I have adopted, together with others, certain plans. But this activity is not actually particularly valuable in relation to any particular class of individuals other than I or to any aspect or aspects of the community as a whole.

Could he conceive of himself as under a duty qua official, i.e. as such an individual or, put otherwise, insofar as his situation is described in terms of one, some or all of these properties, to perform the relevant actions? It is clear to me that he could not. For he should think that there is a normative consideration according to which an individual whose situation is described in terms of one, some or all of the properties we have mentioned is under a duty, and this would be senseless. There is no plausible normative consideration of that sort. There is no plausible normative consideration according to which if, out of prudential considerations of the sort mentioned, one intends together with others to contribute, and contributes, to a group-activity that is not particularly valuable in relation to others or to the community as a whole, one is mutually responsive, one's intentions are accessible, and (all this implies that) one has adopted, together with others, a particular plan, one is under a duty (a categorical requirement that applies irrespective of (some of) one's interests, desires or goals) to perform the relevant actions. The same applies if one considers one of these properties only, or some of them.

Granted, the idea of adopting a plan (and similarly, the idea of intending) for this type of reasons might be relevant to his thinking of himself as being under what might be called a requirement. But no aspect of his situation makes it possible that he thinks, without absurdity, that he is under a *categorical* requirement (a duty).

In effect, consider the individual case. Suppose that I adopt the plan of running 20 minutes to be fit for the London Marathon (or similarly, that I intend that). My adoption of this plan (or my intention) would give rise to some kind of requirement, for adopting a plan to A (or intending to A-ing) is being committed to A-ing. Besides, the requirement is a teleological one, in the sense that it applies only insofar as it satisfies my goal of getting fit for the marathon. Finally, I can extinguish this requirement simply by deciding not to run any more. But my adoption of this plan (or my intending) for this reason cannot be seen as giving rise to a duty. For duties are categorical requirements, requirements that apply regardless of (some of) our own interests, goals and desires, and cannot be extinguished simply by deciding that one is no longer under a requirement.

The same occurs in the collective case. Suppose that I see you running. I adopt the plan of running together with you for 20 minutes to be fit for the marathon (or, similarly, I intend to do this). I begin to run along your side. You do not complain. On the contrary, you begin to match your pace with mine. Assume that, at some point, it is fair to say that you have adopted the plan of running together with me for 20 minutes, and for the same reason as I. Suppose that the rest of Shapiro's conditions are met. In his view, this would be a JIA. We would be running together. But we would not consider ourselves under any duty to keep running. There is no normative consideration such that, if two individuals adopt this type of plan (or if they intend to do this) for prudential reasons of this sort, and act accordingly, each of them has now a duty to perform the relevant actions. My adoption of this plan (or my intention) would only give rise to a teleological requirement in the sense explained. Besides, I can extinguish this requirement simply by deciding not to run any more. The same applies to you.

These objections would be avoided in the collective case if we interpreted the idea of "adopting a plan" in terms of *agreeing to follow a plan*. This could indeed create a duty, and participants could think of themselves, qua agents who have agreed, under a duty to follow through, even if they have agreed to follow the plan for this type of reasons, for there is a plausible normative consideration according to which agreements should be kept. But these alternatives are blocked in the case of Shapiro's model for, according to Shapiro, the elements we have considered are sufficient for there to be an instance of legal practice. Besides, to agree to follow a plan is not the sense of adoption of a plan that Shapiro has in mind. Moreover, he explicitly denies that, for there to be a JIA, there must be an agreement.[139] So, under

---

[139]LPPR 435.

this possible reading of Shapiro's characterization of officials, his model would not capture officials' self-understandings in developed instances of legal practice.[140]

Perhaps Shapiro would add other conditions to characterize officials, or characterize them differently altogether. But he has not done so. So, as it stands, the model does not contain sufficient conditions, at least in relation to developed instances. Moreover, I think that, even if we set aside this objection, Shapiro's conditions would not be sufficient for another reason, namely that some elements are still missing. I shall return to this point later (in Chapter 9).

What about non-developed instances? Suppose that it is argued that, in these instances, officials are those individuals who satisfy properties (a)–(d) above, with the addition that they think that the joint-activity (the creation or maintenance of the system) is actually valuable, primarily, in relation to individuals other than themselves, and in relation to the community as a whole. Could they conceive of themselves as under a duty qua officials, qua individuals who satisfy these properties? Would the conditions be sufficient in this respect? I shall not answer this question now. But I shall suggest a negative response later (in Chapter 6).

4.3.5 Meeting the Third Test

Recall the objection from disagreement. I conceived of a possible instance of legal practice, D, where the criteria of legality are conceived of as properties that pick out sets of norms defined by a certain property that do not overlap. The objection states that, in D, there is disagreement about some of the criteria (C3 or C4). Some officials claim that it is their duty to apply norms that satisfy C3, while others deny it and claim that it is their duty to apply norms that satisfy C4. They ground their assertions to that effect by appealing in part to the practice itself, and they debate about this issue endlessly.

According to Shapiro, for there to be an instance of legal practice it is necessary that most officials at least look to the same criteria (that is his definition of the J of law). Accordingly, participants could not appeal to their practice to ground their assertions to the effect that C3 (or C4) should be applied, for in Shapiro's view there would not be such practice. On Shapiro's view the only kind of disagreement that is admitted is disagreement about the rules that pass the tests or criteria, not disagreement about the tests or criteria themselves. Moreover, according to Shapiro most officials must solve their disagreements; otherwise legal practice would disappear

[140] On the other hand, if we appealed to the idea of a rule of adjudication to see who are officials according to Shapiro (that is, if we appealed to Shapiro's idea of there being a plan adopted by participants, for prudential reasons of the sort considered, picking out those individuals who have the jurisdiction – I submit, the power – to determine whether the rules that satisfy the criteria have been followed), it is clear that similar considerations would apply. Besides, officials could not conceive of themselves as under a duty qua officials for independent reasons. The construal "as an individual who, together with others, has adopted a plan according to which I have *power* to decide that p, I have a *duty* to decide that p" is senseless.

(for it would stop being a JIA). By contrast, in D, participants' disagreement about what some of the criteria themselves are remains unsolved, and their failure to solve this disagreement does not imply that there is no legal practice any more. So on this view there is no explanation of this type of disagreement. It is in fact impossible.

4.4 Conclusion

Shapiro's account of legal practice is defective, for it does not meet our tests. Nevertheless, a positive lesson can be extracted from our assessment.

Shapiro's model of collective intentional activities, if applied to groups which act with no normative unity, is flawed, essentially, because it contains superfluous conditions. Nonetheless, once we remove these unnecessary conditions, we are left with the idea of there being a number of individuals who intend to contribute to a group-activity, an idea which Shapiro borrows from Kutz. I think that this condition could be necessary for there to be a group which acts with no normative unity, as long as the problem of its apparent uninformative circularity is removed. If so, this could be the starting point to provide a model of the intentional activities of this type of group.

The positive lesson, I suggest, is also an important one. Providing an account of the intentional activities of groups with *no* normative unity could be the first step towards providing a general account of intentional collective activities. And the latter seems to be promising as a starting point to build an account of legal practice. For legal practice is the practice of members of a particular other-regarding institution (the Judiciary) and, as we saw, this institution is a group which acts intentionally. So it seems that an account of the intentional activities of groups can be helpful as an account of legal practice.

In the remainder of this study I shall attempt to show that this suggestion is correct. But the argument will proceed in stages. I shall begin with the intentional activities of groups with no normative unity. They will be the focus of the next Chapter.

Chapter 5
Kutz on Collective Intentional Activities. Building an Alternative Model: Groups Which Act with No Normative Unity

5.1 Overview of the Chapter

The idea according to which, if there is an instance of a collective intentional activity, there are several individuals who intend to contribute to a group-activity (an idea that Shapiro borrows from Kutz), could indeed, I claimed, be a necessary element of the intentional activities of groups with no normative unity. The problem is its apparent uninformative circularity. But if this seeming difficulty were overcome, this could be the starting point to provide a model of the activities of groups with no normative unity.

I shall present Kutz's account of collective intentional activities, which is based on the idea of intentions to contribute (Section 5.2), and argue that, under one interpretation of his model (one that, I should add, it seems that Kutz would disavow), the problem of uninformative circularity would be removed. Still, the model could be improved. So I shall propose an alternative model of the activities of groups with no normative unity (Section 5.3).

5.2 Kutz's Model

Kutz begins by noticing that there are many types of collective intentional activities. They may vary depending on the intricacy of the tasks involved (compare walking together with building a skyscraper), their cooperative spirit (compare playing football with our pushing the car out of the snow bank), and many other factors.

Despite this variety, Kutz thinks that a model that identifies the common element in all types of collective intentional activities can be construed. We shall see below what his model is. For the moment suffice it to say that he does not consider as necessary conditions such as "intentions that we J", mutual responsiveness, or common knowledge, the type of conditions that appear in Bratman's or Shapiro's models. We saw that this is correct, for such conditions need not be present. Kutz does not deny that conditions such as these are normally present. In fact, he acknowledges that some forms of collective intentional activities cannot be properly understood unless one brings them in, in addition to the conditions of his own model. For instance,

R.E. Sánchez Brigido, *Groups, Rules and Legal Practice*,
Law and Philosophy Library 89, DOI 10.1007/978-90-481-8770-6_5,

walking together is a clear instance of a type of intentional activity ascribable to a group. If two agents are walking together then each agent must, *inter alia*, be matching his pace with the other. This type of case cannot be understood appropriately, he acknowledges, unless one brings in, perhaps among others, ideas such as mutual responsiveness. Yet mutual responsiveness does not appear in all cases of collective intentional action, and thus the model should not consider that condition as necessary. So Kutz's labels his strategy "minimalistic".[141] The minimalistic strategy, as I understand it, consists in proposing necessary conditions for there to be any type of collective intentional action. But it also consists in providing sufficient conditions for there to be the simplest type of instance, while not denying that the model has to be supplemented by adding further conditions if it is to capture what takes place in many forms of collective intentional activities which are, in an intuitive sense, more complex. I think that this strategy is promising, so let us inspect Kutz's minimalistic model.

Kutz's model states this: *there is an instance of an intentional collective activity if, and only if, members of a group (a set of individuals) are acting with overlapping participatory intentions.*[142]

Consider the idea of a *participatory intention*, the key notion of the model. A participatory intention, or a contributory intention, is an intention, Kutz claims, to do one's part of a collective act. It has therefore two representational components: individual role and collective end. By "individual role", Kutz means the act an individual performs as a contribution to a collective end. A "collective end" is, according to Kutz, the object of a description that is the causal product of different individuals' acts (such as the movement of a heavy object) or is constituted by different individuals' acts (such as dancing a tango); a collective end is, in other words, a state of affairs whose realization depends on several agents acting together.[143] Kutz adds that the following idea is already implied in his notion of a participatory intention: when participants display participatory intentions, they are disposed towards the other's possible knowledge of that.[144] For, he argues, it seems impossible for a participant to conceive of his act as contributing to a collective end while also intending that his contribution never become known:

> If I do intend that my contribution to some collective end be secret, for example surreptitiously stuffing a ballot box to help a candidate, then the natural thing to say is not that I am doing my part of our electing the candidate, but rather that I am acting as a rogue, trying to get my candidate elected.[145]

Consider now the idea of *overlap*: it must be the same joint enterprise in which agents participate intentionally. According to Kutz, intentions overlap

---

[141] *C* 74–75, 89–90.

[142] *C* 89, 94, 103–104.

[143] *C* 81–82.

[144] *C* 93. See *C*77, 274 for a more refined version of this idea.

[145] *C* 93.

> ...when the collective end component of their participatory intentions refers to the same activity or outcome and when there is a nonempty intersection of the sets of states of affairs satisfying those collective ends.[146]

So, for instance, I may intend that we go together to a friend's house for a quiet dinner, while you intend that we go there for a surprise party. If we act accordingly, while our going to the surprise party is not jointly intentional, our going to our friend's house is. As Kutz clarifies, overlap is always a matter of degree, given that on many occasions there are differences in each agent's conceptions of the group-act.

So these are the main elements of Kutz's model. Notice that ideas such as common knowledge, or mutual responsiveness, are completely absent from the picture. There is no denial that some cases cannot be understood adequately unless one brings in these ideas. But the model is minimalistic; it could be coupled with these conditions to capture these intuitively more complex cases. In fact, notice that the Bratmanian "intentions that we J" (or intentions that the group J) are absent from the picture too. An agent who has a participatory intention does not intend, in any relevant sense, that the group J. He simply intends to do his part of a collective act. In fact, he need not even act so as to achieve the collective end. Consider an example to illustrate this. Suppose that Steven wants John to paint the front of the house and Mark to paint the rest. He wants this because, he thinks, by their doing this the house will end up being painted, and the house needs to be painted badly. John and Mark, each for his part, get to know Steven's plan. John sets out to paint the front, and Mark sets out to paint the rest. Each decides this because, let us suppose, each knows that Steven is a grateful person, and that most likely each will be rewarded by him if each does this. So John begins to paint the front, and Mark to paint the rest. They see each other, and each conceives of what they are doing as their doing their parts of their painting the house together; besides, both perform these actions intentionally. Each now, we can say, intends to contribute. In other words, each displays participatory intentions. But each does not care about the house being in the end painted. Each simply intends to do his part, for each thinks that it is their doing this which will be rewarded by Steven.

Of course, there are cases, Kutz recognizes, where this is not so, where the agents intend that the collective end be achieved. These are cases where participants "intend that we J" (or "intend that the group J"), or, as Kutz puts it, where participants share a "group-intention". Kutz claims that "when agents act so as to realize the collective outcome, to the extent of aiding others in their contributions, we should attribute to them the group-intention to achieve that collective end".[147]

---

[146] *C* 94.

[147] *C* 97. This construal needs, I think, to be revised. When one intends "that the group J", it seems that one intends more than merely intending to do one's part so as to realize the collective outcome to the extent of aiding the others. One also intends that the others do their parts. The latter, nevertheless, may seem problematic. How can I intend something that is not up to me? The problem is only, I think, apparent. My intention *that* you do your part is not really puzzling, for we can intend things different from our own actions. For instance, I can intend that my son go to

Notice that intentions "that we J" are intentions to do one's part of J-ing plus some extra conditions. So these cases can be captured by adding further conditions to the model, in accordance with the minimalistic strategy. In sum, the model is far less demanding than Bratman's and Shapiro's models.

Some clarifications are necessary before proceeding. Firstly, to claim that agents intentionally perform their parts does not imply that the parts are completely specified. They may not. If they are not, Kutz claims, participatory intentions present agents with problems of practical reasoning. The agents must reason backwards from the nature of the group-act to an understanding of what each should do if the group-act is to be achieved:

> If the decomposition of the act is obvious, then no deliberation is needed: I see you trying to push your car out of the snow bank, so I get behind the bumper and push too. But if the goal is complex, or the roles are unobvious, then deliberation may be necessary ... If we are to have a picnic, then we need drinks, sandwiches, and a blanket; I ought to bring one of these; I have a nice blanket and the others do not; everyone realizes this; therefore I ought to do my part of bringing a blanket in order to promote our having a picnic.[148]

Secondly, the model is too narrow because it assumes that only acts performed by all members may be re-described as acts of the group. Yet there are collective actions which may be just the actions of a single member. For instance, when a company's representative signs a contract to acquire property, it is the company that has acquired property. But Kutz suggests that these are, intuitively, more complex cases. Normally they occur because groups can incorporate devices by which the acts of one member count as the act of the group.[149] Although Kutz does not elaborate this idea, I think that such devices normally consist of the adoption of special rules by members to that effect. The minimalistic model can also capture these cases by adding conditions that refer to this type of device.

5.3 Assessing Kutz's Model

Our first test of a theory of legal practice that claims that it has the structure of intentional collective activities requires that the theory should (a) propose an account of collective intentional action, (b) such that it captures the main features I mentioned. If we were to build a model of legal practice by employing Kutz's model, it should meet this test. Let us see whether this is so.

---

school if I see his actions as in someway affected by me (see *FI* 116). Similarly I may intend that you perform your part. In short, my intention that "we J" can be understood as my intention *to* do my part and *that* you do yours. For the relation between "intentions to" and "intentions that", see Vermazen (1993, 223).

148 *C* 84.

149 *C* 104–105.

5.3.1 Meeting Condition (a) of the Test

Condition (a) demands that the account be clear, simple, not uninformatively circular, etc. One problem with Kutz's account is that it states that there is a *collective* intentional activity if, and only if, a set of individuals are acting with overlapping participatory intentions. But a participatory intention is an intention to do one's part of a *collective act.* The content of these intentions have, as Kutz puts it, a collective-end component. And Kutz insists that the content of the participatory intentions is "irreducibly collective". So it seems that our requirement is not met. We are trying to understand collective intentional action, and a model that claims that collective intentional action must be understood in terms of intentions to do one's part of a collective act seems uninformatively circular.

Kutz is aware of this problem but, he claims, the worry of circularity is "more methodological than substantial". In his view, "collective intentional activities cannot be made sense of except in collective terms".[150] So he asserts:

> What we need, then, is not an analysis that tries to show how each instance of collective action is built out of noncollective materials, but rather a genealogical account that shows generally how the capacity to engage in collective action emerges out of capacities explicable without reference to collective concepts.[151]

To see how this genealogical account would work, Kutz distinguishes between executive and subsidiary intentions. An executive intention is an intention whose content is an activity or outcome conceived as a whole (e.g. playing chess). It also plays a characteristic role in generating, commanding or determining other intentions in order to achieve that outcome (e.g. moving the rook, the knight, etc). A subsidiary intention is an intention generated and rationalized by an executive intention, whose content is the achievement of a part of the total outcome or activity.

So Kutz claims that

> . . . the content of executive intentions can be irreducibly intentionalistic, and even jointly intentionalistic, so long as the subsidiary intentions they command have nonintentional objects. Accordingly, when I play chess, my subsidiary intentions can be explicated without relying on the notion of joint intentionality, such as intending to move my queen in response to the threat of your rook. In learning to play chess, I first conceive of the elements of the game in nonjoint terms: the knight moves so and so; it is best to open with pawns; and if you threaten my queen, I should check your king. As I learn to play, these constituent elements of chess come to be represented and internalized as 'my playing chess', or, alternatively, 'my doing my part of our playing chess together'. By such a bootstrapping process, the collective joint activity thus becomes the object of an agent's executive intention, having been built out of noncollective elements.[152]

This argument is, I think, intriguing. Firstly, it is unclear what Kutz means when claiming that the worry of circularity is "more methodological than substantial". Secondly, it is also unclear what the role of Kutz's genealogical account is.

---

[150] *C* 86.

[151] *C* 86.

[152] *C* 87–88.

The distinction between executive and subsidiary intentions is plausible. The intention to get involved in a collective act may be an overarching intention (an executive intention) that may command and give rise, when coupled with means-end reasoning, to more specific (or subsidiary) intentions. But Kutz's executive intentions are characterized in collective terms, and the problem is how to remove the concern of uninformative circularity. Does he think that a genealogical account would dispel the concern? This is unclear to me. But if that is what he means, it seems that he is wrong. If a genealogical account of the capacity of forming executive intentions of this sort were available, it would be an account of the *origin* of such capacity. The output of such an account should have this kind of form: "our capacity to form *executive intentions to engage in collective action* emerges out of capacities explicable without reference to collective concepts". It is clear that the output of a genealogical account employs the concept of collective action without clarifying it. It only explains, if successful, from where it comes. But it does not elucidate the concept itself. So the concern of uninformative circularity still remains. Thirdly, and most importantly, it is unclear why Kutz needs a genealogical explanation in order to defuse the problem of circularity in the first place. The problem of circularity is, I think, only apparent.

Suppose that I conceive of a particular state of affairs: that this house be painted. I conceive of certain actions as standing in an instrumental relation to this state of affairs. Say, getting the brushes and the paint, scraping, painting the front first, the back next, and so on, such that, if these actions are performed, the state of affairs will likely be brought about. Of course, the state of affairs might be brought about otherwise, by performing other actions, and I recognize this. But this is how I conceive of the matter now. Put otherwise, I conceive of a state of affairs the bringing about of which involves performing these actions. Suppose that I decide to perform these actions myself. I plan in advance what to do: the first day I will paint the front, the second day the back, etc. It is like dividing labour among my inner-selves. Something similar might happen if, instead of deciding to perform these actions myself, I decide to hire two painters to paint it. I divide labour among them, and assign tasks to each such that, if my plan is followed, the state of affairs (that this house be painted) will likely be brought about. There is no significant difference when the agents are you and I. Just as I can divide labour among my inner-selves, and between the two painters, you and I can divide labour among ourselves. If we do this, each of us will see our own actions, and the actions of the other, as standing in an instrumental relation to the state of affairs (that this house be painted). So, paraphrasing Kutz, we can say that some collective ends are just states of affairs the bringing about of which is conceived of as involving the actions of two or more individuals. These actions can be conceived of as the parts each is to perform in order to bring about the state of affairs.

This definition of some collective ends does not employ any collective notion. It only claims that there are states of affairs the bringing about of which is conceived of as involving the performance of certain acts by several individuals, an idea with which we are very familiar. And with this idea we can characterize at least some participatory intentions. Some of them can be characterized as intentions to perform certain acts that the agent conceives as, together with the actions of other agents, standing in an instrumental relation to the bringing about of a state of affairs. I think there is no uninformative circularity involved here.

Some collective ends, and hence some participatory intentions, cannot be so understood nevertheless. They refer to states of affairs of which it can be said, not that their bringing about is conceived of as involving the actions of several individuals, but as *constituted* by the performance of certain acts by several individuals. Suppose that an assembly receives a guest, and that its members want to honour him by offering a toast. Let us assume that, in their community, there is a common conception of what counts as "an assembly offering a toast". Say, it consists of each member of the assembly, when prompted by one of the members, facing the guest and raising his or her glass of wine for a couple of seconds as a way of showing respect to the guest. In this community this counts as the assembly offering a toast. Paraphrasing Kutz again, we can say that it is a state of affairs the bringing about of which is seen as constituted by the actions (and attitudes) of several individuals. Notice the difference with the other type of collective ends. Here the actions do not stand, in any plausible sense, in an instrumental relation to the state of affairs. Besides, it is not possible that the relevant individuals think of the state of affairs as achievable in ways other than their performing the relevant actions and displaying the relevant attitudes. So their intentions to do their parts of their giving a toast (a collective action) are just intentions to perform certain actions (coupled with certain attitudes) that, together with the actions (and attitudes) of the others, are seen as constitutive of the bringing about of a particular state of affairs. Again, I think there is no uninformative circularity involved here.[153]

These two characterizations of participatory intentions seem to cover all cases. We can use them to suggest a model of collective intentional action that, allegedly, does not face the problem of uninformative circularity. My suggestion is this:

> There is a collective intentional activity if, and only if, there is a set of individuals (defined extensionally or intensionally) such that:
>
> a) each conceives of a state of affairs the bringing about of which involves, or is constituted by, the performance of certain actions (and the display of certain attitudes) by all members of the set;
> b) their conceptions of this state of affairs overlap;
> c) each intends to perform these actions (and displays the relevant attitudes), and each conceives of these actions (and attitudes) as related in the way described to the state of affairs;
> d) and each executes his or her intention, such that the state of affairs mentioned in (b) obtains.

[153] Similarly for more complex cases. Playing chess and dancing a tango are activities that involve two individuals. The state of affairs where you and I play chess, or dance a tango, are states of affairs the bringing about of which is constituted by our doing certain things (and displaying certain attitudes). There is nothing mysterious about this. It simply follows from the concept of playing chess or dancing a tango.

Condition (c) can be put otherwise too: each intends to perform these actions, and conceives of performing them under the description "my doing my part of the bringing about of the state of affairs". In other words, each intends to do his or her part. I shall say that when, and only when, an individual satisfies condition (a)–(c), he or she has an overlapping participatory intention.

To illustrate the model consider the case of Mark and John above, who learn about Steve's plans and want to be rewarded by him. Each conceives of a state of affairs, i.e. that the house be painted. It is a state of affairs the bringing about of which is conceived of by them as involving the performance of certain actions by each of them (John painting the front, Mark painting the rest). Their conceptions of the state of affairs actually overlap. Each intends now to perform the relevant actions (John to paint the front, Mark the rest). But it is not the case that each merely intends to perform these actions. Each sees his performing these actions as standing in a contributory relationship to the state of affairs; put otherwise, each sees his performing these actions under the description "my doing my part of the bringing about of the state of affairs". This does not imply, nevertheless, that each has as his goal that the house be painted, i.e. that the state of affairs be obtained. Each simply intends to do his part, for this is what they think will be rewarded. If that were the case, and if each executed his intention (if each acted in accordance with, and because of, his intention), then it is proper to say that there is a collective intentional activity: this set of individuals are painting the house jointly. And it seems clear that there is no uninformative circularity involved.

Let me now make one clarification. In the most general sense, a group is a set of individuals defined extensionally (e.g. Mark and John) or in terms of a certain property (vg the red-haired people). The model uses this general notion at a general level: it understands a group that acts intentionally as a set of individuals defined intensionally, i.e. as a set of individuals who satisfy properties (a)–(d). Of course, when the set is defined intensionally, it must be understood that the properties in question are properties other than properties (a)–(d).

From the model we can extract a test of membership, i.e. a test that establishes when an individual is a member of a group which acts intentionally. An individual is a member of such group if, and only if, there is a set of individuals (defined intensionally or extensionally) such that: (i) he conceives of a state of affairs the bringing about of which involves, or is constituted by, the performance of certain actions (and the display of attitudes) by him and by the other individuals of the set; (ii) his actions (and attitudes) are seen by these other individuals as, together with their own actions (and attitudes), related in that way to the state of affairs; (iii) his conception of the state of affairs overlaps with the other individuals' conceptions of the state of affairs; (iv) he intends to perform the relevant actions, which he conceives of as related in the way described to the relevant state of affairs, and the other individuals of the set satisfy these conditions as well; (v) he carries out his intention, and so do the other individuals of the set, such that the state of affairs configured by their overlapping conceptions obtains. This test is in accordance with the truism that a group of any type is the set of all its members. For the set of all the individuals who satisfy the conditions just mentioned form the group which acts intentionally.

I think that the model is well oriented. Notice the following point in this connection. There is a recognizable use of the pronoun "we" that refers to the members of a group which acts intentionally. For instance, when Mark and John satisfy all these conditions (when they are members of a group which acts intentionally), they could claim "we are painting the house" (and if they use "we" this presupposes, at least, that they believe that they form a group which is acting intentionally). Here "we" refers to them, i.e. the members of the group which acts intentionally.

So the model is plausible. It avoids, I think, the problem of uninformative circularity. And it meets, I believe, the other standard requirements (consistency, clarity, etc) that condition (a) of our test contains. Perhaps it is in essence Kutz's model. But given his insistence on the "irreducible collective" character of the content of participatory intentions (a view that the model I have just outlined denies) and his appeal to a genealogical strategy to avoid the concern of circularity (a strategy that the model I have just outlined does not employ), I am unsure as to whether Kutz would accept it. So let us label this model the "alternative model".

Notice that this model is a model of the activities of groups with no normative unity. Members do not believe that they are under any duty qua members.

5.3.2 Meeting Condition (b): Groups Which Act with No Normative Unity

Are Kutz's conditions in effect necessary for there to be groups of this type? Kutz states that the idea of a participatory intention should be understood as already implying that participants are favourably disposed towards the others' possible knowledge of their participatory intentions. Recall that he supports this view by discussing the case of the individual who surreptitiously stuffs the ballot. Is this correct?

I think that the general idea is incorrect. We can conceive of scenarios where agents are involved in a collective intentional action and where they are not disposed favourably towards the others' possible knowledge of their participatory intentions. Recall the three employees of a company who intend to do their parts of overthrowing the director in the hope that the others do their parts. Each believes that the others have these intentions. But they are unsure about this. They do not really know it. In addition, each thinks that, if the others actually knew about her intentions, they will be tempted to report it to get a promotion, for overthrowing the director is a second-best outcome compared with the first-rank preference of being promoted. So none of them is disposed favourably towards the others' possible knowledge of his intentions. Yet if these set of individuals executed their intentions and if, as a result, the director is overthrown, I see no reason to deny that this group has overthrown the director. So we need not understand the idea of a participatory intention as already implying that participants are favourably disposed towards the others' possible knowledge of their intentions.

The case of the individual who surreptitiously stuffs the ballot does not show otherwise. Kutz claims that the natural thing to say is not that this individual is doing his part of electing the candidate, but rather that he is acting as a rogue, trying to get his candidate elected. It is true, I think, that this individual is not doing his part of electing the candidate. But this is true not because he is not disposed favourably towards the others' possible knowledge of his intentions. Rather, he is not doing his part of electing the candidate because his stuffing the ballot is not a part of the collective intentional action of getting the candidate elected in the first place. The action of electing the candidate is constituted by valid votes, not by surreptitiously stuffing ballots.

In short, the idea that participants are favourably disposed towards the others' possible knowledge of their intentions, which Kutz considers as already implied in the concept of a participatory intention and hence as a necessary element for there to be a collective intentional activity, is incorrect. So I shall understand the alternative model I have sketched as not implying that these dispositions obtain necessarily. This gives us an additional reason to treat both models as clearly distinct.

So our inquiry has led us to the following result: there is an instance of the intentional activity of a group with no normative unity if, and only if, the clauses of the alternative model I have sketched obtain.

This account is also minimalistic. There is no denial that additional conditions (such as mutual responsiveness, or common knowledge, or the idea that agents intend not only to do their parts, but also that the group act)[154] should be introduced to capture more complex cases. Besides, just as Kutz claims, that members intentionally perform their parts is not to claim that the parts need be completely specified. If they are not, the agents are faced with problems of practical reasoning, namely what one should do as part of the group-act. Furthermore, this characterization of this type of collective intentional activities is also too narrow. For there are cases where the acts of one member of the group count as the act of the group. But these seem, as Kutz suggests, more complex cases, where members have devices (such as the adoption of special rules) by which the acts of one member count as the act of the group (as in the example of the company's representative who signs a contract). And the account can capture them by adding further conditions that make reference to this type of devices.

Although built on Kutz's model, the alternative account represents a departure from his approach. It construes the idea of participatory intentions in a way which it is not clear that he would defend. And it rejects the idea that an agent who displays a participatory intention must be favourably disposed towards other participants' knowledge of this. The alternative account meets, I think, our test in relation to groups which act with no normative unity.

---

[154] In fact, there can be cases where some intend to do their parts only, whereas the others intend that the group act.

5.3.3 Meeting Condition (b): Groups Which Act with a Normative Unity

We have evaluated Kutz's model by considering groups which act with no normative unity, and in doing so we have developed an alternative account. What about groups which act with a normative unity?

Kutz recognizes that this is a familiar type of collective action, but he says very little about it: "because joint action often occurs in a context of implicit or explicit agreement, other's expectations are raised, generating obligations of trust and reciprocity".[155] In a footnote, he refers to Bratman's argument in support of this idea.[156]

Notice that the response is in accordance with the minimalistic strategy: if we add further conditions to the initial model, more complex cases would be captured. The response is also suggestive. It seems particularly suitable for the activities of groups with a normative unity of type (II). For instance, agreements to do A seem to create duties regardless of whether one thinks of doing A as particularly valuable. But the suggestion must be elaborated. For one thing, it is not the case that agreements create obligations because expectations are raised. More will be said on this point later.

Our alternative account says nothing of the activities of this type of groups. The following chapters will be devoted to them.

5.4 Conclusion

I have claimed that the alternative account, which is built on Kutz's idea of a participatory intention, would capture the activities of groups with no normative unity. It seems that, to capture the activities of groups with a normative unity, we need to incorporate new elements to the picture.

In the next chapter I shall propose an account of the activities groups with a normative unity of type (I). I will try to show that this account, if coupled with additional conditions, would capture some instances of legal practice, namely those which are non-developed.

---

155 *C* 85.
156 *C* 275–276.

Chapter 6
The Activities of Groups with a Normative Unity of Type (I). Non-developed Instances of Legal Practice

6.1 Overview of the Chapter

I shall propose now, first, an account of the activities of groups with a normative unity of type (I) (Section 6.2). Next, by relying on such account, I shall propose an account of non-developed, other-regarding institutions in general (Section 5.3). Finally, by relying on the latter account, I shall propose a model of non-developed instances of the institution in which we are interested, the Judiciary. This will lead us to a characterization of the practice of members of the Judiciary so conceived. Put otherwise, this will lead us to a characterization of the structure and content of non-developed instances of legal practice (Section 5.4). I shall conclude by examining whether this account meets our three tests (Section 5.5).

6.2 The Alternative Account and the Activities of Groups with a Normative Unity of Type (I)

In groups which act with a normative unity of type (I), I claimed, participants consider themselves as under a duty qua members of the group, and this depends on their thinking of the group-activity as valuable in relation to individuals other than themselves. The alternative account of the activities of groups with no normative unity can, I think, be coupled with further conditions, in accordance with the minimalistic strategy, to capture this type of activities.

Consider this proposal:

> There is an intentional activity of a group with a normative unity of type (I) if, and only if, there is a set of individuals (defined intensionally or extensionally) such that:
>
> (a) each of them conceives of a state of affairs the bringing about, involves, or is constituted by, the performance of certain actions and the display of certain attitudes by all members of the set;
> (b) their conceptions of this state of affairs overlap;

R.E. Sánchez Brigido, *Groups, Rules and Legal Practice*,
Law and Philosophy Library 89, DOI 10.1007/978-90-481-8770-6_6,

(c) each intends to perform the relevant actions (and displays the relevant attitudes), and conceives of these actions (and attitudes) as related in the way described to the state of affairs;
(d) each executes his intentions and, as a result, the state of affairs mentioned in (b) is being achieved;
(e) *each believes that the previous conditions obtain, and that the state of affairs being brought about is valuable in relation to individuals other than themselves;*
(f) *each thinks that a normative consideration which makes reference to the value of the state of affairs (a normative consideration according to which everyone who is in a position of, together with others, bringing about a state of affairs that is valuable for individuals other than themselves, should do his part) is applicable to them.*[157]

Consider the model in general. It is just a version of the model of the intentional activities of groups with no normative unity deployed in the previous chapter: it only contains some additions, which are highlighted in italics, namely clauses (e) and (f). This has two implications.

First, it is clear that there is a group which acts intentionally with a normative unity of type (I) if, and only if, conditions (a)–(f) obtain. And it is clear that, from this characterization, we can extract a test of membership. An individual is a member of this sort of group if, and only if, there is a set of individuals (defined intensionally or extensionally) such that: (i) he conceives of a state of affairs the bringing about of which involves, or is constituted by, the performance of certain actions (and the display of attitudes) by him and by the other individuals of the set; (ii) his actions (and attitudes) are seen by the others, together with their own actions (and attitudes), as related in the way described to the state of affairs; (iii) his conception of the state of affairs overlaps with the conceptions of the other individuals; (iv) he intends to perform the relevant actions, and so do the other individuals; (v) he carries out his intention, and so do the other individuals; (vi) he believes that the previous conditions obtain and conceives of the state of affairs that is being achieved as valuable in relation to individuals other than the members of the set; the same applies to the other individuals of the set; (vii) he thinks that a normative consideration which makes reference to the value of the state of affairs (according to which everyone who is in a position of, together with others, bringing about a state of affairs that is valuable for individuals other than themselves, should do his part) is applicable to him; the same can be said of the others. The set of all individuals who satisfy these properties form the group which acts with a normative unity of type (I).

[157] Recall that, throught, when referring to attitudes such as believe/think/conceive/regard etc, I mean actual or counterfactual attitudes.

Second, there is no denial that, just as happened with the model of the activities of groups with no normative unity, additional conditions (such as mutual responsiveness, or common knowledge, or the idea that agents intend not only to do their parts, but also that the group act) should be introduced to capture what takes place in more complex cases. To claim that members intentionally perform their parts is not, besides, to claim that the parts need be completely specified. If they are not, the agents are faced with problems of practical reasoning. Furthermore, this characterization of this type of collective intentional activities is too narrow. For there are cases where the acts of one member of this type of group count as the act of the group. But as said these are more complex cases. They obtain when there are special mechanisms among members (such as the adoption of special rules) to that effect, and the model can capture them by adding further conditions that refer to them.

Consider the model in particular now. The only difference between this model and the model of the intentional activities of groups with no normative unity deployed in the previous chapter are clauses (e) and (f). They are introduced to capture the fact that, when there is an activity of a group with a normative unity of type (I), members conceive of themselves thus: they believe that they have certain duties qua members of the group and this depends on their thinking that the group-activity is valuable in relation to individuals other than themselves.

These self-understandings have several pre-theoretical features. They presuppose that these individuals believe, at least, that there is a group which acts and that they are members. Besides, they depend on members' conceiving of the group-activity as particularly valuable in relation to individuals other than themselves. Finally, they have certain content. *Inter alia*, when a member believes that he has a duty qua member of the group which acts, he believes that, as a member of the group (as a person described in terms of a particular property or properties only, i.e. his being a member or, to put it otherwise, his belonging to a particular kind of group), he ought (where the "ought" brings in the idea of there being a duty) to do certain things. And he so believes because he thinks that there is some general normative consideration (according to which, if one satisfies one, some or all of these properties – i.e. those which add up to his being a member –, then one has a duty to do certain things) that is applicable to him.

To establish whether the model captures these self-understandings we have to see the situation from the point of view of members, as they see it. And the best way of doing so consists of going, in a rough and ready way, through the clauses of the model dispensing, when appropriate, with those components that make reference to attitudes such as "*believe/conceive* etc that...", and considering the content of these attitudes only. If we follow this strategy we notice that members see their situation somewhat along these lines:

> There are several individuals and myself; there is a state of affairs the bringing about of which involves, or is constituted by, me and the rest of the members of the set performing certain actions (and displaying certain attitudes); I intend to perform the relevant actions, and the others intend likewise; we are bringing about the state of affairs, and this state of affairs is valuable in relation to individuals other than us; in short, we form a group which acts and whose activity is valuable in the way described, and I am a member of this group;

this means, in particular, that I satisfy a special property: I am in a position of bringing about, together with the rest of us, a state of affairs which is valuable for individuals other than us; and since there is a normative consideration according to which everyone who satisfies that property should do his part, I ought to do my part.

I think that this captures well participants' self-understandings. First, it captures the fact that the self-understandings (they think "I am under a duty qua member of this group") presuppose, at a minimum, that the agents believe that there is a group which acts and that they are members. This is precisely what our model entails, as our construal of how our individual sees his situation shows: "... in short, we form a group which acts and whose activity is valuable in the way described, and I am a member of this group".

Second, it accounts for the fact that participants' self-understandings depend on their considering the group-activity as particularly valuable in relation to individuals other than themselves. That is precisely what our model entails, as our construal of how our individual sees his situation shows: "... and this state of affairs is valuable in relation to individuals other than us ...".

Thirdly, it captures the fact that these self-understandings have a certain content. Our individual is a member of this type of group. This means that he satisfies several complex properties (see our test of membership above). But it is one particular aspect of his membership, as he sees it, i.e. it is his satisfying some of these properties, which explains his conceiving of himself as under a duty. What explains his self-understanding is his believing that his actions (and attitudes), together with the actions (and attitudes) of the others, stand in an instrumental relation to, or are constitutive of, the bringing about of a state of affairs that is being obtained, that this state of affairs is valuable in the way described, and that there is a normative consideration that imposes on any individual who is in this position (a position of bringing about, together with others, a state of affairs of the sort described) a duty to do his part. That is why our construal of his position goes "... I am a member of this group; this means, *in particular*, that I satisfy a *special* property: I am in a position of bringing about, together with the rest of us, a state of affairs which is valuable for individuals other than us; and since there is a normative consideration according to which everyone who satisfies that property should do his part, I ought to do my part." I have characterized the normative consideration in an abstract and unrefined way deliberately, to allow for the possibility of members thinking of more much more specific or refined versions of it. But despite its abstract character and lack of refinement, the normative consideration is, on its face, plausible. And it is a *duty-imposing* normative consideration, for it imposes a requirement that applies irrespective of (most of) the interests, goals, and desires of the relevant individuals.

To illustrate the model we could simply modify one of the examples of the activities of groups which act with no normative unity. Recall the case of the painters. Participants did not conceive of themselves as under any duty there. But suppose that we change the scenario. For instance, suppose that participants are painting the house and that they conceive of this state of affairs as particularly valuable in relation to individuals other than themselves: the house needs to be painted because it is going to be a rest-home where elderly people will be accommodated. That is, condition (e) above is met. Notice, nevertheless, that this condition alone does not yet suffice. For the case might be such that, despite members thinking of the state of affairs as particularly valuable in the way described, they do not yet consider themselves as under a duty qua members to do their parts. That is why condition (f), which demands that they think that the relevant normative consideration applies, is necessary.

Given that, to capture these self-understandings, we needed clauses (e) and (f), it follows that these clauses are necessary. And I think that these clauses, together with the rest, are also sufficient. In short, our model seems to capture adequately what happens when there is an intentional activity of a group with a normative unity of type (I).

Before concluding let me make one clarification. I claimed above that some groups which act are acting-groups which display a normative unity of type (I) *to a certain degree*, where only *most* members think that they are under a duty. The model can be modified to capture these cases. We only need to replace the "each" that appears in clauses (e) and (f) with a "most" (the "most" is intentionally vague), thus obtaining clauses (e') – "most believe that. . ." – and (f') – "most think that..." – which are identical to the first two save for these minor modifications. So the model should claim that there is a group which acts intentionally *with a certain degree of normative unity of type (I)* if, and only if, clauses (a)-(b)-(c)-(d)-(e')-(f') are met.

6.3 Other-Regarding, Non-developed Institutions

I claimed, in Chapter 1, that there is a recognizable sense of the term "institution" which picks out certain items, namely certain types of groups. I distinguished between other-regarding and self-regarding institutions of this sort. I shall focus on other-regarding institutions only, for ultimately we are concerned with the Judiciary, which is an institution of this type. In fact, I shall focus on one of the two sub-types of other-regarding institutions, namely on the non-developed instances, putting aside, for the moment, developed instances. In non-developed institutions, we should recall, (most) members conceive of the group-activity as valuable in relation to individuals other than themselves, and in relation to (some aspect(s) of) the society as a whole. And they would not conceive of themselves as under a duty qua members if they thought otherwise.

So I claimed, in Chapter 1, that these institutions have certain pre-analytic features. Firstly, if there is an other-regarding, non-developed institution, then there is a group which acts intentionally for a significant period of time only if (most of) its members follow, and are disposed to follow, some rule(s) for a significant period of time. Secondly, if there is an institution of this sort, (most) members of the group think of the activity as purporting to be valuable in relation, primarily, to non-members and in relation to (some aspect(s) of) the community or society as a whole. Thirdly, if there is an institution of this sort, (most) members of the group just described (i.e. the group characterized by the two foregoing features) think that they have a duty qua members of such group (although in many cases they think that they have a duty qua members of the institution), and this depends on their thinking of the group-activity as actually valuable in relation to individuals other than themselves, and in relation to (some aspect(s) of) the society as a whole.

It is clear, then, that institutions of this sort are particular kinds of groups which act intentionally (see especially the first feature). And that they are groups which act intentionally with a normative unity of type (I), when all members think that they have a duty qua members, or groups which act intentionally and which display *a certain degree* of normative unity of type (I), for there are cases where only *most* members think that they have a duty qua members (see the two other features).[158] So we can rely on the models of groups deployed in the previous section to propose a theoretical characterization of these institutions. We only need to expand them in some respects. Consider the following proposal:

> There is an other-regarding, non-developed institution if, and only if, there is a set of individuals (defined intensionally or extensionally) such that:
>
> (a) each of them conceives of a state of affairs the bringing about of which is *constituted* by the performance of certain actions (and the display of certain attitudes) by all members of the set: *their following, and intending to follow, some rule(s) for a significant period of time;*
> (b) their conceptions of this state of affairs overlap;
> (c) each intends to *follow the rule(s), and conceives of his following the rule(s)* as related in the way described to the state of affairs; *his intentions are publicly accessible*;
> (d) each executes his intentions for a significant period of time and, as a result, the state of affairs mentioned in (b) obtains;
> (e) either: (i) each believes that the previous conditions obtain, and that the state of affairs being brought about is valuable, primarily, in relation to a set of individuals other than themselves *and in relation to (some aspect(s) of) the life of the community as a whole*; or (ii) most believe that;
> (f) either: (i) each thinks that a normative consideration that makes reference to the value of the state of affairs (according to which everyone who is in a position of, together with others, bringing about a state of affairs that is valuable in relation to individuals other than themselves, *and to (some aspect(s) of) the life of the community as a whole,* should do his part) is applicable to them; or (ii) most think that.

Consider the model in general. It is simply a combination of two slightly modified versions of the model of the activities of groups with a normative unity of type (I) and of the model of the activities of groups with a certain degree of normative

[158] It seems that not all other-regarding, non-developed institutions are groups which act *with a certain degree* of normative unity of type (I). There might be cases where all must think that they have a duty qua members for the group to qualify as an institution. For instance, cases where, if one individual did not think that he has a duty qua member, the rest would not consider him a member.

unity of type (I) deployed in the previous section. The differences are highlighted in italics. For these institutions are groups which act intentionally of a particular type (this is what clauses (a)–(d) attempt to capture). And they are groups which act intentionally *with a (certain degree of) normative unity of type (I)* (this is what clauses (e) and (f)) attempt to capture). This has two implications.

Firstly, we can extract from the model a test to establish when an individual is a member of an other-regarding, non-developed institution. I shall not deploy, nevertheless, for it can be easily construed by following the strategy that we followed before. Secondly, this model is minimalistic. There is no denial that additional conditions (such as mutual responsiveness, or common knowledge, or the idea that the individuals intend not only to do their parts, but also that the group act) should be introduced to capture what takes place in more complex cases. This characterization is, besides, too narrow. For there are cases where the acts of only one member of this type of group count as the act of the group. But, as said, these cases seem to be more complex cases where there are special mechanisms among members to that effect, and they can be captured by adding clauses.

Consider the clauses in particular now. The idea that there is a set of individuals is clearly necessary, for institutions of this type are groups, and this requires that there be a set of individuals.

Clause (a) demands that participants conceive of a state of affairs the bringing about of which is constituted by the actions and attitudes (their intending to follow, and following, some rule(s) – which, I assumed, involves acting on a special kind of reason – during a significant period of time) of all members of the set.

I think that claiming that participants think of the bringing about of the state of affairs as something which is *constituted by* (not as something that merely involves) the actions and attitudes of the members of the set is correct. For if they thought of the bringing about of the state of affairs as something which merely involves the actions of all, this would imply that the actions are seen as standing in a sort of instrumental relation to the bringing about of the state of affairs, as if its existence could be conceived of independently of the relevant actions. And the latter seems not to be the case with institutions. It seems that the achievement of relevant state of affairs (the institutional activity) could not be conceived of independently of the relevant attitudes and actions.

Consider now the idea of intentions. One pre-theoretical feature of these institutions is that members must be disposed to follow some rule(s). Our clause proposes a theoretical understanding of these dispositions. They are construed as intentions, which are, we assumed, special types of mental states that involve a commitment (and hence a disposition) to act in a certain way. In this case, to follow some rule(s). It construes the dispositions in such terms because these institutions are groups which act intentionally and, as I have already argued, nothing counts as a group of that sort unless members have formed the relevant intentions. And since the state of affairs is something the bringing about of which is seen as partly constituted by these attitudes (intentions), this is why clause (a) incorporates the idea.

Focus now on clause (b), which requires overlap in participants' conceptions of the state of affairs. I think that this clause is also necessary. These institutions are groups which act intentionally and, as already argued above, nothing counts as a group of that sort unless there is overlap among members' conceptions of the state of affairs. Notice that this clause implies that there is overlap in their conceptions of the rule(s) too, for it is their following the rule(s) which is partly constitutive of the bringing about of the state of affairs.

Condition (c), which demands that participants intend to follow the rule(s), is also necessary. One pre-analytic feature of these institutions, we claimed, is that its members must be disposed to follow some rule(s). The model construes these dispositions, for the reasons mentioned above, as intentions. Besides, it is not the case that they are merely disposed to follow the rule(s). Rather, they conceive of their following the rule(s) as constitutive of the bringing about of the relevant state of affairs. Put otherwise, each conceives of his following the rule(s) as his doing his part of the achievement of a collective end. It must be so, for these institutions are groups which act intentionally and, as argued before, nothing counts as a group of that sort unless members display these intentions. The public accessibility feature of these intentions, which I shall understand as meaning that each participant is disposed to disclose his intention to the others, seems also a necessary feature. If they kept their intentions in secret, these institutions would be, I submit, unrecognizable.

Clause (d) only states explicitly that, as a result of participants executing their overlapping participatory intentions for a significant period of time, the relevant state of affairs obtains. As argued above, there is no group which acts intentionally, and hence no institution, unless this is the case.

Clauses (e) and (f) are introduced to capture, together with the other clauses, the pre-analytical feature according to which, when there is an institution of this type, all members (or most members) conceive of themselves in a particular way: they believe that they have certain duties qua members of a particular type of group which acts.

Now it is quite obvious that these clauses are fit for the task. For there is no significant difference between participants' self-understandings when the individuals form an institution of this type and when they form a group which acts with a normative of type (I). After all, these institutions *are* particular kinds of groups with a normative unity of type (I). And there is no significant difference between clauses (e) and (f) of our model and the clauses of our model of groups with a normative unity of type (I) deployed in the previous section, which captured participants' self-understandings. So the same considerations that we mentioned when discussing that model apply here, and I shall not repeat the argument.

Notice, just to illustrate, how participants see their situation in our institutions once we follow the strategy used before (that is, by going, in a rough and ready way, through the clauses of our model dispensing, when appropriate, with those components that make reference to attitudes such as "*believe/conceive* etc that...", and considering the content of these attitudes only). If we follow this strategy we notice that members of our institutions see their situation somewhat along these lines:

> There are several individuals and myself; there is a state of affairs the bringing about of which is constituted by me and the other individuals intending to follow, and following, some rule(s) for a significant period of time; I intend (and this is no secret) to follow this rule or rules, I follow them, and the others intend and act likewise; we are bringing about the state of affairs, and this state of affairs is valuable, primarily, in relation to individuals other than us, and in relation to (some aspect(s) of) the life of the community as a whole; in short, we form a group which acts and whose activity is valuable in the way described, and I am a member of this group; this means, in particular, that I satisfy a special property: I am in a position of bringing about, together with the rest of us, a state of affairs which is valuable in the way described; and since there is a normative consideration according to which everyone who satisfies that property should do his part (follow the relevant rule(s)), I ought to do my part (I ought to follow the relevant rule(s)).

This way of understanding their situation is almost identical to the way in which members of a group with a normative unity of type (I) see their situation, as shown in the previous section. After all, to insist, these institutions *are* particular kinds of groups with a normative unity of type (I). So the same considerations apply.

The only point worth considering here is this. As said, when there is an institution of the kind we are interested in, participants believe that they have a duty qua members of a particular group (not necessarily qua members of an institution). Our model captures this feature. The model does not entail that participants believe there is an institution, i.e. a group as defined by conditions (a)–(f), and that they are members of an institution so defined. That is why our construal goes "... in short, we form a group which acts whose activity is valuable in the way described, and I am a member of this group", and not "... in short, we form an institution, and I am a member of this institution". For participants need not have the concept of an institution. Of course, participants normally have the concept, and are normally aware that there is an institution and that they are members. Put otherwise, they are aware that conditions (a)–(f) obtain. And this is why they conceive of themselves "as a member of this institution I ought to...". But this need not be the case (I shall mention an example below). Recall that the model is minimalistic. That is, it does not deny that further conditions may be required to capture what happens in more complex cases. The model focuses on the simplest ones; once we understand them, we can understand the complex ones. And this aspect of complex cases can be captured by adding clauses, in accordance to the minimalistic strategy.

Given that clauses (e) and (f), together with the other ones, are indispensable to capture the presence of these self-understandings in the right way, these clauses are necessary. And they are, I think, also sufficient for there to be an institution of this type.

Consider an example now. Suppose that an individual notices that children from a poor background need to be nourished adequately. He thinks that, given this and other circumstances (say, he has a lot of free time and he is relatively well-off), he is under a duty to remedy this situation. But he cannot remedy this situation alone. The situation is so bad that he needs several individuals acting, and being disposed to act, in concert for a significant period of time. He therefore designs a plan, i.e. a set of rules to be followed by several individuals, including him, for a certain period of time (how meals are to be cooked, served, and so on). He conceives of the scenario where these individuals abide by his plan as a state of affairs the bringing about of which is constituted by the actions (and attitudes) of all of them, and as a state of affairs which, if obtained, would be valuable in relation to the children, and indirectly to the life of the community as a whole. Many learn of his plan and show up. Each forms the intention to follow it, and this is clear to all. Each of them thinks that their actions and attitudes are constitutive of the bringing about of the would-be state of affairs, and their conceptions of the state of affairs overlap. In other words, clauses (a) and (b) of our model are met. In fact, most think that this state of affairs, if achieved, would be valuable in the way described, and that a normative consideration that makes reference to the state of affairs being valuable in this way (according to which everyone who is in a position of bringing about, together with others, a valuable state of affairs of this sort, should do his or her part) is applicable to them. But this group does not act yet. Suppose now that they begin to follow their parts of the plan, that this situation persists for many years, and that they all believe that this is the case. Naturally, since most thought, before executing their intentions, that the state of affairs that could be brought about would be valuable in the way described, now that the state of affairs is being obtained most think of it as valuable in the way described. So clauses (c)–(f) of our model are also met. These individuals form, in other words, a particular type of group which acts and which displays a normative unity of type (I) to a certain degree. We have arrived at a point in the story where it is clear, I submit, that there is an institution in this neighbourhood. Say, a charity. And it is a point where conditions (a)-(f) are met. So the model seems to capture well what takes place in these institutions. (This example shows clearly, I think, that members need not be aware that there is an institution of this type, i.e. a group defined in terms of conditions (a)–(f), for them to belong to one.)

So the model seems adequate. These institutions, of course, might become more complex. Consider this possibility.

Suppose that in our charity members want to feed more children than the group has managed to nourish so far, and more adequately. But to do this they need more individuals participating. They need more members. So they conceive of a second state of affairs. It is a state of affairs the bringing about of which will be constituted by the performance of certain actions and the display of certain attitudes by *all* the relevant individuals (the initial members, and the new would-be members): their following, and intending to follow, the plan. Of course, they all understand that the would-be members might be less committed than they are, and might not follow the plan. But the situation is such that, if they do not follow it, this will not hinder the achievement of the first state of affairs, i.e. the state of affairs which is being obtained now, which is still acceptable. So suppose that they adopt a special rule to incorporate new members. For instance, a rule according to which, if an individual shows a disposition to participate and is seen as fit for the job, he will count as a member. Here this simply means: "we will see his actions and attitudes as partly constitutive of the bringing about of the second state of affairs". Suppose that some individuals show up, and that they are incorporated. Here this simply means: everyone, the new individuals included, understands now that their actions and attitudes will be seen as partly constitutive of the bringing about of the second state of affairs. The new individuals are not active members yet, for they do not perform the relevant actions. At this stage they are, so to speak, "formal" members. So the first state of affairs is being obtained. But the second state of affairs would be obtained if (and only if) the formal members did their parts, i.e. if (and only if) they became active members.

The possibility of incorporating new members just described is, I think, quite common. Notice that, when the new individuals have just been incorporated but not performed the relevant actions yet, there are two groups which are inter-related. That is, there is a set of individuals who satisfy conditions (a)–(f) of the model (the initial members) which is related in a particular way to another set of individuals (those who have been incorporated, i.e. the formal members). Due to the incorporation of new members, we can say that both groups form the non-developed, other-regarding institution. This idea is not captured by the model as it stands, for according to it an institution of this type is a set of individuals who satisfy conditions (a)–(f). And here there are two sets of individuals (two groups) which are interrelated, and only one of them satisfies those conditions. Moreover, according to the model, the new individuals are not members of the institution, for they do not satisfy our test of membership above: they do not execute their intentions.

This does not represent any particular problem, nevertheless, for this case is more complex. The model focuses on the simplest cases, and can be expanded to capture more complex cases. It can be expanded to capture the sense in which all these individuals form the institution. The expanded model should simply claim that, in this sort of complex case, "institution" refers to a complex group formed by two sub groups. One of them is a set of individuals described in terms of conditions (a)–(f) suggested by the minimalistic model, the other is a set of individuals who, due to the adoption of special rules, have been incorporated in the sense described. This is simply an expanded model, for it employs clauses (a)–(f). And from this expanded model we can extract an expanded test of membership. An individual is a member of this sort of institution if, and only if, there is a set of individuals such that he: (i) either satisfies the conditions mentioned in our test of membership above, or (ii) has been incorporated in the way described (he is a formal member); but (iii) most of these individuals must satisfy our test of membership above; otherwise the institution would vanish.

These remarks are important for the following reason. In my initial approximation to non-developed, other-regarding institutions I claimed that one of their features (see the first feature above) is that they are groups which act intentionally only if (most of) its members follow, and are disposed to follow, some rule(s). I employed the "most" (which is intentionally vague) and used the brackets because, in some cases, there is an institution of this type (and hence a group which acts intentionally) where certain individuals count as members of the institution (and hence as members of the group which acts intentionally) even if they are not disposed to follow, or even if they do not follow, the relevant rule(s). The model does not capture these cases. For it entails that, in all cases, these institutions are groups which act only if *all* their members follow, and are disposed to follow, some rule(s).

And it entails that, in all cases, an individual is a member of an other-regarding, non-developed institution only if he follows, and is disposed to follow, the relevant rule(s).

Cases where we claim that there is an other-regarding, non-developed institution (and hence a group which acts intentionally) and where only most members are disposed to follow, and do follow, some rule(s) – and therefore cases where certain individuals count as members even if they do not follow, or even if they are not disposed to follow, the relevant rule(s) – are, I believe, more complex cases. The case of the charity is one of such cases. The new individuals count as members because of a special rule to that effect. They have not followed the plan yet. So they count as members even if they have not followed the plan yet. And we can claim that here there is an institution (and hence a group which acts intentionally) where only *most* of its members are following some rule(s). But this case can be captured, I have suggested, by expanding the model. Here "institution" refers to a complex group formed by two subgroups which are inter-related, namely the sub group of the initial members plus the sub group of formal members. Only the first sub group acts intentionally, the second has not acted intentionally yet. So the claim that here there is an institution (and hence a group which acts intentionally) where only most of its members are following some rule(s) simply means: there is a complex group (formed by two sub groups which are inter-related, i.e. the initial, active members, and the new, formal members) part of which acts intentionally (namely the first subgroup); so only most members of the complex group (namely the initial members) are following the relevant rules.

I think that we can generalize. All cases where we claim that there is an other-regarding, non-developed institution (and hence a group which acts intentionally) and where only most (not all) members (are disposed to) follow some rule(s) – and hence cases where an individual counts as a member regardless of whether he is disposed to follow, or follows, the rule(s) – are more complex cases, where "institution" refers, in part, to a complex group (a set of individuals defined in terms of certain properties) part of which (a sub group of the complex group) acts intentionally. Accordingly, these cases can be captured by expanding the model. And the fact that an individual counts as a member of the institution (the complex group) even if he does not follow, or is not disposed to follow, the rule(s), can be captured by extracting from the expanded model an expanded test of membership. Or, at any rate, I cannot think of any example to the contrary.

So the minimalistic model seems adequate. It captures all the simplest cases of other-regarding, non-developed institutions, and can be expanded to capture more complex cases.

These institutions can become even more complex. For instance, in our charity participants might become aware that they form an institution and adopt a rule of the form "an individual counts as a member of this institution only after procedure X is followed". Suppose that all the former members have left, and that others have been incorporated through the procedure. All of them are formal members now but, let us assume, they are also doing their parts. They are active members too. Suppose now that some of them have left, and that new individuals are incorporated through the procedure to replace them. They count as members (as formal members) that very moment, even if they have not followed the plan yet. This case is even more complex, not least because participants have adopted a rule that makes reference to the institution itself, a possibility that is not captured by the minimalistic model. But here, again, "institution" refers in part to a complex group (a set of individuals defined in terms of certain formal properties) part of which (namely the sub group of formal and active members) acts intentionally. So this sort of complex case can be captured by expanding the model. And from it we can extract an expanded test of membership. Notice that the expanded test of membership should state that an individual is not a member of a complex group of this sort unless: most of the other individuals of the set conceive of a state of affairs the bringing about of which is constituted by their actions and attitudes (their following the plan); have overlapping conceptions of the relevant state of affairs; intend, publicly, to follow the relevant plan; execute their intentions; and think of the state of affairs that is being obtained as valuable in the way described such that a normative consideration of the type described above is applicable to them. For if these conditions were not met the whole group would not be an other-regarding, non-developed institution. And hence an individual could not count as a member of the institution.

The situation might become more complex in other ways. But I shall not consider further complexities, for these institutions seem rare. They cannot survive the possibility of alienation. They are non-developed. Recall our thought-experiment. When envisioning an institution, suppose that most of its members think of the activity as valuable in the sense described. Suppose now that each of the relevant members stops thinking, individually, of the activity in this way. If, for that reason, each of them would stop thinking of himself as under a duty, then the institution is a non-developed one. In fact, we should say that the institution *was* an institution, for a necessary condition for the existence of any institution is that (most of) its members think of themselves as under a duty qua members. This is what happens in our model. If most of the relevant members realized that the group-activity is not in effect valuable in the way described, they would stop thinking of themselves as under a duty qua members, and hence the institution would vanish that very moment. Few institutions seem to be of this type.

6.4 Non-developed Instances of the Judiciary

We have at our disposal, I think, enough material to sketch a model of non-developed instances of the Judiciary. On the one hand, we have the results of our previous inquiry of other accounts. Raz's views are particularly relevant in this respect. When inspecting his model, in Chapter 3, I concluded that, although he did not provide a complete characterization of the Judiciary, at least this partial characterization could be attributed to him: there is a group of individuals (most of) whose members follow some rule(s) which require that they evaluate conduct by applying norms identified by criteria contained in it, norms that form a system (they are internally related norms) which is open, comprehensive and supreme. I also claimed that there is reason to think that these conditions are necessary for there to be an instance of the Judiciary. On the other hand, we can avail ourselves of the minimalistic model of other-regarding, non-developed institutions just sketched. This model, if adequately coupled with Raz's conditions, should be helpful to provide an appropriate characterization of non-developed instances of the Judiciary. Consider the following proposal.

> There is a non-developed instance of the Judiciary if, and only if, there is a set of individuals (defined extensionally or intensionally) such that
>
> (a) each of them conceives of a state of affairs the bringing about of which is constituted by all of them performing certain actions (and displaying certain attitudes): *intending to follow, and following, a rule or rules which require that the conduct of members of the community be evaluated according to norms that satisfy certain criteria, norms that form a system (they are internally related norms) which is open, comprehensive and supreme;*
> (b) their conceptions of this state of affairs overlap;
> (c) each intends to follow the rule(s), and conceives of his following the rule(s) as related in the way described to the state of affairs; his intention is publicly accessible;
> (d) each executes his intention for a significant period of time and, as a result, the state of affairs mentioned in (b) is being brought about;
> (e) either: (i) each believes that the previous conditions obtain, and consider the state of affairs that is being brought about as valuable, primarily, in relation to individuals other than themselves, and in relation to the life of the community as a whole; or (ii) most believe that;
> (f) either: (i) each thinks that a normative consideration which makes reference to the value of the state of affairs (which requires that everyone who is in a position of, together with others, bringing about a state of affairs that is valuable in relation to individuals other than themselves, and in relation to the life of the community as a whole should do his or her part) is applicable to them; or (ii) most think that.

This model of the Judiciary is just a more specific version of the minimalistic model of non-developed, other-regarding institutions sketched in the previous section. It only contains some additions, which are highlighted in italics. So each of the clauses, putting aside the particular way of describing the state of affairs, should be understood accordingly. Besides, if the Judiciary is an other-regarding institution, if there are non-developed instances of the Judiciary (as I claimed there might be), then the clauses, putting aside the particular way of describing the state of affairs, must be individually necessary and jointly sufficient to capture non-developed instances of the Judiciary.

It should also be clear what the particular characterization of participants' conceptions of the state of affairs is. These ideas are, essentially, the same as Raz's, and I have already described what Raz's idea of a system of internally related norms, etc, which appears in our description of participants' conceptions of the state of affairs, involves.

Besides, from the model we can extract a general characterization of officials, when the Judiciary is a non-developed institution. But I shall not do so here, for the characterization is very easy to construe.

Finally, the explanation of why members of other-regarding, non-developed institutions in general conceive of themselves as under a duty qua members of a particular type of group which acts put forward above applies here as well, so I shall not repeat the argument.

This model is adequate to capture some of the cases mentioned in my initial characterization of non-developed instances of the Judiciary, but not all of them. In some cases there is a non-developed instance of the Judiciary and yet *only most* (not all) members (are disposed to) follow the relevant rule(s); and in some cases (most) members think of themselves *as under a duty qua members of the institution* (and not merely qua members a particular type of group which acts). But these cases are more complex cases and, as I have suggested above, they can be captured by expanding the model just sketched, which is minimalistic.

I shall not discuss the model more, for most of the work has been done in the previous section.[159] But the main reason for not discussing the model more is that these instances of the Judiciary seem very rare. They are non-developed instances. And more often than not the Judiciary is a developed institution, not a non-developed one. In fact, I would say that all actual instances of the Judiciary are developed ones. In other words, in actual instances of legal practice it is possible that most officials regard themselves as under a duty qua members even if they do not think of the activity ascribable to the group as particularly valuable. Put otherwise, in actual instances of legal practice the Judiciary is an institution that can survive the possibility of alienation. Recall the thought-experiment. Assume that most members of the American Judiciary (officials) think of the activity as valuable. Suppose now that each of them is sitting at his desk and that each stops thinking of the activity in this way. It seems clear to me that each of them would still consider himself as under a duty qua official, despite not thinking of the activity as valuable in the relevant way any more. They would perhaps think that they should resign. But resigning is an act that is thought of as extinguishing their duties qua officials. This presupposes that they still think of themselves as under a duty until resignation takes place. They would not believe that their realization that the activity is invaluable is sufficient to extinguish their duties.

Before concluding let me now return to three issues that I left open in previous chapters and deserve consideration.

Firstly, recall the Hartian account (as deployed in the Postscript) and the conventionalist account. There are several aspects of both models that are incorrect, as I attempted to show. But there is one common element which I did not criticize.

---

[159]That said, I deploy and discuss below (Chapters 9 and 10) an account of *developed* instances of legal practice, and most of the claims I make there by way of discussion are applicable here too.

Putting details aside, both models claim that, when there is an instance of legal practice, members follow the relevant rule *only if others do so*. This element contains, I think, a grain of truth, and hence it could be regarded as necessary. Our model helps us to see that, in a sense, it is. Essentially, if members followed the relevant rule with complete disregard of what others do (i.e. even if they thought that nobody else was following the rule), they could not think of themselves, in so doing, as members of a group. And officials do conceive of themselves as members. Our model retains, then, this aspect of Hart's and the conventionalist account (at least in relation to non-developed instances of legal practice).

Secondly, recall Raz's account. Our model retains many of its elements. But it also helps to show more clearly which elements are missing. I suggested, for instance, that the simplified Razian model would not contain sufficient conditions in relation to non-developed instances. The model in question, let us recall, is this: there is a non-developed instance of the Judiciary if there is a set of individuals who follow some rule(s) (requiring them to evaluate conduct by applying norms identified by criteria contained in it, norms which form a system which is open, comprehensive and supreme) because they think that doing so is valuable, primarily, in relation to individuals other than themselves and to the community as a whole. On this view it suffices, at bottom, that there be a set of individuals who are following a particular type of rule (each for certain reasons). And I suggested that we would not treat a set of individuals so defined *as a group which acts intentionally*, and hence as an institution. I suggested that something would be missing. We can now see what. For our model shows that several elements are absent from the picture. The requirements that members of the set conceive of their following the rule(s), and of the system, as a state of affairs the bringing about of which is constituted by their actions and attitudes, that they intend to follow the rule(s), and that they conceive of these actions as contributions to the state of affairs in a way which is publicly accessible, are absent. And these are the elements which explain in what sense the Judiciary is a group which acts intentionally. Moreover, the view we discussed does not require that members believe that the relevant normative consideration is applicable. So it does not account for the fact that it is a group which acts intentionally *with a normative unity of type (I)*.

Finally, let us come back for a moment to Shapiro's account. Our model also retains many aspects of it. But it also shows which elements are missing. I suggested, for instance, that one way of reading his model (which claims that a non-developed instance of the Judiciary exists if there is a group of individuals who satisfy the conditions of his model – they intend to contribute by way of meshing subplans, etc – plus the condition that they intend to contribute because they think of the group-activity as valuable in the required way) would not contain sufficient conditions to capture non-developed instances. We can see now see why. Several elements are absent too. This reading of Shapiro's model employs the idea of a unified system, a group of norms that satisfy the same criteria, but not the idea that these norms form a special kind of system which is open, comprehensive and supreme. And it does not require that members conceive of their following the rule(s), and of the system, as a state of affairs the bringing about of which is constituted by their actions and attitudes. Nor does it require that they believe that the relevant normative consideration is applicable.

In short, from the model just sketched we can extract a particular view of the content and structure of legal practice, when legal practice is understood as the practice of members of a non-developed instance of the Judiciary. The *content* of the practice is this: there is a group which regularly evaluates the conduct of members of the community by applying norms that satisfy certain criteria, norms that form a special kind of system. The *structure* of the practice, i.e. the attitudes that participants display, is quite complex: they see their doing this (where "their doing this" is tantamount to "our group doing this") as constituted by a complex set of attitudes and actions, and they think that a normative consideration that makes reference to the value of such state of affairs requires that they perform the relevant actions.

6.5 Meeting the Tests

We can examine now whether our account meets our three tests. The first test requires from a theory that claims that legal practice is a collective activity that it propose an account of collective intentional action that captures the main features of collective intentional actions. I have already attempted to show, in the previous chapter, that this test is met in relation to the intentional activities of groups with no normative unity. In this chapter I have tried to show that an extended model can be used to capture the activities of groups with a normative unity of type (I). We still have, nevertheless, to propose a model of the activities of groups with a normative unity of type (II). So the test is met in part.

Our second test requires of a theory of legal practice that it provide a characterization of its content, and of its structure, such that conceiving of the practice in these terms captures its main features, namely that it is the practice of members of an institution (a group with the special features I mentioned in Chapter 1).

Recall that the first conditions are understood as bringing in standard requirements, such as consistency, non-circularity, etc. In particular, the favoured category of practices (the practice in terms of which legal practice should, according to the theory, be understood) cannot be characterized using the notion of an institution in an un-analyzed way. I have provided a characterization of legal practice's content and structure, when legal practice is the practice of members of non-developed instances of the Judiciary, which, I have attempted to show, is adequate in this respect. In particular, the account does not characterize the favoured category of practices using the notion of an institution in an un-analyzed way. On the contrary, it relies on an analysis of this notion. So these requirements, in relation to non-developed instances at least, are met. Nevertheless, we still need an account of developed instances. So this aspect of the test is met in part.

The test also requires that the theory furnish us with necessary and sufficient conditions for there to be an instance of legal practice. It seems to me that the conditions mentioned in the account are, in relation to non-developed instances, necessary.

And they also seem sufficient. The theory entails that, if there is a non-developed instance of legal practice as characterized by it, there is an instance of the practice of members of an institution, a (complex) group of individuals (part of) which acts intentionally (it evaluates the conduct of members of the community by applying certain norms). It also entails that (most of) its members are following some rule(s). Finally, it entails that, if there is a non-developed instance of legal practice, (most) members of the institution intelligibly conceive of themselves as under a duty qua members, and that this depends on their considering the activity as particularly valuable in the way described. The intelligibility feature is explained in the right way. Of course, we have still to provide an account of developed instances. So this aspect of the test is met only partially.

Thus, our second test is met only partially because we have proposed an account of non-developed instances of legal practice only. We still need a theory of developed instances.

Our third test requires that a theory of legal practice should provide a characterization of legal practice that explains why in D officials disagree about what some of the criteria of legality are (they all agree that they should apply norms that satisfy criteria C1 and C2, but disagree about whether they should also apply norms that satisfy criterion C3 or C4); when they disagree, they count their social practice as grounding their assertions as to what the criteria that should be applied are. Each believes that his view is sounder, and the disagreement proves endless.

If D were a non-developed instance of legal practice, this disagreement (as to whether C3 or C4 ought to be employed) would be unintelligible. For these instances of the practice obtain only if there is at least one rule in the group, one shared rule, which requires that they evaluate conduct by applying certain criteria, and the only rule which is shared in any relevant sense according to our model is the rule whose content is exhausted by participants' overlapping conceptions. So participants could not claim that C3 (or C4) is the criterion to be applied by appealing in part to the practice itself. For in D there would be no shared rule, and hence no practice, to that effect. Consequently this test is not met.

6.6 Conclusion

I have proposed an allegedly adequate account of non-developed instances of legal practice. But there is no explanation of developed instances of legal practice yet. We need an account of the latter for, as we claimed, few instances of legal practice (if any) are non-developed.

Developed instances of legal practice are the practices of members of developed instances of the Judiciary. A developed instance of the Judiciary is in part a group which acts intentionally, (most of) whose members conceive of themselves as under a duty qua members even if they do not think of the group-activity as particularly valuable in relation to individuals other than themselves, or in relation to the community as a whole. So a developed instance of the Judiciary is, it should be clear, a particular group which acts and which displays a (certain degree of) normative unity of type (II). Thus, we could attempt to provide an account of developed instances of the Judiciary by relying on an account of the activities of groups with a normative unity of type (II).

We have already seen some possibilities suggested by Bratman and Kutz in this respect: to incorporate into thc picturc the idea that participants have agreed, or promised, or that they have created legitimate expectations, or something along such lines. Before exploring these possibilities we shall inspect very briefly one prominent account, Gilbert's, which is based on a different idea. If correct, it would explain the activities of groups with a normative unity of type (II)[160] and, accordingly, it might enable us to build an account of developed instances of the Judiciary.

[160]For reasons of space, I shall ignore the other prominent account of collective intentional activities that, if correct, would perhaps capture the activities of groups with a normative unity of type (II), namely Tuomela's. See nevertheless n 176 below.

Chapter 7
Gilbert's Account of Collective Activities

7.1 Overview of the Chapter

I shall present the core idea of Gilbert's account first (Section 7.2). I shall then assess it and, while doing so, I shall suggest a first approximation to an alternative (Section 7.3). This will pave the way towards a proper account of the activities of groups with a normative unity of type (II), to be developed later.

7.2 Gilbert's Account

For Gilbert, if two or more people are involved in a collective activity, they form what she labels "the plural subject of a goal". Thus, if two people are on a walk together, they form the plural subject of the goal of walking together. The notion of a plural subject is a technical notion introduced in her earlier writings, and her characterization of it is somewhat intriguing. But in her later work she attempts to clarify it in these terms: two or more people constitute the plural subject of a goal if, and only if, they are jointly committed to accepting the goal of J-ing "as a body".[161] Her account of collective activities can be put thus:

> Two or more people are involved in the collective action of J-ing if, and only if, they are jointly committed to accepting the goal of J-ing as a body and each one is acting in a way appropriate to the achievement of that goal in the light of the fact that each is subject to the joint commitment.[162]

[161] *LT* 8; CJC 73–74.

[162] This follows from the previous considerations and from Gilbert's contentions in Gilbert (2002, 68). For reasons of space, I am deliberately ignoring Gilbert's views as to how joint commitments arise: namely if, and only if, it is population common knowledge that each has expressed individually, intentionally, and openly his or her readiness to be jointly committed to accepting the goal of J-ing as a body (CJC 87–88, 92–93; her detailed construal of each of these technical notions – population, common knowledge, etc – appears in OSF Chapter 4). Suffice it to say here that, if the contentions I put forward below are correct, these technical notions are superfluous to understand collective intentional action.

R.E. Sánchez Brigido, *Groups, Rules and Legal Practice*, Law and Philosophy Library 89, DOI 10.1007/978-90-481-8770-6_7,

Consider, first, the general idea of being *jointly committed* to accepting the goal of J-ing as a body. According to Gilbert, two or more people can be jointly committed to many different things as a body. They can be jointly committed to intending something as a body, to upholding a decision as a body, to planning something as a body, etc. In the case of collective actions, agents are jointly committed to accepting or endorsing the goal of J-ing as a body.

The basic idea is that agents join forces toward the achievement of the goal by each committing himself or herself together with others in a particular way, i.e. by becoming "jointly committed". The main properties of a joint commitment are these: (a) it involves more than one person and, special cases aside, the creation of a joint commitment requires the participation of all parties (the "special cases aside" qualification is introduced because there might be cases where there are special background understandings, involving all the parties, that allow for the creation of a joint commitment by some proper subset of the parties only); (b) each party is answerable to all parties for any violation of the joint commitment; (c) normally, the joint commitment is not rescindable by either party unilaterally, but only by the parties together; (d) each party is committed through the joint commitment; one may speak of associated individual commitments; the content of these individuals commitments is to promote, to the best of one's ability, the object of the joint commitment; (e) these individual commitments are interdependent: one's commitment cannot exist independently of the other's commitment; (f) the dependent individual commitments come into being simultaneously at the time of the creation of the joint commitment; finally, (g) if individuals are jointly committed, relevant entitlements and obligations will be in place, and we can expect the parties to know this.[163]

Thus, the example above of Jack and Sue walking together would be construed by Gilbert in part as Jack and Sue being jointly committed. This, according to Gilbert, would explain the pre-analytic features we considered. For instance, we noted that, if Jack inadvertently draws ahead, Sue will see herself as being in a position to criticize him mildly, or rebuking him, and that this suggested that they conceive of themselves as under a duty qua members of the group. This feature would, on Gilbert's view, be captured by properties (b) and (g). We also noticed that if Jack wishes not to walk together anymore, he will think that he needs to seek (in some way or another) for Sue's acquiescence, for her approval, in order to call the joint project off. This feature would be captured, on Gilbert's view, by property (c). Besides, although we did not focus on this, it seems that this would be a normal way of starting a walk together: A: "Would you like me to go with you?"; B: "Yes, please do". It seems that this feature would be captured, on Gilbert's view, by properties (a) and (f).

Consider now the content of the joint commitment, namely that of *accepting or endorsing the goal of J-ing as a body*. Gilbert claims that joint espousal of a goal can be interpreted roughly as follows: "the relevant joint commitment is an instruction to the parties to see it that they act in such a way as to emulate the best they can a

[163] See especially CJC 77–79, 90–91.

single body with the goal in question".[164] This way of describing the content of the joint commitment is meant to capture in a generic way, according to Gilbert, what is achieved by becoming jointly committed: "a binding together of a set of individual wills so as to constitute a single, 'plural will' dedicated to a particular goal".[165]

7.3 Assessing Gilbert's Account

Recall that a theory of collective activities should, according to our test, propose an account of collective intentional action such that it captures the main features of collective intentional action which we mentioned. As said, the account must be clear, simple, not uninformatively circular, consistent, etc. Besides, since there are two main types of collective intentional activities (the activities of groups with a normative unity -of type (I) and of type (II)- and the activities of groups with no normative unity), the conditions put forward by the theory should be actually necessary and sufficient for there to be a group which acts with no normative unity and a group which acts with a normative unity. I demanded that, for the conditions to be sufficient in relation to groups which act with a normative unity, a particular requirement should be met: the account must entail not only that participants' beliefs to the effect that they are under a duty qua members are not absurd, but also explain why this is so. I assumed that an explanation of this involves the following. Given that members' beliefs that they are under a duty qua members of the group are grounded on the belief that there is something about being a member such that, when coupled with a normative consideration or considerations, then one has a duty to do certain things, the theory should specify what these normative considerations are. These normative considerations cannot be just any considerations. They should be capable of giving rise to a duty.

Gilbert's model entails, *inter alia*, that all groups which act are groups with a normative unity. For in her view there is a group which acts only if members are jointly committed; and, by definition of being "jointly committed", this entails that they are under a duty to act accordingly (qua members of the group). This is, I think, incorrect. There are cases, we saw, of groups acting intentionally where members do not conceive of themselves as under a duty qua members, such as the picnic example. Bratman, Shapiro and Kutz also acknowledge this, as we noticed. Moreover, I proposed an account of these groups (groups which act with no normative unity) in Chapter 5 which, I argued, is correct. It is clear, then, that Gilbert's account does not meet our test.

Her account could be conceived, nevertheless, as designed to capture the activities of groups with a normative unity only, and in what follows I shall assume that this is so.

---

[164]Gilbert (2002, (n 162) 67).

[165]*LT* 185.

Consider, then, the key notion of her analysis, namely the idea of joint commitments. Let us begin with the idea of joint commitment irrespective of its content (i.e. putting the idea of "being jointly committed to A-ing *as a body*" aside). We can claim safely that, if individuals are jointly committed, then the following takes place by definition (see properties (a)–(g) of joint commitments above): several agents are each individually committed in a particular way; each commitment is interlocked with the others (the individual commitments are interdependent, are arrived at simultaneously, and cannot be rescinded without the concurrence of all); this gives rise to duties to act in accordance with the commitments.

This does not seem to capture all cases. We can think of groups which act with a normative unity where this type of commitments does not obtain. I suggested, in the previous chapter, some examples. Recall the case of painters who want the house to be painted because it is going to be a rest-home for elderly people, the individuals intend to perform the relevant actions, and hence they are committed to doing them. The commitments are interdependent in some sense, for they all concern actions which, taken together, are related in a special way to a state of affairs the bringing about of which is seen as involving, or as being constituted by, the actions and attitudes of members (and which is considered by them as being valuable in relation to individuals other than themselves). But these commitments need not have been arrived at simultaneously. For instance, one of the relevant individuals might intend to perform the relevant actions first, in the hope that others will join him. We need not think of these commitments as not rescindable without the concurrence of others either. For example, the joint action might be taking place and one of the relevant individuals might simply change his mind as to the valuable character of the activity and opt out. He does not need the concurrence of all to do this in any sense. The conditions put forward by Gilbert seem, then, too demanding. In fact, in the previous chapter I built an account to capture this type of activities (the example I have just mentioned included) which does not mention the type of conditions that Gilbert brings in as necessary. But there is one aspect of her account where it goes seriously wrong. For she thinks that it need be the case that participants *be* actually obligated. And there is no reason to think that. It is easy to conceive of collective actions where individuals believe that the activity is valuable, but are completely wrong about it. They may think that the activity is valuable, and in part because of this consider themselves as under a duty, but they can be mistaken about this. In fact, they might recognize their error. Our account admits this obvious possibility. Gilbert's account does not. It requires, not only that they think they are obligated, but also that they be actually obligated (for in her view joint commitments do in fact create duties). Moreover, we saw that there might be groups which act and which exhibit a normative unity of type (I) to a certain degree. In those cases it is not the case that *all* conceive of themselves as under a duty. It suffices that most do. By contrast, Gilbert requires that all members be jointly committed, and hence that all members conceive of themselves as (and actually be) under a duty. This is clearly too demanding, especially in large groups.[166]

[166]Cf Baltzer (2002, 8)

In short, there are groups which act with a (certain degree of) normative unity of type (I), an analysis of which I sketched in the last chapter, where Gilbert's main conditions are not met. So the idea of joint commitment is not necessary to understand this type of groups.

It may be the case, however, that the joint-commitment-approach is an adequate construal of groups which act with a normative unity of type (II), where participants conceive of themselves as under a duty qua members even if they do not think of the activity as particularly valuable in relation to individuals other than themselves. Could that be so?

One reason in favour of a negative answer is that the account demands too much, for it rules out the obvious possibility of participants thinking that they are under an obligation but being mistaken about this, and of their coming to recognize this. On Gilbert's account this could not be so. Once you are jointly committed, you are under an obligation.

But we can put this objection aside. The account is problematic for a deeper reason.[167] The problem is that we do not know exactly what a joint commitment is. Gilbert refuses to break down the notion, and this makes it unclear. This concern may be defused by arguing that a joint commitment is just a set of individual commitments which satisfy the properties mentioned above (see conditions (a)–(g)): basically, they are interdependent, arrived at simultaneously, not rescindable without the acquiescence of others, and they give rise to duties. Here the central notion would have been broken down into other notions. But these notions are still mysterious. This is so not because the idea of being individually committed to doing something is not familiar to us. On the contrary, we commit ourselves to different courses of action. For instance, as Bratman claims, when we intend to A we are committed to A-ing. Nor are the notions mysterious because we could not imagine a mechanism by which two or more agents can commit themselves with others such that their individual commitments become interlocked in the way described. For we could conceive of such a mechanism. The notions are mysterious because, just as individual commitments do not create duties (for instance, if I intend to do A, it does not follow that I have a duty to do A necessarily), a meshing set of individual commitments does not create duties. So on this reading the account is incorrect. For it would be absurd for participants to conceive of themselves as under a duty qua members of the group, i.e. qua individuals who are committed in the way described. Accordingly, this feature of the phenomenon in which we are interested would not be captured, and hence our test would not be met.

Perhaps Gilbert is not talking of individual commitments as we normally understand them. She may have captured a phenomenon (joint commitments) that is unique, and for that reason her explanatory strategy may be different. Joint commitments may be phenomena that consist of a singular and characteristic combination of properties. A joint commitment may be a meshing set of "individual commitments". The latter are like the individual commitments with which we are familiar,

---

[167]The remarks that follow provide an additional reason for thinking that Gilbert's account is inadequate as an account of groups which act with a normative unity of type (I).

with the only difference that they mesh in the particular way described above and that, when that is the case, duties to act in accordance with the commitments arise. Insofar as the notion of joint commitment can be broken down into other notions that are familiar to us, it can be broken down to a certain extent only. This, in fact, seems to be Gilbert's idea.[168]

But the idea is still problematic, for it remains mysterious. What is special about joint commitments that duties arise necessarily? Gilbert claims that this is so not because of prudential reasons, such as self-interest or convenience, and this seems correct. Prudential reasons of that type alone do not ground duties. We considered, for instance, the walking-together example, where participants think of themselves as under an obligation to perform the relevant actions even if the applicable prudential reasons (Jack was walking simply to stretch out after a heavy dinner) no longer apply. On the other hand, it is not so, Gilbert suggests, because the activity is considered particularly valuable in relation to others either.[169] This might well be the case too, if we have in mind groups which act with a normative unity of type (II). Gilbert's explanation of why duties arise out of joint commitments is that this is so analytically. That is, because it is part of the concept of being jointly committed. This occurs of necessity.[170]

This is, I believe, inadequate. To see why notice, first, that the idea that once one is jointly committed one becomes, without further ado, obligated, is counterintuitive. Surely certain restrictions should apply. Any reasonable person would claim, for instance, that if one is seriously coerced to become jointly committed no obligation appears. But this is not so according to Gilbert. She claims explicitly that, even if one is seriously coerced to become jointly committed (she mentions the example of somebody forcing another to become jointly committed by putting a gun to his head), one becomes obligated.[171] This sounds extremely odd, to say the least. The reasons for this run deep. The idea is counterintuitive, in part, because explanations of duties should have a certain form: they must involve normative argument, argument that brings in normative considerations, of what is good, valuable, worthwhile, etc. The other part of the explanation of why the idea is counterintuitive is, I believe, that there are no normative considerations that ground the creation of duties when one is seriously coerced into an arrangement, and this is so, ultimately, because there is no value being promoted. This reveals what the general problem with Gilbert's explanation is. It is problematic because it is not of the relevant form. According to her, duties arise of necessity, without further ado.

It seems that Gilbert wants to find support for her view that joint commitments necessarily create obligations in the fact that we recognize the existence of obligations of a certain form (essentially, obligations created by people, which exist until rescinded by the relevant individuals, and which persist even if there are

---

[168] CJC 88.

[169] *LT* 181.

[170] CJC 90–91; *LT* 351–352.

[171] *LT* 351–352.

reasons – such as purely prudential reasons of the sort described – against performance) in situations which, pre-analytically, can be described as people becoming jointly committed.[172] But this is still not the right type of explanation.

Suppose, nevertheless, that we accept that joint commitments create duties because it is part of the concept itself that that is so, without requiring an explanation of the sort mentioned. The idea of joint commitments would still be problematic. For there is some pressure, for Occamist reasons if you like, not to introduce new theoretical constructs in any field of inquiry unless strictly required. And it seems that there is no need to introduce the idea of joint commitments. All the main features of the phenomenon that Gilbert intends to capture at a pre-analytical level by employing the concept of joint commitment can be explained, in principle, in other terms.

One could argue, for instance, that they can be explained thus: there is a group which acts with a normative unity of type (II) if, and only if, there is a set of individuals, defined intensionally or extensionally, such that: (i) each conceives of a state of affairs the bringing about of which involves, or is constituted by, the performance of certain actions (and the display of certain attitudes) by all the members of the set; the relevant actions are the actions which each has *agreed* (explicitly or implicitly) to perform; (ii) each has an overlapping conception of the state of affairs, (iii) each intends to perform the relevant actions (and displays the relevant attitudes), and conceives of these actions (and attitudes) as related in the way described to the state of affairs; (iv) each executes his intentions and, as a result, the state of affairs mentioned in (ii) is brought about; and (v) each thinks that the previous conditions obtain.

As we shall see, this model needs to be completed and elaborated. So it is a first approximation only. But the point is that all the main features of the phenomenon that Gilbert attempts to capture seem to be captured by employing the idea of agreements, a notion with which we are familiar, and dispensing with the idea of joint commitments, which is a new theoretical construct. In effect, agreements, under any plausible construal, are ways of voluntarily undertaking obligations. In this sense the relevant obligations are created by the parties. Accordingly, participants can conceive of themselves as under an obligation qua members of the group, i.e. qua individuals who have agreed. When agreements are reached, the parties think that they have become obligated regardless of the applicability of purely prudential reasons. The obligations are not thought of as depending on whether the thing one has agreed to is particularly valuable either. The obligations are also thought of as arrived at simultaneously (when one agrees, no party becomes obligated first), and normally the agreement is not rescindable unilaterally. And since participants intend to fulfil the agreement, they are committed to performing the relevant actions.[173]

---

[172]E.g. *LT* 178–184, 293–295, 351–352.

[173]Notice that it is not the case that agreements are considered binding – and in fact, I argue briefly later, they are not – without any type of restrictions, e.g. when serious coercion takes place. So this alleged aspect of the situation is not captured by my alternative explanation. But it was never part

Some argue, incorrectly in my view, that the statement "if you agree to do A, you have a duty to do A" is analytic. Others argue in a different way. They claim that agreements create duties because there is a normative principle according to which agreements should be kept, and attempt to show that this principle is valid for certain normative reasons. The point is that, whatever your view as to the binding character of agreements, the idea is familiar to us. The notion of joint commitments is not.

Gilbert is aware of the parallel between agreements and joint commitments, but she rejects the idea that joint commitments can be replaced by the idea of agreements. Her main reason is that, in her view, agreements themselves are instances of joint commitments. They are instances of being "jointly committed to upholding a decision as a body".[174] Her rejection, nevertheless, brings us back to all the problems I have mentioned. And, besides, agreements ought to be understood otherwise, as I shall attempt to show later.

I have objected to the idea of joint commitments, setting aside the way in which Gilbert understands its content. But if one considers that issue further problems appear. Collective action is explained in terms of individuals being jointly committed to accepting the goal of J-ing *as a body*. As noted, the relevant joint commitment is, Gilbert claims, an instruction to the parties to see it that they act in such a way as to emulate as best they can a single body with the goal of J-ing.

This characterization of the content of the joint commitment is, I think, metaphorical and not very illuminating.[175] How does it work, for example, in the case of two people walking together? Do they think of themselves as committed to seeing it that they act so as to emulate a single body that has the goal of walking? Does the body have the goal that its parts walk together? That seems too artificial and outlandish. We do not normally think of ourselves in terms of parts of a body constituted by other agents. Accordingly, one aspect of our test (which requires the account to be clear) is not met. Notice by contrast that, if we bring in the idea of participants having agreed to perform certain actions which are thought of as standing in an instrumental relation to, or as being constitutive of, the bringing about of a particular state of affairs (such as walking together), the obscurity would be dispelled.

7.4 Conclusion

The central notion of Gilbert's account (the idea of joint commitment) does not capture cases of groups which act with a normative unity of type (I). It could be conceived of as a possible construal of groups which act with a normative unity of

---

of the pre-analytical data anyway: the idea that one becomes obligated even when one is forced seriously into an arrangement is completely counterintuitive (and indeed incorrect).

[174] *LT* 292–296.

[175] Nevertheless, it is Gilbert's preferred formulation in her latest writings. *LT* 8, 204, 353; Gilbert (2000, 41).

type (II), but it is an obscure notion on several counts, and it could be replaced by a simpler and more familiar notion (the idea of agreements). I have suggested a first approximation to a model of this type of groups based on that idea.[176] But it needs to be elaborated and tested. In order to do so, it will be convenient, first, to take a look at agreements. This will be the task of our next chapter.

[176]As claimed (n 160), I have ignored Tuomela's account of collective intentional activities. His views are extremely complex, and appear in an enourmous variety of works. In Tuomela (1995), one of his latest writings where he attemtps to unify his stance, he offers an account of groups which act intentionally where participants think they have a duty qua members based on the idea of an agreeement. That model looks similar to the first approximation I have suggested here. There are, nevertheless, important differences, which I discuss these issues in a work in progress. Suffice it to say here, firstly, that Tuomela employs the notion of a "we-intention", which is not, as an intention to contribute is, a standard intention, but an intention of a different nature: it is an intention "in the we-mode" (see especially Chapter 3 of Tuomela (1995); cf *C* 88–89). That notion is, I think, to some extent uninformatively circular. Besides, if my contentions in Chapters 6 and 9 are correct, we-intentions (a new theoretical construct) are unnecessary to understand the activities of groups with a normative unity. Intentions to contribute (which are standard intentions) are a better tool. Secondly, Tuomela requires (1995, 125–126) that participants "mutually believe" that each has a we-intention (roughly, for two participants A and B, (i) A believes that B has a we-intention; (ii) B believes that A has a we-intention; (iii) A believes that (ii); (iv) B believes that (i); and so on). If my contentions in Chapters 6 and 9 are correct, this is unnecessary. Thirdly, Tuomela claims that agreements create obligations because of Scanlon's principle of fidelity (1995, 421). I argue in the next Chapter that this is incorrect. Finally, a model based on the idea of agreements does not capture cases of groups which act with a normative unity of type (I) (this follows from my contentions in Chapter 6), nor does it capture, as I shall argue in Chapter 9, all cases of groups which act with a normative unity of type (II).

Chapter 8
On Agreements

8.1 Overview of the Chapter

Most theories of agreements assume that agreements are conditional promises, or exchanges of conditional promises, and attempt to explain what it is to agree and why agreements may be binding by explaining what it is to promise and why promising may be binding. They also attempt to solve another problem, the treatment of which will be relevant for our purposes: they try to establish how the content of agreements is determined. Three main views are held in this respect. It is maintained either that the content of an agreement is determined by taking into account all the mental states of the parties, such that only if the parties have the same relevant mental states has an agreement been reached (the subjective view), or by considering the mental states that were communicated by one party to the other regardless of whether the party had in effect the relevant states (the objective view), or by considering certain mental states as relevant, but not others (the mixed view).

I shall begin by discussing the standard model of agreements, according to which agreements should be understood in terms of promises. It can be fleshed out in different ways, for there are many different accounts of promising available in the literature. I shall assess some of them, those which I think are representative of the main strands and assessment of which will pave the way towards a correct account of promising. The latter will enable us to fill in the standard model in a particular way (Section 8.2). I shall claim later that, despite its initial appeal, the standard model so understood should be dismissed because agreements cannot be understood in terms of promises. So I shall sketch an alternative account (Section 8.3). It has implications as to how the content of agreements is determined that show that neither the subjective view, nor the objective view, nor the mixed view is correct (Section 8.4).

8.2 The Standard Model

There is a difference between entering into an agreement and agreeing with somebody about something (as when both you and I agree that chocolate is delicious). We are concerned with the first sense only. Consider two simple, paradigmatic cases:

R.E. Sánchez Brigido, *Groups, Rules and Legal Practice*,
Law and Philosophy Library 89, DOI 10.1007/978-90-481-8770-6_8,

(1) Jerry: "I'll do A if you do B".
Mary: "Ok".
(2) Peter: "Why don't you do A and I'll do B?"
Mark: "Fine".

These agreements have several pre-theoretical features. Entering into an agreement is a way of undertaking an obligation by performing certain acts. Uttering "I agree" is one such act, but it is neither necessary (consider the examples) nor sufficient (consider "I agree with you that chocolate is delicious"). Normally, both parties undertake obligations (like in case 2), but not necessarily (like in case 1). The obligation is owed to the other party, and she is put in a special position: she has a right to demand conformity as long as the agreement stands. Normally, when the agreement is such that both parties acquire obligations (like in case 2), the relevant obligations are acquired simultaneously (neither party becomes obligated first).

The standard model holds that simple agreements (like case 1) are conditional promises, and that more complex agreements (like case 2) are an exchange of conditional promises.[177] Thus, case (1) is construed as a conditional promise made by Jerry to the effect that he will do A if Mary does B that has been accepted by Mary. Case (2) is more complex. It cannot be reconstructed as an exchange of this sort: Peter: "I promise to do A"; Mark: "I promise to do B". For Peter would become obligated first, thus not meeting the simultaneity feature. But, in principle, it seems that it could be reconstructed in other ways. For instance: Peter: "I promise this: I'll do A if you promise to do B"; Mark: "On condition that you promise this: you will do A if I promise to do B, I promise to do B". Once Mark has promised, and since the condition of his promise is fulfilled, both would have acquired each of their obligations simultaneously.[178]

The standard model is appealing because of the correspondence between some of the pre-analytical features of agreements and those of conditional promises or exchanges of promises. Promising is a way of undertaking an obligation by performing certain acts. Uttering the words "I promise" is neither necessary (consider "I give you my word") nor sufficient (consider "I promise that it was not my fault"). The obligation is owed by the promisor to the recipient, and she is put in a special position (she can demand compliance) as long as the promise stands (until she releases the promisor). Conditional promises structured in a special way seem to be a device to acquire obligations simultaneously too.

---

[177] Cf among others Robins (1984, 105–106); Lewis (1969, 34, 45, 84); ONR 202-203; *MF* 173–175; P Atiyah also refers to the view that equates agreements with an exchange of mutual promises as the common view, both in and outside the law. See also Atiyah (1981, 204–205, and 1986, 11–12). Cf also Coote (1988, 91).

[178] This is one of the ways, among others, in which Gilbert claims that the standard model could reconstruct the exchange to capture the simultaneity condition (*LT* 313–338). I shall take no stance as to whether this, or other possible construals, are correct. For even if they are the standard model fails, I shall claim below, on other counts.

The standard model has, nevertheless, to be brought into sharper focus. First, it has yet to clarify what promising is. To promise seems in part to communicate something to somebody. But we still need to know what is involved in this act of communication. Second, the standard model has to explain why promising (an act that consists in part of communicating something) may be a means by which agents may bind themselves.

I shall consider two main views that attempt to answer these questions. Each fleshes out the standard model in different ways.

8.2.1 *The Practice View*

This view claims that to promise is to perform certain actions that, given a social practice of promising, count as a way of undertaking an obligation to perform an action (until the recipient releases the promisor). The practice consists in part of a set of rules that are, in Searle's terminology,[179] constitutive of what is to make a promise. These rules define which acts count as undertaking an obligation, just as the rules of soccer stipulate that performing certain acts counts as scoring a goal. When the practice is justified in the relevant way, performing the relevant acts in effect creates obligations of the kind considered. In other words, a promise is valid if the practice of promising is justified.

Rawls' views are the paradigmatic example of this position. He claims that the constitutive rules specify that, if one performs certain acts, one is to do something unless certain excusing conditions obtain. According to Rawls, for this practice to give rise to actual obligations, two conditions must be met. First, the practice should satisfy his two principles of justice. Very roughly, the rules must be such that both the promisor and the promisee are free and equal at the time the promise is made. Second, the parties must have satisfied the principle of fairness, according to which one must do one's part in supporting a just practice of promising that generates benefits that one has accepted.[180] The general idea is that, if I have accepted the benefits of an entrenched and just practice (e.g. the fact that this practice enables cooperation), I must do my fair share (keep my word) when my turn comes.

There are several objections against this view. We are familiar with a distinction between making a promise and a promise being binding or valid. Some promises are invalid. They are promises, but they do not create an obligation (e.g. a promise to kill your annoying neighbour, to play Russian roulette, etc). Other promises are valid, i.e. they in effect create obligations. The practice view does not do justice to this distinction. On the practice view, just as according to the constitutive rule of soccer performing certain acts counts as scoring a goal, according to the constitutive rule of promising performing certain acts counts as undertaking an obligation.

---

[179]Searle (1969, 33–35).

[180]Rawls (1971, 112, 344–348). For other versions of this conception: Hart (1958, 101–103); Murphy (25–31); Kolodny and Wallace (2003, 119, 148–154).

In other words, in this view the statement "promising creates an obligation" is analytic.[181] But then it does not make sense to distinguish between a promise and a valid promise, just as it does not make sense to distinguish between a goal and a "valid" goal. Notice that this renders dubious the idea of requiring that the practice meet extra conditions for promising to create a "real" obligation.

Suppose that the previous objection is overcome. The practice view claims that it is this practice, when certain additional conditions are met, that justifies the existence of actual obligations. Rawls' appeal to the value of fairness is a typical example of this strategy. As seen, the general idea is that one must do one's part in supporting a just practice of promising that generates benefits that one has accepted. But this seems problematic. Even if one has accepted the benefits that accrue from the practice, it seems one could legitimately break some promises. Breaking a trivial promise, for instance, cannot be plausibly conceived of as undermining the practice. The cooperative scheme might well survive without this promise being kept. Yet we do regard breaking this promise as wrong. Besides, we can conceive of agents who have not had the opportunity to enjoy the benefits of the practice (and hence have not accepted any benefit) and still acquire an obligation by promising. This view seems to have no resources to explain why this is so.

These obstacles are not perhaps decisive. More sophisticated arguments may be available. A conclusive objection against any version of the practice view should show that one could plausibly conceive of a person performing certain acts that, despite the absence of any practice of promising, would be recognisable as a (valid) promise. This is what the second view of promising, which I shall label "the intention conception", claims.

8.2.2 The Intention Conception

This conception focuses on the idea of promising in isolation of the possible presence of a practice of promising. It focuses on an idealised context, where no practice of promising exists, so as to show that if an agent were in such a context he could in effect succeed, despite the absence of any practice of the relevant kind, in performing certain acts that we would regard as a (binding) promise. Of course, promising practices are important. But this conception claims that the obvious importance of such practices can only be explained once the idea of promising itself has been explained.

The intention conception conceives of promising as communicating a particular kind of intention, and it purports to show why such communication may create an obligation. There are two main variants of this conception. I shall label them "the expectation account" and "the normative power account".

---

[181] Cf PO 213.

8.2.2.1 The Expectation Account

This account holds, roughly, that she who promises communicates to the recipient an intention to perform an act being aware that she is creating an expectation that the act will be performed. I shall focus on Scanlon's version of this account, which is perhaps the most sophisticated one along these lines.[182]

Scanlon claims that the reason why promises ought to be kept is, roughly, that they are a mechanism that enables people to give and receive assurance (which is a special way of creating expectations), and that being able to do this is valuable. It gets matters settled, and this in turn enables us to plan our activities in advance and to coordinate our actions. More precisely, Scanlon claims that the reason why promises ought to be kept is related to a principle which embodies this value, the "principle of fidelity" (PF). PF reads as follows: if (1) A voluntarily and intentionally leads B to expect that A will do X (unless B consents to A's not doing X); (2) A knows that B wants to be assured of this; (3) A acts with the aim of providing this assurance, and has good reason to believe that he or she has done so; (4) B knows that A has the beliefs and intentions just described; (5) A intends for B to know this, and knows that B does know it; (6) B knows that A has this knowledge and intent; then, in the absence of some special justification, A must do X unless B consents to X's not being done.[183]

According to Scanlon, promising is only one special way in which one may provide this kind of valuable assurance. Its special character lies on the kind of reason that the promisee has for believing that the promisor will perform: when promising to do X, one provides the desired assurance only if one persuades the recipient of one's intention to do X, and one persuades the recipient of one's intention in a particular way, i.e. one indicates one's awareness of the fact that not fulfilling the promise 'would, under the circumstances, ... be morally wrong, ... disallowed by the kind of moral reasoning that lies behind principle F'.[184] So when I say "I promise", according to Scanlon, I do several things: a) I claim to have a certain intention to do X; b) I make this claim with the clear aim of getting you to believe that I have this intention, and in circumstances in which it is clear that if you do believe it then the truth of this belief will matter to you; c) I indicate to you that I believe and take seriously the fact that, once I have declared this intention under the circumstances, and have reason to believe that you are convinced by it, it would be wrong for me not to fulfil my intention.

The first difficulty of this account is the concern of circularity. As Scanlon puts it, promising creates an obligation only if it persuades the recipient of the speaker's

---

[182] I shall concentrate on Scanlon (1990), but see also Scanlon (1998, Chapter 7). Other versions include: MacCormick (1972, 59, 61–62); Brandt (1979, 286–305); Narveson (1971, 207, 214–221); Stoljar (1988, 193, 193–194); cf also Ardal (1968, 225, 234–237). It will be clear, I hope, that my criticisms against Scanlon's approach apply to any version of the expectation account as broadly defined in the text.

[183] Scanlon (1990, 199, 206–208).

[184] Scanlon (1990, 211).

intention to do A. But it can only do that if it gives the recipient reason to believe that the speaker has reason to do A. This reason is, on the analysis proposed, the speaker's awareness of the fact that it would be wrong to fail to follow through having promised. But it would be wrong only if promising created an obligation, and it creates an obligation only if it gives the recipient reason to believe that the speaker has reason to do A.[185]

Scanlon's response to the problem is this. He asks us to suppose that I, the would-be-promisor, abide by "the principle of due care" (DC), and that you, the would-be-promisee, believe that I am DC-abiding. DC reads:

> One must exercise due care not to lead others to form reasonable but false expectations about what one will do when one has good reason to believe that they would suffer significant loss as a result of relying on these expectations.[186]

Given this, Scanlon claims, you have to reason to believe that I would not attempt to persuade you that I have an intention to do A unless I actually had a settled intention to do A. So, he claims, suppose that I do the following: (i) I give you good reason to believe that I am attempting to persuade you that I have a settled intention of doing A, and that I know that, if you are persuaded, the truth of this belief will be important to you; and (ii) I lead you to believe that I know and take seriously the fact that, under the circumstances, it would be wrong for me to attempt this unless I really had that intention. By doing this, Scanlon concludes, I give you reason to believe that I have a settled intention to do A, and hence reason to believe that I will do A.[187] Thus, clause (1) of PF would be met. I would have given you reason to believe that I have a reason to do A without invoking PF, i.e. without invoking the fact that an obligation has been created by promising. This would avoid the problem of circularity. And if the other clauses are met, an obligation to do A would have allegedly been created.

This response is ingenious but, I think, unconvincing. It is a concession of defeat, for as shown above Scanlon himself admits, before addressing the objection of circularity, that the promisor persuades the promisee of her intention by indicating her awareness of the fact that *not fulfilling the promise* would be wrong, not by indicating her awareness of the fact that *claiming to have an intention if she did not have such an intention* would be wrong. Besides, it does not follow from my doing (i)–(ii) above that I give you reason to believe that I will do A. I only give you reason to believe that I have an intention to do A (for it is in the public domain that I am DC-abiding, and hence that I would not attempt to persuade you that I have a certain intention unless I actually had it). But I might have formed that intention on a whim, or because of reasons of very little weight that I know might be easily overridden. And I can change my mind on a different whim, or if the reasons are overridden. So, if you are reasonable,[188] you could not believe that I will do A, and hence I would

---

[185] Scanlon (1990, 212).

[186] Scanlon (1990, 204).

[187] Scanlon (1990, 213).

[188] I am assuming, as Scanlon is, that the parties are reasonable.

not have led you to expect that I will do A. Accordingly, PF would be inapplicable, for clause (1) would not be met.

Scanlon might reply that this objection ignores the fact that I would have not just persuaded you that I have a *mere* intention to do A; for the argument states that I would have persuaded you that I have a *settled* intention to do A. But for this reply to work, the latter should mean "an intention that I think is supported by stringent, very weighty reasons that I think will not be overridden". And if that is so most cases of promising would not be captured. For promises to do A are normally made and requested when the parties think that the would-be promisor has no independent reason for doing A.[189] And this is the case because of a more general feature of promising, namely that the promisor is aware that he will, by promising, acquire a duty to do A even if he has no independent reasons for doing A, even if doing A is not, in and of itself, particularly valuable. Scanlon himself admits this:

> Typically a promise is asked for or offered when there is doubt as to whether the promisor will have sufficient motive to do the thing promised. The point of promising is to provide such a motive.[190]

Secondly, Scanlon does not provide an adequate account of what promising is. As shown, he claims that, when I say "I promise", I (a) claim to have a certain intention (b) in order to persuade you that I have this intention, such that it is clear to me that, if I persuade you, the truth of this belief will matter to you, and (c) I indicate to you that I believe that, once it is clear to me that you are persuaded, it would be wrong for me not to fulfil my intention. This suggests that he thinks that these conditions are, at least, necessary for there to be a promise. But it seems clear that they are not. For instance, Jake might promise to do A despite not having persuaded the recipient of his intention to do A (say, because everyone knows that Jake always fails to honour his promises). Besides, one can promise to do A and know that the recipient will not consider one's doing A as something desired or welcome, so long as it is not considered as unwelcome (the latter would be, arguably, a case of threatening, not of promising). Consider an example by Raz: Paul promises his father never to smoke despite his father's protestations that he sees nothing wrong in smoking; Paul makes the promise in order to strengthen his resolve, and the father reluctantly accepts his son's undertaking as a favour to him.[191] Moreover, both Jake and Paul might have actually created an obligation by promising. Accordingly, Scanlon's necessary conditions for there to be a *binding* promise (that an expectation the promisee cares about has in effect been created) are not met. Scanlon's argument is that these are "impure", non-typical cases of promising, and admits that PF needs to be revised to deal with them.[192] But the claim makes sense only if one assumes that PF captures the typical cases. And as seen in the previous paragraph it does not.

---

[189] This objection is roughly equivalent to Kolodny's and Wallace's (2003, 139–154). Along similar lines, Pratt (2001, 142, 152–153); Murphy (22).

[190] Scanlon (1998, 322).

[191] PO 213–214.

[192] Scanlon (1990, 216–217).

Besides, although Scanlon has not explicitly provided an account of the sufficient conditions for there to be a promise, we can attribute to him a specific view. He thinks that if conditions (a)–(c) above are met such that principle F applies, then one ought to fulfil one's intention. This suggests that conditions (a)–(c), in conjunction with some of or all the clauses of the antecedent of principle F, contain the sufficient conditions for there to be a promise. Yet this cannot be so. We regard promising as a way of voluntarily undertaking an obligation, and hence promising must consist of performing certain acts that are performed as a means of thereby acquiring an obligation. An individual whose conduct is captured by conditions (a)–(c) such that principle F applies does not communicate her intention as a way of thereby acquiring an obligation, and hence is not promising. She only indicates her awareness of the fact that not fulfilling the intention would be morally wrong. But this does not mean that she communicates her intention as a means of thereby acquiring an obligation. One might act being aware of the consequences of one's act without these acts being performed as a means of giving rise to these consequences.

In short, PF seems not to be the ground for holding that promises ought to be kept. Besides, there is no adequate construal of what promising is.

8.2.2.2 The Normative Power Account of Promising

The normative power account of promising is developed by Joseph Raz. I shall present, first, a very rough outline of his notion of normative powers. Secondly, I shall present Raz's characterization of promises which, I think, is essentially adequate. Nonetheless, it does not explain promising practices, and it seems subject to counterexamples. So, thirdly, I shall attempt to show that the model can be expanded to avoid these difficulties. It is here where some of Raz's contentions have, I think, to be abandoned.

Normative Powers

Normative powers should be distinguished from physical and mental abilities to bring about a state of affairs, and from the ability to influence other people's beliefs. Normative powers can be generally defined as the power to bring about a particular type of normative change.[193] It is an ability instantiated when, for instance, one makes vows, takes oaths, or consents (and, as we shall see, when one promises).

A normative change is the alteration of a normative situation, i.e. of the totality of reasons which apply to a particular person. Thus, a normative change may appear through the creation of new reasons for action (of whatever kind) or the cancellation of such reasons. The exercise of a normative power must bring about a particular type of normative change: it must at least create (or cancel) reasons of a particular kind, i.e. duties or obligations. But not every act of bringing about this

---

[193] *PRN* 98–99.

type of normative change is the exercise of a normative power. For instance, injuring somebody intentionally brings in a normative change in that it generates, other things being equal, a duty to compensate, but it is not the exercise of a normative power. What explains the difference between the change of a normative situation where no normative power is exercised (as in this example) and the change effected by the exercise of a normative power (as in the case of somebody taking an oath of allegiance, or consenting to be operated, or, as we shall see, promising) is this: an act is the exercise of a normative power when, and only when, there is a justified norm that confers the power to obligate oneself (and to dissolve the bond).[194] There are, for instance, norms conferring upon us the power to make oaths, to make vows, and to consent (and, as we shall see, to promise). What justifies the relevant norm is that it promotes a value. The general value at stake is the value of being able to create, if one wishes to do so, special normative relationships. Put otherwise, it is the general value of being able to shape, to a limited extent, our moral world by voluntarily creating special binding relationships.[195] And Raz suggests that being able to bind oneself in this way (i.e. being able to create special binding relationships) is valuable because 'it is desirable ... to have a method of giving grounds for reasonable reliance in a special way, not necessarily by intending to induce reliance but by intending to bind oneself'.[196] Let us now consider this general view, which I think is correct, as applied to promises.

Normative Powers and Promising

Raz characterizes promises thus: an agent P (the promisor) promises an agent R (the recipient) to do A if, and only if, P communicates to R, in circumstances C, an intention to undertake, by that very act of communication, an obligation to do A and to invest R with a right to its performance (conditional on R's acceptance or non-rejection) and until R releases P.[197]

Notice that this characterization avoids the difficulties of the previous accounts. It does not rely on the existence of a practice of promising, for one might promise without this practice existing. Besides, one might promise to do A even if the recipient is not persuaded of one's intention to do A, and even if one knows that one's doing A is not something the recipient will consider desirable or welcome (so long as one knows that it will not be considered unwelcome). It also captures well the idea that promises, when conceived in the idealized way in which we are envisaging them here, are ways of voluntarily undertaking obligations.

---

[194] This is oversimplistic as a rendering of Raz's approach but is, I think, essentially correct: VONP 87–89, 92–98; cf *PRN* 102–106.

[195] ONR 201; PO 228; cf *PRN* 102–105.

[196] VONP 101; cf *MF* 95–96.

[197] PO 211. Circumstances C concern marginal conditions (the agent is not joking, suffering from delusions, etc).

Performing these acts (the acts mentioned in the characterization of promising just proposed) creates an obligation when, and only when, it is the exercise of a normative power, that is, when and only when there is a valid norm conferring upon us such power. The promising principle, i.e. the familiar principle according to which "promises ought to be kept", is such a valid norm. Given that, according to the promising principle, when an agent performs these acts (when she promises) she is obligated to do something (to deliver the thing promised), the principle can be seen as conferring upon agents the possibility of binding themselves by performing certain acts if they so wish (by promising), and in that sense the principle is a power-conferring norm.[198]

The principle is valid because it is valuable to enable people to create this type of binding relationship, a relationship where one party is bound to another if the recipient accepts such that she has a right to demand compliance until she releases the first party. When one promises to do A one indicates to the recipient one's awareness of the fact that one will acquire an obligation if she accepts and until being released. This enables one to give assurance on the performance of the act, even if (it is in the public domain that one thinks that) one has no previous independent reason for doing A. And this is a valuable thing, for as a result of that assurance the recipient can rely upon one's doing A until she releases the promisor. Promising does not create an obligation because it provides assurance. It provides assurance because it creates an obligation. It is a device that enables people to do this.

(The foregoing considerations apply to promising in the context we are envisioning, i.e. in the idealised context. As we shall see, promising can take place in other contexts, and here, I think, other values might (also) be in play.[199] For instance, when promising takes place within an on-going relationship such as friendship, this ability might be valuable for other reasons. It might have an expressive character: promising might be an expression of an appropriate attitude towards some of the values that friendship embodies.[200] Being supportive to one's friends' initiatives is valuable. This value is partly constitutive of friendship, and promising to help one's friend with one of his initiatives – i.e. binding oneself in this special way – might be an appropriate way of expressing one's respect for this value.)

To be complete the normative power account should spell out the promising principle more, but I shall not do so here. My purpose was to characterize what a promise is and to explain why promises may be binding, and the foregoing account, I think, fulfils such a purpose. Some considerations should, nevertheless, be made.

Firstly, it is clear that the principle not only reads "if one promises to do A one ought to do A", but also (at least) "if, in circumstances C, one promises to do A, and if one's undertaking is accepted (or not rejected) by the recipient, until the recipient releases one, one ought to do A". Notice that releasing is itself the exercise of a normative power, a power to dissolve the bond.

---

[198] ONR 202; VONP 87–89; *PRN* 105.

[199] The same applies, I think, to other forms of voluntary undertakings, such as consent, vows, etc.

[200] Raz defends a similar view in relation to consent (*MF* 87–88).

Secondly, the principle should be construed as containing qualifications on the content of the promise itself. There are valid and invalid promises, and at least some invalid promises are such because of their content (e.g. a promise to kill your annoying neighbour, to play Russian roulette, etc). The normative power account has resources to complete the principle as containing such qualifications. Having the ability to create binding relations based on immorality is not valuable, and this is why a promise to perform an immoral act is invalid.[201]

So the normative-power account of promising seems adequate. Since it gives an account of promising without relying on the existence of promising practices, it contains a decisive objection against the practice view. And it characterizes (binding) promises in a way that overcomes the difficulties of the expectation account.

Promising Practices and Difficult Cases

The account has yet to explain promising practices. They can be defined, I believe, as special kinds of social rules. That is, as rules which are practised by most members of a group to the effect that certain acts count as promising, when promising is understood in the idealised sense considered above (i.e. in the absence of such practices) and which are regarded as valid – as promoting a value – insofar as they are generally practised. The value at stake is their enabling to obtain certain goals for everyone's benefit. Thus, they may be seen as helping to: (a) make the ability to bind oneself easier and quicker to exercise by determining which acts counts as promising; e.g. by stipulating that uttering the expression "I promise" is a way of communicating the relevant intention; (b) make determinate certain normative implications that may be seen as so debatable that it is better to have a fixed answer (e.g. there might be social rules as to what are the rights of third parties).[202] This characterization of promising practices has not been, to my knowledge, explicitly defended by Raz, but I think it fits well with his approach.

Let us consider now cases that seem to impugn the adequacy of this account of promising.

There are many scenarios where an agent is regarded as having promised and yet the conditions mentioned in the definition above are not met. Lying promises are a case in point. A lying promise to do A is considered a promise to do A, albeit an insincere one, i.e. the insincere promisor performs certain acts but not as a means of thereby obligating herself to do A. When rebuking the insincere promisor for not doing A, the recipient claims that she has obligated herself because she promised, regardless of whether she performed the relevant acts as a means of obligating herself or not.

One way of dealing with this sort of case is to deny that they are cases of promising. This seems to be the route taken by Raz himself. He claims that the insincere "promisor" has not promised. The recipient would be in reality invoking a principle

---

[201] ONR 201; *MF* 173.

[202] Cf Lamond (1996, 145–147).

of estoppel, according to which the putative promisor is prevented from denying that he has promised on the grounds that he has induced reliance.[203]

Such a view is, I think, unsatisfactory. It conflicts with the natural reaction of the promisee ("but you promised!"), and with the fact that we think of lying-promises as promises, albeit insincere ones. Besides, the recipient might demand compliance regardless of whether she relied on the insincere promisor. So she need not be invoking a principle of estoppel. Finally, similar cases abound, and explanations in terms of principles such as the principle of estoppel seem implausible. Consider the case of James.

Absent-minded as he is, James thinks that his five-year old niece's birthday is on the 19th when in fact it is on the 18th. He commits himself to take her to go to the zoo on the 19th, and tells her that he will take her to the zoo on her birthday. When he takes notice of his confusion, he acknowledges that, despite his intention to bind himself to go with her on the 19th, he should go with her on the 18th. He claims that that is so because he has promised. Yet James did not intend to bind himself to go on the 18th. No principle of estoppel, or other similar doctrine, seems applicable. James does not think that he is prevented from denying that he has promised to go on the 18th. He simply thinks that he has promised to go on the 18th. Perhaps it could be claimed that James has promised because there are practices of promising to the effect that certain acts count as promising regardless of whether the mental states are present. But, let us assume, this is not the case. Moreover, this is not what James thinks. He would claim that whether there are practices of this sort or not is completely irrelevant.

The problem of cases that seem to be cases of promising despite the relevant mental states being absent appears because we have construed the notion of a promise by considering an idealised context. We have put aside the fact that promising normally takes place within the framework of on-going relationships (among friends, colleagues, relatives, neighbours, and so on), which are seen as partly constituted by certain values and norms, such that they shape the ways in which one can promise, when promising is conceived in the idealised way.

James thinks that his intention is actually irrelevant because he conceives of his relationship with his niece as having certain features. In his view the uncle-niece relationship is such that it requires that the uncle should attach special importance to the birthdays of his niece; it also requires that the uncle conduct himself in such a way that his niece learn that promises are not to be made without thinking carefully what is being promised; one has to exercise this power responsibly. The relationship as such, James think, requires that his act counts as promising even if the stringent conditions, when promises are conceived in the idealised way in which we have been envisaging them so far, are not met. Moreover, he conceives of the relationship as requiring this regardless of promising practices, that is, even if there were no promising practices at all.

[203] Raz (1982, 916, 935).

James might be wrong, but his position is intelligible. And this is so because, when promising takes place within the framework of different relationships (which are seen as embodying distinct values and as partly constituted by norms), these relationships may mould the way in which one can promise: they may require that performing certain acts counts as promising, when promising is conceived of in the idealised way, regardless of whether all the ideal conditions for promising mentioned above are met.

This also explains the case of an insincere promise. For when the recipient rebukes the insincere promisor for not doing A on the ground that she has promised to do A, regardless of whether she intended to obligate herself, the recipient is invoking a particular conception of promising. She is invoking the existence of either a promising practice or of a special relationship according to which the promisor's acts count as promising, when promising is understood in the idealised way.

The picture is now complete. Let us consider whether this account of promising, which helps to flesh out the standard model of agreements in a particular way, would provide a good explanation of agreements.

8.3 Assessing the Standard Model: Agreements Reconsidered

Recall that, according to the standard model (now fleshed out in terms of the normative power account of promising), an agreement is a conditional promise or an exchange of conditional promises. It seems that the standard model so fleshed out cannot provide a satisfactory account of agreements.

When an agent enters into an agreement, he makes an offer to the other party. And when he makes an offer, he proposes to undertake an obligation. But he also reasonably thinks the offeree will consider this welcome. This is, I think, part and parcel of the idea of making an offer, and that agreeing involves making an offer is, I think, also part and parcel of the idea of agreeing.[204] If that is so, when an agent enters into an agreement, she is not promising. For, as argued above, an agent might promise to do something and need not think of the undertaking as being welcome to the recipient.

The objection is not, of course, conclusive, for an advocate of the standard model could claim that agreeing is in part making a promise, though a particular kind of promise, namely a promise where the undertaking is thought of as welcome to the recipient. After all, many promises are of this sort. So let us focus on other difficulties of the standard model which, I think, are conclusive.

Notice, firstly, that one way in which agreements cease to exist is by mutual rescission. Mutual rescission can be reconstructed as the shared normative power to cancel the agreement: a power that cannot be exercised unilaterally but need to be exercised by all the parties who have agreed such that, once exercised, both parties' obligations are put to an end simultaneously. The presence of this power is, I

[204] Bach and Harnish (1979, 51); Lamond (1996, 158, 161).

think, in the nature of agreements as well, to the point that it is natural to think that neither party, except in special circumstances (on which see below), can cancel the normative consequences of an agreement unilaterally.

For instance, consider cases like (1) above, where only one party acquires an obligation. Suppose that Sylvia and Rachel work together at the office and are invited to the birthday of a common colleague, who lives outside the city. Suppose that they agree that Rachel will buy the present if Sylvia buys the tickets to get there. Rachel loves to buy presents and hates to organize trips, and Sylvia is in exactly the opposite position. They do not know this about each other, however, for they are not friends, just acquaintances. Suppose now that Sylvia has already bought the tickets but no longer wishes the agreement to stand (for whatever reason, or for no particular reason). It seems quite clear that she cannot simply decide to cancel the arrangement. Rachel would react adversely, saying something of the sort "but we agreed!". Notice that she would invoke the fact that they have agreed as still grounding the existence of an obligation, regardless of Sylvia's wishes. Rachel could also appeal to additional reasons, such as the fact that she has agreed because she loves to buy presents, or because she has an exquisite taste in buying presents. But she does need not do so for her position to be intelligible, and in fact these would be *additional* reasons, grounded on the fact that the agreement still exists. The standard model cannot capture this aspect of agreements. For according to the standard model, Silvia would in effect be able to cancel the normative consequences of the arrangement unilaterally if she wished to do so. After all, she is the recipient of the promise, and she can release the promisor at will.

An advocate of the standard model cannot avoid the objection by claiming that, in cases like (1), agreeing consists of making a certain type of promise (one where the undertaking is believed to be welcome to the recipient) such that the recipient cannot release the promisor, and thus cannot cancel the arrangement unilaterally. A "promise" where the recipient cannot release the promisor if she wishes is not a promise. As seen, when a promise is made, the recipient has the power to cancel the normative arrangement unilaterally. This is part of the concept of promising. By contrast, when an agreement takes place, one of the parties does not have that power (except on special circumstances, on which see below).

Secondly, recall case (2), where Mark and Peter both acquire obligations (Mark to do A, Peter to do B). Suppose that, before Mark had the opportunity to do A, he sees Peter taking an airplane, and that this means that he cannot do B. Peter has already failed to fulfil his obligation. Suppose, in addition, that Peter has done so unjustifiably. In short, suppose that Mark knows that Peter has unjustifiably failed to fulfil his obligation before he (Mark) had the opportunity to fulfil his. There is an important sense, I think, in which Mark's position has changed. Mark may not be seen as obligated as before. This is not because his obligation was conditional (for that is not the case), and not, let us assume, because the agreement has become pointless.

Margaret Gilbert refers to a similar scenario to object to the standard model. In her view, Peter's defection has nullified both his and Mark's obligations. The agreement has ceased to exist. Gilbert claims that, however one attempts to refine the standard model, it will always be the case that, since each of the promises exchanged generates its own obligations, there is no way of showing that unilateral unjustified defection of one promise nullifies the agreement as a whole.[205]

The attack affects the standard model but, I think, is wrong in the diagnosis. The diagnosis is wrong because it is based on the incorrect assumption that the agreement ceases to exist when there is unilateral unjustified defection. If that were so, Mark would not be in a position to criticize Peter for defecting on the ground that he has violated the agreement. For if the agreement ceases to exist when there is unilateral unjustified defection, it would be senseless to invoke the agreement (which *ex hypothesi* does not exist any more) to criticize the defecting party. Moreover, *pace* Gilbert, it is important to notice that Mark himself is still obligated (although not as before). Unless the applicable reasons change, Peter can still criticize him if he (Mark) defects when the opportunity for doing A arises, on the ground that his failing to fulfil his obligation does not justify Mark's failing to fulfil his. This presupposes that the agreement still stands. Furthermore, Mark can well go on and do A, while later demanding compensation from Peter (for he would have spent time, and perhaps other valuable resources, in doing A). This also presupposes that the agreement still stands.

Yet Gilbert's attack on the standard model hits the mark because in effect Mark's position has changed, and the standard model cannot explain in what sense this is so.

Mark's position has changed, I believe, in this sense: he is still under an obligation, but he can cancel the arrangement in the face of unjustified defection if he wishes. In other words, he has an option. He can either exercise the power to nullify the whole arrangement, or not do this but rather go on and fulfil his obligation (thus creating a right to demand compensation). On the standard model, since each promise generates its own obligations, there is no way of understanding why Mark would have that power. Unjustified breach of the promise by Peter to Mark does not give Mark the power to cancel the obligation he has created by promising to Peter. If Peter fails to fulfil his promise, there is no way of explaining why Mark would have the power to cancel his own obligation, the obligation he has created by promising something to Peter. When promising, only the recipient (Peter) can release the promisor.

Can an advocate of the standard model avoid the objection by claiming that, in cases like these, agreeing consists of an exchange of certain types of promises (promises where the undertakings are believed to be welcome to the recipients) such that one of the promising parties can release *herself* if the other party fails to fulfil her obligation? Clearly, the answer should be negative. As seen, when a promise is made, only the recipient has the power to cancel the normative arrangement unilaterally. The promisor has no such power. This is part of the concept of promising. So, although some promises are such that the undertaking is believed to be welcomed by the recipient, an exchange of "promises" where one of the parties can release herself if the other party fails to fulfil her obligation is not an exchange of promises.

Finally, recall that the standard model assumes that one party may acquire obligations only after communicating her intention to undertake an obligation if the

[205] *LT* 316–330.

other accepts *on condition that the other do something*. That is why it conceives of agreeing as a *conditional* promise (or as an exchange of *conditional* promises). Yet there are cases where parties agree by one of them simply communicating her intention to undertake an obligation in the relevant way if the other accepts, not by communicating her intention to undertake an obligation if she accepts *on condition that the other do something*.

Suppose that Geoffrey and Steven have a common friend who needs to be informed of a piece of bad news. After debating, Geoffrey offers to convey the bad news himself (after all, somebody has to do it), and Steven accepts Geoffrey's offer. It seems clear to me that they have agreed that Geoffrey will convey the bad news and that, in order to agree, Geoffrey has made an offer that was accepted, but *not subject to the condition that Steven do some other thing*. In other words, there are cases of agreeing where this conditional aspect, an aspect that the standard model deems necessary, is completely absent.

An advocate of the standard model would perhaps deny that Geoffrey and Steven have reached an agreement. Geoffrey, the reply would go, has simply promised Steven that he will convey the bad news. But this is not the case. If that were the case, Steven would be in a position to cancel the arrangement unilaterally, i.e. to release Geoffrey from his obligation. For instance, he could release him and decide to convey the bad news himself. But he is not in such a position. Geoffrey could perfectly claim that Steven is not able, without his acquiescence, to opt out. Steven has no power to cancel the arrangement unilaterally.

The foregoing considerations show that the standard account of agreements is incorrect. Agreements cannot be construed as conditional promises or exchanges of conditional promises.

To propose an alternative account of agreements one should begin by focusing on the case of Geoffrey and Steven first, for it is the simplest one. If one focuses on idealised situations (i.e. regardless of agreeing practices and putting aside the fact that agreeing might take place within the framework of on-going relationships), one can say that two agents agree to do something, in the simplest cases like this, when, and only when:

1) one of them communicates to the other her intention to undertake, by that very act of communication, (a) an obligation to perform an action such that the undertaking is believed to be welcome by the recipient, and such that both parties will share the power to cancel the obligation; (b) if the other party accepts;
2) and the recipient accepts.

The first clause characterizes an offer. Notice that, just as there is a valid promising principle that promises ought to be kept, there is a valid principle that agreements ought to be kept: a principle that states that, if two parties agree, then the agreement ought to be fulfilled. This principle is also a power-conferring norm, and it enables us to create certain types of binding relationships. The considerations about the validity of the promising principle that we mentioned above apply, *mutatis mutandis*, to the agreeing principle: the principle is valid because it enables us to create binding relationships of a special kind (with normative consequences similar, but not identical, to the normative consequences of promising: here the binding relationship can be put to an end only if all the parties decide so), and this is in turn valuable because it enables us to provide and receive this kind of valuable assurance.

For more complex cases like (1), where only one party acquires an obligation on condition that the other do something, one can say that two parties agree when, and only when:

1) one of them makes an offer subject to the condition that the other party perform a certain action;
2) and the recipient accepts.

In turn, more complex cases where two parties (X and Y) become obligated, like case (2), can be construed thus: (1) X makes an offer to do A subject to the condition that Y makes an offer to do B; (2) Y makes an offer to do B and accepts X's offer subject to the condition that X accepts hers; (3) X accepts Y's offer. These restrictions are necessary to account for the fact that, when agreeing, the obligations are acquired simultaneously. The qualification related to the power to cancel the obligations unilaterally in the face of unjustified defection should be taken as read.

Let us label the foregoing model "the alternative model". It seems to provide a good explanation of agreements. It can also explain practices of agreeing: practices of agreeing are rules which are practised by most members of a group (and are regarded as valid only if most practise them) to the effect that certain acts count as agreeing, when agreeing is conceived of in the idealised way we have just considered.

The same applies to agreements that take place within the framework of special relationships. When agreeing takes place within the framework of different relationships with distinct values and which are partly constituted by norms, they mould the way in which one can agree (when agreements are conceived in the idealised way): they may require that performing certain acts counts as agreeing, when agreeing is conceived of in the idealised way.

The picture is now complete. It has several implications as to how the content of agreements (and also of promises) is determined. Let us consider how most accounts deal with this problem first.

8.4 The Content of Agreements

According to the subjective view, for there to be an agreement to do A, the intentions of the parties must coincide.[206] The difficulties of this view seem obvious, for there are plenty of counterexamples. Consider cases where one party makes an ambiguous offer. The individual intended to bind himself to do A, but becomes aware that the

[206] Cf Treitel (2003, 1); Atiyah (1979, 407–408, 731–733).

recipient will reasonably think that he intended to bind himself to do B because the context clearly supports that view. So he acknowledges that he agreed to do B, despite not having the intention to obligate himself to do B. The same applies to many other cases, like blunders, mistakes as to the identity of the other party, errors about the nature of the thing proposed, and so on. In many cases of this sort an agreement has been reached and, contrary to the subjective view, the intentions do not coincide.

According to the objective view, whether one has agreed to do something depends on whether the parties have performed some actions that count as agreeing as defined by a practice of agreeing, regardless of whether the intentional states are present.[207] This view is "objective" only in the sense, I would say, that it is not subjective. And it is also unsatisfactory. As noticed, there might be agreements without practices of agreeing. Most importantly, counterexamples abound. Agreeing practices may require some intentions to be present.

According to the mixed view, some mental states are relevant while others are not. Endicott's views are a good example of this approach.[208] He claims that whether the parties have agreed to do A is determined by the meaning of the conduct by which the parties agreed as interpreted by a reasonable person. The only "subjective" aspect of agreement is that the parties must do intentionally what counts as entering into an agreement to do A. For instance, in Endicott's view, if X reasonably thinks that she is signing an autograph (not a form of contract), then she has not agreed to anything, even if Y, a reasonable person, would interpret her conduct otherwise (e.g. because Z arranged things so that everything looked to Y as if X was signing a contract).[209]

This view is also subject to counterexamples. In some cases the "subjective" aspect that it requires may not be met and yet an agreement has been reached. For instance, there might be (justified) agreeing practices which, while providing a remedy against Z for misleading X, stipulate that X has acquired an obligation by merely signing a form of contract, even if X reasonably thinks that she is signing an autograph, in order to enable third parties like Y to perform transactions rapidly and without bothering about X's mental states. In other cases no "objective" aspect is required. For instance, Peter acts in a way that leads his intimate friend, John, to think that he has agreed to do A, where Peter's doing A is something that both of them consider relatively unimportant. John thinks that Peter has agreed to do A because that is what a reasonable person would make of Peter's conduct. John begins to act accordingly and, when Peter notices this, he promptly claims that he had no intention to bind himself. So John apologizes and claims "I am sorry, I thought you agreed to do A, but obviously I was wrong". It seems clear that Peter has not agreed to anything, so the objective aspect that the view considers indispensable is absent.

---

[207] Along these lines, see Goddard (1987, 263); Langille and Ripstein (1997, 63).

[208] Endicott (2000).

[209] Endicott (2000, 152–153, 157, 162–163).

One could attempt to provide more sophisticated arguments in favour of each of these views, but the result will always be, I think, unsatisfactory. It is clear that sometimes we adopt the "objective" view, sometimes the subjective view, and sometimes the mixed view.

The reason is that agreements normally take place within the framework of ongoing relationships or agreeing practices that are thought to promote certain values. These relationships and practices may require that certain acts count as agreeing (when this notion is construed in isolation of these relationships and practices). They may demand that the subjective view be adopted. That is the case of the friends, where agreeing requires the presence of all the relevant mental states because the relationship as such requires that one takes into special consideration what a friend intends. The relevant practices may require that the "objective" view be adopted, as in the case of the contract signed by mistake, such that one has agreed regardless of whether all the mental states are present. In other cases, the mixed view is appropriate. That would be the case if James, who is confused about dates, had offered his niece to go to the zoo on her birthday and she had accepted.

Perhaps the best way of establishing when one has promised or agreed to do A, where promising or agreeing takes place within the framework of special relationships or promising or agreeing practices, is in these terms: an individual has promised or agreed to do A, when promising or agreeing takes place within the framework of special relationships or promising/agreeing practices, when, and only when, the relevant practices, or the relevant relationships, require that his or her actions count as promising or as agreeing to do A (where promising or agreeing is understood in the idealised sense). Whether somebody has promised or agreed to do A in these contexts is, then, an objective question in the following sense: it depends on what the practices or relationships require, and what the practices or relationships require is something that is independent of what the parties to the alleged arrangement think in this respect. In fact, we can claim that, in these scenarios, the promise or agreement to do A does create obligations to do A when, and only when, the relationships or the promising/agreeing practices, which require that the relevant acts count as promising or agreeing to do A, are in effect valuable. That is, when a value is in effect promoted by the relevant relationship or practice requiring that.[210]

This explains all cases, and shows that neither the "objective" view, nor the subjective view, nor the mixed view is correct.

8.5 Conclusion

I have proposed an account of agreements. With this conception of agreements at hand we can return to our first approximation to the activities of groups with a normative unity of type (II) suggested in the previous chapter.

---

[210] These considerations also apply, *mutatis mutandis,* to other forms of voluntary undertakings, such as vows, consent, etc.

Chapter 9
The Activities of Groups with a Normative Unity of Type II. Other-Regarding, Developed Institutions. Developed Instances of the Judiciary

9.1 Overview of the Chapter

We can now see whether the first approximation to the activities of groups with a normative unity of type (II) suggested in Chapter 7 can be used to propose an account of activities of this sort. I shall claim that, though well oriented, it can be a starting point only. So I shall deploy an alternative model (Section 9.2). By relying on it, I shall propose an account of other-regarding, developed institutions (Section 9.3). And based on the latter account I shall suggest a model of developed instances of the Judiciary (Section 9.4).

9.2 The Activities of Groups with a Normative Unity of Type (II)

Consider this proposal:

> There is an intentional activity of a group with a normative unity of type (II) if, and only if, there is a set of individuals (defined extensionally or intensionally) such that:
>
> a) each conceives of a state of affairs the bringing about of which involves, or is constituted by, the performance of certain actions (and the display of certain attitudes) by all members of the set; *the relevant actions are the actions which they have agreed (explicitly or implicitly) to perform;*
> b) their conceptions of this state of affairs overlap;
> c) each intends to perform the relevant actions (and displays the relevant attitudes), and conceives of these actions (and attitudes) as related in the way described to the state of affairs;
> d) each executes his intentions and, as a result, the state of affairs mentioned in (b) obtains;
> e) *each thinks that the previous conditions obtain, and that a normative consideration according to which agreements should be kept is applicable to them.*

R.E. Sánchez Brigido, *Groups, Rules and Legal Practice*,
Law and Philosophy Library 89, DOI 10.1007/978-90-481-8770-6_9,

Let us inspect this account in general. The model is identical to the model of the activities of groups with no normative unity deployed in Chapter 5, save for some minor differences (which are highlighted in italics), namely the second part of clause (a) and clause (e). This has two implications.

Firstly, it is clear that there is a group which acts with a normative unity of type (II) if, and only if, conditions (a)–(e) obtain. From this we can extract a test of membership. An individual is a member of such a group if, and only if, there is a set of individuals (defined intensionally or extensionally) such that: (i) he conceives of a state of affairs the bringing about of which involves, or is constituted by, the performance of certain actions (and the display of attitudes) by him and by the other individuals of the set; the relevant actions are the actions which they have agreed (explicitly or implicitly) to perform; (ii) his actions (and attitudes) are seen by the others, together with their own actions (and attitudes), as related in the way described to the state of affairs; (iii) his conception of the state of affairs overlaps with the conceptions of the others; (iv) he intends, and so do the others, to perform the relevant actions; (v) he executes his intentions, and so do the others, and the state of affairs configured by their overlapping conceptions is being achieved; (vi) he thinks that the previous conditions obtain, and that a normative consideration according to which agreements should be kept is applicable to him; the same applies to the others. The set of individuals who satisfy these properties form the group which acts with a normative unity of type (II).

Secondly, there is no denial that one might need to appeal to further conditions (such as mutual responsiveness, or common knowledge, or the idea that agents intend not only to do their parts, but also that the group act) to understand more complex cases. Notice for instance that the characterization is too narrow, for there might be special cases such that particular mechanisms among participants, to the effect that the acts of one member of the set count as the act of the group, are present. But as suggested before these cases are more complex and can be captured by adding extra conditions to the model.

Consider the model in particular now. Since it is almost identical to the model of the activities of groups with no normative unity deployed in Chapter 5, save for the second part of clause (a) and clause (e), I shall consider these two clauses only and the way in which they affect the reading of the other clauses.

Clause (a) states that the relevant actions (those which are deemed as standing in an instrumental relation to, or as being constitutive of, the bringing about of the relevant state of affairs) are the actions that members have agreed to perform. Some clarifications are needed.

Firstly, I claimed that we can conceive of agreements in an idealised context, or within the framework of agreeing practices, or within the framework of special relationships. The clause should be interpreted as contemplating all such possibilities.

When the agreement has taken place in an idealised context, the clause should be interpreted, in accordance with our account of this type of agreements, as stating that each of the members has put forward (tacitly or explicitly) a (conditional) offer that has been accepted to the effect that he should perform certain actions (actions that are conceived of as standing in an instrumental relation to, or as being partly constitutive of, the bringing about of the relevant state of affairs), such that the relevant individuals share the normative power to cancel the whole arrangement if they so wish (except in special circumstances).

In turn, when the agreement has taken place within the framework of agreeing practices or special relationships, the clause should be interpreted as stating something different. Practices of agreeing are, I claimed, rule(s) to the effect that certain acts count as agreeing, when agreeing is conceived of in the idealised way, which are followed by most members of a group, and which are deemed valid because they are thought of as promoting a value which can be instantiated only if they are generally practised. (And they are in effect valid if, and only if, they in effect promote a value which can be instantiated in that way.) Something similar happens with agreements arrived at within the framework of special relationships. Participants might be friends, colleagues, relatives, neighbours, fellows, and so on. These relationships are partly constituted by norms. They might demand, I claimed, that certain acts counts as agreeing, when agreeing is understood in the idealised way. (And these norms are valid if, and only if, they in effect promote a value within the relationship). Thus, when this clause states that participants have agreed, and when the agreement envisaged is one that has taken place in any of these two contexts, the clause should be interpreted as stating that the relevant practices or relationships require that participants' actions count as agreeing.[211] Whether a particular agreement has been reached in these contexts is, then, an objective question in the following sense: it depends on what the practices or relationships require, and what they require is something that is independent of what the parties to the agreement think in this respect.

Secondly, since the bringing about of the state of affairs is deemed as involving, or as being partly constituted by, the actions that they have agreed to perform, this clause implies that each participant's conception of the state of affairs makes essential reference to the agreement they have reached. Each thinks that there is a state of affairs the bringing about of which involves, or is constituted by, the performance of such-and-such actions, but each thinks of those particular actions under the general description "the actions we have agreed to perform".

Clause (b), which requires overlap in participants' conceptions of the state of affairs, has already been discussed.

Clause (c), which states that participants intend to perform the relevant actions, has also been discussed already. But notice that, since the actions in question are the actions that participants have agreed to perform, the clause implies that they intend to fulfil the agreement they have reached.[212] Given the considerations above,

---

[211] There might be cases where participants think that they have agreed but, in reality, no agreement has been reached. To capture these possibilities clause (a) should be construed as (a)': "... they *think* that they have agreed...". I do not state this in the model explicitly because the possibility is far-fetched.

[212] When the model is construed in terms of clause (a)', i.e. "they think that they have agreed...", clause (c) should be construed as implying that participants intend to fulfil the agreement they think that they have reached.

when the agreement has taken place within the framework of agreeing practices or special relationships, this should be understood as implying that they intend to fulfil the particular normative arrangement that, according to the relevant practices or relationships, they have reached.

Finally, clause (e) involves the idea that the individuals think that the agreement they have reached is valid, i.e. that it does generate obligations. If we think of cases where the agreement takes place in an idealised context (where no practices of agreeing exist, and where the parties are not linked by special relationships), the clause states that they think that the valid normative principle according to which agreements should be kept applies to them. If, as happens normally, the agreement takes place in a non-idealised context, the situation is somewhat different. As seen, an agreement reached within the framework of agreeing practices or special relationships generates obligations if, and only if, the relevant practices or relationships (which are partly constituted by norms to the effect that certain acts count as agreeing and are supposed to foster certain values) are in effect valuable (i.e. they do promote certain values). So, in these situations, the clause brings in the idea that they think that the agreeing practices or relationships are in effect valuable.

Let us consider, then, whether the model captures the fact that these individuals think of themselves as being under a duty qua members of the group even if they do not conceive of the group-activity as particularly valuable in relation to individuals other than themselves. Recall that these self-understandings have several features. They presuppose that the agents believe that they form a group which acts and that they are members. Besides, they obtain even if members do not conceive of the group-activity as in effect particularly valuable in the way described. Finally, they have a certain content. *Inter alia*, when a member believes that he has a duty qua member, he believes that, as a member of the group (as a person described in terms of a particular property or properties only, i.e. his being a member or, put otherwise, his belonging to a particular kind of group), he ought (he has a duty) to do certain things. And he believes so because he thinks that there is some general normative consideration (according to which, if one satisfies one, some or all of these properties – i.e. those which add up to his being a member – then one has a duty to do certain things) which is applicable to him.

To establish whether the model captures these self-understandings we have to see the situation from the point of view of members. And the best way to do this consists of going, in a rough and ready way, through the clauses of the model dispensing, when appropriate, with those components that make reference to propositional attitudes (such as "*believe that...*") and considering the content of these attitudes only. If we follow this strategy we can see that members see their situation somewhat along these lines:

> There are several individuals and myself; there is a state of affairs the bringing about of which involves, or is constituted by, me and all the others performing certain actions (and displaying certain attitudes); these actions are the actions that we have agreed to perform; I intend to perform, and perform, the relevant actions, and hence I intend to fulfil the agreement, and the rest of us intend and act likewise; we are bringing about this state of affairs; in

short, we form a group which acts, and I am a member of this group; this means, in particular, that I satisfy a particular property: I have agreed to perform some actions that stand in an instrumental relation to, or are partly constitutive of (together with certain attitudes), the bringing about of this state of affairs; and since there is a normative consideration according to which agreements should be kept, I ought to perform the relevant actions.

This seems to capture well all the features of participants' self-understandings. First, these self-understandings presuppose that the relevant individuals believe that there is a group which acts, and that they are members. This is precisely what our model entails, as our construal of how our individual sees his situation shows: "...in short, we form a group which acts, and I am a member of this group".

Second, it captures the fact that participants' self-understandings – that they are under a *duty* – obtain even if they do not consider the activity as particularly valuable in the way described. The normative consideration mentioned in clause (e), i.e. that agreements should be kept, is a plausible normative consideration and, as I have tried to show in Chapter 8, this normative consideration is duty-imposing. Accordingly, the "ought" in question ("...I ought to perform the relevant actions") brings in the idea that duties are involved. Besides, this normative consideration demands that one performs the relevant actions regardless of whether the action one has agreed to perform is, in and of itself, particularly valuable.

Third, the model captures the fact that these self-understandings have a certain content. Our individual is a member of this type of group. This means that he satisfies several complex properties (see our test of membership above). But there is one particular aspect of his membership, as he sees it, i.e. it is his satisfying some of these properties, which explains his conceiving of himself as under a duty, namely that he satisfies conditions (i) and (vi) above. That is, what explains his self-understanding is his believing that: (i) there is a state of affairs the bringing about of which involves, or is constituted by, the performance of certain actions (and the display of attitudes) by him and by the other individuals of the set; the relevant actions are the actions they have agreed (explicitly or implicitly) to perform; (vi) a normative consideration according to which agreements should be kept is applicable to him. That is why our construal of his position goes "...I am a member of this group which acts; this means, *in particular*, that I satisfy a *special* property: I have agreed to perform some actions that stand in an instrumental relation to, or are partly constitutive of (together with certain attitudes), the bringing about of this state of affairs; and since there is a normative consideration according to which agreements should be kept, I ought to perform the relevant actions".

So the model seems to capture well what takes place. To illustrate it we only need to modify one of the examples of the activities of groups with *no* normative unity considered before. Recall the case of the painters discussed in Chapter 5. Participants did not think that they were under any duty there. But suppose now that participants have agreed to perform their parts. That is, assume that condition (a) above is met. If that were the case, and if condition (e) – together with the others – were also met, the group would become a group which acts with a normative unity of type (II).

The reason why participants might have agreed may vary depending on the setting. But prominent among these reasons is the fact that agreements are ways of creating, voluntarily, obligations that will accrue regardless of whether one thinks that the thing one has agreed to do is particularly valuable, thus assuring that one's part will be performed regardless of what one thinks in this respect (such that, if not performed, the relevant individuals will have acquired a right to demand compliance and compensation in some way). The difference in this respect with the activities of groups with no normative unity, and with groups which act with a normative unity of type (I), is, therefore, more than relevant. For one thing, in those cases members have no special right to demand compliance, or compensation.

Now one difficulty with the model is that it does not capture cases where not all members think that they have a duty qua members. In other words, it is not a model of groups which act with *a certain degree of normative unity of type (II)*. But the model can be easily modified to capture these cases. Clause (a) should be replaced with clause (a'): each conceives of a state of affairs the bringing about of which involves, or is constituted by, the performance of certain actions (and the display of certain attitudes) by all members of the set; the relevant actions are the actions which *most* have (explicitly or implicitly) agreed to perform. And clause (e) should also be replaced with clause (e'): *most* think that the previous conditions obtain, and that a normative consideration according to which agreements should be kept is applicable to them. So we could say that there is a group which acts intentionally *with a certain degree* of normative unity of type (II) if, and only if, there is a set of individuals such that conditions (a'), (b), (c), (d) and (e') are met.

Is this account correct? I think that it still needs elaboration. It contemplates a possibility, perhaps a very common one, but by no means the only one.

Agreements are voluntary undertakings. But they are not the only kind of voluntary undertaking. Promises, for instance, are another type of voluntary undertaking which I explored in some detail. They exhibit, I claimed, certain important differences with agreements. But they are relatives of the same family. And it could be the case that some groups which act with a (certain degree of) normative unity of type (II) are groups where members have promised, instead of having agreed, to perform their parts. Promises have, despite their differences with agreements, the same relevant and general features that would account for the fact that members conceive of themselves as under a duty qua members despite their not thinking of the joint activity as particularly valuable in the way described. For, as argued in Chapter 8, the normative consideration according to which promises ought to be kept is plausible; it is, when applicable, a duty-imposing one; and it demands, when applicable, that the action be performed regardless of whether the action one has promised to perform is particularly valuable. For instance, in the case of the painters mentioned above it could perfectly be the case that participants, instead of having agreed, had promised (tacitly or explicitly) to perform the relevant actions. The normative consequences would be somewhat different, but the activity of the group would still be the activity of a group with a normative unity of type (II).

In fact, there are cases where participants have neither agreed nor promised and, nevertheless, there is a group which acts with a normative unity of type (II). Some groups are normatively structured by participants making vows before the others, and making vows is also one way of voluntary undertaking obligations. This normally occurs in a ritualized setting, where the individual undergoes a significant change of normative status. Some gangs are examples of groups structured in this way. Of course, I shall not propose an analysis of vows. My point is only that vows, although at a pre-analytical level distinct from promises and agreements in some respects, are also forms of voluntary undertakings[213] They are also relatives of the same family. At a pre-theoretical level, they also share with promises and agreements the same general and relevant characteristics that would account for the fact that members of the group, if vows were included in the picture, would conceive of themselves as under a duty qua members even if they do not think of group-activity as particularly valuable: the normative consideration according to which vows made before others ought to be kept is a plausible one; it is a duty-imposing normative consideration; and, when applicable, it demands that the action which one has vowed to perform be performed regardless of whether it is particularly valuable.

Moreover, agreements, promises and vows are but examples of voluntary undertakings. There are others, such as making oaths, or consenting. Despite there being differences at a pre-analytical level among them (which I shall not explore), all of them exhibit, as forms of voluntary undertakings, the same general and relevant characteristics. And there might be activities of groups with a normative unity of type (II) where, for instance, participants have made an oath, or have consented, to perform the relevant actions.

To capture all these possibilities we should generalize. We could modify the model a bit, especially clause (a), thus obtaining a model of this sort: "There is a group which acts with a normative unity of type II if, and only if, there is a set of individuals (defined extensionally or intensionally) such that: (a) each conceives of a state of affairs the bringing about of which involves, or is constituted by, the performance of certain actions (and the display of certain attitudes) by all members of the set; the relevant actions are the actions which *they voluntarily undertaken (implicitly or explicitly) the obligation to perform*; (b)...".

Still, the model would not have yet sufficient descriptive coverage. Recall one of the considerations that Bratman and Kutz mentioned, namely the presence of acts of purposive creation of expectations. As argued in Chapter 8, one could create expectations of this type without having voluntarily undertaken an obligation. So participants might have led, purposively, other members to expect that they will participate and, under a suitable moral principle which they deem applicable, these acts of purposive creation of expectations may ground the existence of obligations to perform the relevant actions, regardless of whether participants think of the relevant actions as, in and of themselves, particularly valuable. I shall not propose any

[213]For an analysis along Razian lines of vows and their normative differences with promises (Lamond 1996, 127–129). Cf Robins' (1984, 14, 85–87, 96–104).

particular account of the moral principle according to which certain acts of purposive creation of expectations create duties. Scanlon's principle of fidelity may be the starting point to provide a construal of it.[214] My only point is just that this principle is a plausible normative principle. That this principle, if applicable, creates duties. And that, when applicable, it creates duties that bear upon one's behaviour regardless of whether the relevant actions are, in and of themselves, particularly valuable.

Yet even if we add this idea to the account it would still have insufficient descriptive coverage. The normative considerations according to which voluntary undertakings should be honoured, or according to which one should perform the actions that one has purposively led others to expect that one will perform, have something in common. They require that the relevant actions be performed regardless of whether they are, in and of themselves, particularly valuable. We can label these normative considerations "content-independent normative considerations". A normative consideration, we can say very abstractly, is content-independent if there is no direct connection between the action which, according to the normative consideration, one ought to perform, and the particular value of the action considered alone.[215] And it seems that normative considerations which make reference to voluntary undertakings or to acts of purposive creation of expectations are not the only normative considerations of this type. The normative principle according to which one must obey, within certain limits, legitimate authorities is, Raz has argued persuasively,[216] a content-independent normative consideration too. And it might be the case, for instance, that participants conceive of a state of affairs the bringing about of which partly involves, or is constituted by, the actions that an authority they consider legitimate has commanded them to perform.

It is not my intention to examine content-independent normative considerations, although I have explored some of them already (when analyzing agreements and promises). I only want to stress that we recognize their existence and plausibility; that groups of the type we are considering might be structured around normative considerations of this general sort; and that this would explain why participants consider themselves, qua members of the group, under a duty even if they do not think of the relevant actions, and correspondingly of the group-activity, as particularly valuable in the way described.

I have mentioned three content-independent normative considerations, namely those which make reference to voluntary undertakings, to the purposive creation of expectations, and to legitimate authorities. But there might be others, and one should leave this possibility open. Perhaps the best way to do so is by proposing a very general and abstract characterization of the activities of groups with a normative

---

[214]The principle should be further elaborated. It should not entail that leading another individual, purposively, to expect that one will perform an intrinsically immoral act (say, kill innocent children) creates a duty to follow through.

[215]This is only a coarse adaptation of Raz's characterization of content-independent reasons. Cf VONP 95; *MF* 35–36.

[216]VONP 95; *MF* 35–36.

unity of type (II). My suggestion is that they obtain if, and only if, the following conditions are met:

There is a set of individuals (defined extensionally or intensionally) such that:

a) each conceives of a state of affairs the bringing about of which involves, or is constituted by, the performance of certain actions (and the display of certain attitudes) by all members of the set; the relevant actions are the actions which, together with certain facts (e.g. the fact that they are the actions which they have voluntarily undertaken the obligation to perform; or have purposively led the others to expect that they will perform; or have been ordered to perform by a particular authority), appear in the antecedent of a content-independent normative consideration;
b) their conceptions of this state of affairs overlap;
c) each intends to perform the relevant actions (and displays the relevant attitudes), and conceives of these actions (and attitudes) as related in the way described to the state of affairs;
d) each executes his intentions and, as a result, the state of affairs mentioned in (b) obtains;
e) each thinks that the previous conditions obtain, and that the content-independent normative consideration mentioned in (a) is in effect applicable to them.[217]

From this model we can build a model of groups which act and which display a normative unity of type (II) to a certain degree only. We only need to modify clauses (a) and (e). Clause (a) should be replaced with clause (a'): each conceives of a state of affairs the bringing about of which involves, or is constituted by, the performance of certain actions (and the display of certain attitudes) by all members of the set; the relevant actions are the actions which, together with certain facts (e.g. the fact that they are the actions which *most* have voluntarily undertaken the obligation to perform; or have purposively led the others to expect that they will perform; or have been ordered to perform by a particular authority), appear in the antecedent of a content-independent normative consideration applicable to *most*. And clause (e) should be replaced with clause (e'): *most* think that the previous conditions obtain, and that the content-independent normative consideration mentioned in (a) is in effect applicable to them. So we could say that there is a group which acts intentionally with *a certain degree* of normative unity of type (II) if, and only if, there is a set of individuals such that clauses (a'), (b), (c), (d) and (e') obtain.

[217]Notice that this allows for the possibility of groups whose members are not linked by exactly the same normative relation (e.g. some might have agreed, others might have purposively created expectations, etc).

9.3 Other-Regarding, Developed Institutions

Now let us come back to institutions. We are interested in other-regarding, developed institutions. I claimed, in Chapter 1, that these institutions have certain pre-analytic features. Firstly, if there is an other-regarding, developed institution, then there is a group which acts intentionally for a significant period of time only if (most of) its members follow, and are disposed to follow, some rule(s) for a significant period of time. Secondly, if there is an institution of this sort, (most) members of the group think of the activity as purporting to be valuable in relation, primarily, to non-members, and to (some aspect(s) of) the community or society as a whole. And, thirdly, if there is an institution of this sort, (most) members of the group just described (i.e. the group characterized by the two foregoing features) think that they have a duty qua members of such group (and in many cases they think that they have a duty qua members of the institution).

It is clear, then, that these institutions are particular types of groups which act (see especially the first feature). And that they are groups (see the other two features) which act with a normative unity of type (II) – when all members think that they are under a duty qua members – or with *a certain degree* of normative unity of type (II) – when only most members think that.[218] So we could rely on the accounts suggested in the previous section to propose an account of these institutions. Consider this proposal:

> There is an other-regarding, developed institution if, and only if, there is a set of individuals (defined intensionally or extensionally) such that:
>
> a) each conceives of a state of affairs the bringing about of which is *constituted* by the performance of certain actions and the display of certain attitudes by all the members of the set *(their following, and intending to follow, some rule(s) for a significant period of time)*; and the relevant actions are those which, together with certain facts (e.g. the fact that *the rule or rules in question are those which all (or most) of them have voluntarily undertaken the obligation to follow; or have purposively led the others to expect that they will follow; or have been ordered to follow by a particular authority*), appear in the antecedent of a content-independent normative consideration applicable to all (or most) of them;
> b) their conceptions of this state of affairs overlap;
> c) each intends to perform the relevant actions, and conceives of these actions as related in the way described to the state of affairs; *his intentions are publicly accessible*;

[218] It seems that not all other-regarding, developed institutions are groups which act *with a certain degree* of normative unity of type (I). There might be cases where all must think that they have a duty qua members for the group to qualify as an institution. For instance, cases where, if one individual did not think that he has a duty qua member, the rest would not consider him a member.

d) each executes his intentions *for a significant period of time* and, as a result, the state of affairs mentioned in (b) obtains;
e) each thinks (or most think) that the previous conditions obtain, *and that the state of affairs being brought about purports to be valuable in relation to individuals other than themselves, and in relation to (some aspect(s) of) the life of the community as a whole.*
f) each thinks (or most think) that the content-independent normative consideration mentioned in (a) is in effect applicable to them.

Consider the model in general. It is simply a combination of two slightly modified versions of the models of the activities of groups with a normative, and with a certain degree of normative unity, of type (II), which were presented in the previous section. (The differences are highlighted in italics.) For these institutions are groups which act intentionally of a particular type (this is what clauses (a)–(d) attempt to capture). And they are groups which act intentionally *with a normative unity of type (II)* or *with a certain degree of normative unity of type (II)* (this is what clause (f) attempts to capture). This has two implications.

First, from the model we can extract a test to establish when an individual is a member of an other-regarding, developed institution. I shall not deploy the test, nevertheless, for this can be easily done by following the same line of reasoning that we used before. Second, there is no denial that additional conditions (such as mutual responsiveness, or common knowledge, or the idea that agents intend not only to do their parts, but also that the group act) should be introduced to capture more complex cases. Besides, this characterization is too narrow. For there are cases where the acts of only one member of this type of group count as the act of the group. But as said this seem to be more complex cases where there are special mechanisms among members to that effect, and they can be captured by adding clauses that refer to these mechanisms.

Consider the model in particular now. There is no need to discuss all the clauses, for this model is almost identical to the model of other-regarding, *non*-developed institutions deployed in Chapter 6, save for some modifications. So I shall consider the relevant differences only.

Focus on clause (a). The only difference with the relevant clause discussed in the previous section is that the bringing about of the state of affairs is deemed as partly *constituted* by the performance of certain actions: their following certain rule(s), namely the rule(s) all of them, or most of them, have agreed to follow, or have been order to follow, etc. So each thinks of the bringing about of the state of affairs as partly constituted by their following some rule(s), namely the rule(s) which all of them, or most of them, have agreed to follow, or have been ordered to follow, etc. Each thinks that the bringing about of the state of affairs is partly constituted by the performance of such-and-such actions, but each thinks of those particular actions under the general description "the actions which consist of following the rule(s) which all of us, or most of us, have voluntarily undertaking the obligation to follow, or have been ordered to follow, etc". The distinction between the "all" and the "most" is necessary in order to distinguish between cases where the institution is a group which acts and which displays a normative unity of type (II) and cases where it displays a normative unity of type (II) to a certain extent or degree.

Condition (b), which demands overlap in participants' conceptions, has already been discussed.

Condition (c), which demands that participants intend to perform the relevant actions, has also been discussed. But notice that, since the relevant actions consist of following the rule(s) which (most of) these individuals have agreed to follow, or have been ordered to follow, etc, this is what they intend: to follow the rule(s) that they (all or most) have agreed to follow, or have been commanded to follow, etc. The public accessibility feature of these intentions, which means that each is disposed to disclose his intention to the others, seems also a necessary feature of these institutions. If each kept his intention in secret these institutions would be, it seems clear to me, unrecognizable. And when clause (d) claims that they execute their intentions, they should be understood as intentions that have the content just described.

Condition (e) requires that (most) participants conceive of the state of affairs which is being brought about as purporting to be valuable in a particular way. This clause is also necessary to account for one of the pre-analytical aspects of these institutions mentioned above. But notice that this clause does not deny that participants might consider the state of affairs as in effect valuable. It only stresses that they need not.

Clause (f) is introduced to capture, together with the other clauses of the model, the fact that either all participants (in the case of institutions which are acting-groups displaying a normative unity of type (II)), or most participants (in the case of institutions which are acting-groups displaying a certain degree of normative unity of type (II)), consider themselves as under a duty qua members of a particular type of group which acts even if they do not think of the group-activity as particularly valuable in the way described.

It should be quite clear that these clauses are fit for the task. For there is no significant difference between participants' self-understandings when the individuals form an institution of this type and when they form a group which acts with a normative of type (II). After all, these institutions *are* particular kinds of groups with a normative unity of type (II). And there is no significant difference between the relevant clauses of the model designed to capture that sort of group, which was discussed in the previous section, and our model of these institutions. So the same considerations apply here as well.

Notice, just to illustrate, how participants see their situation in our institutions once we follow the strategy used before (that is, by going, in a rough and ready way, through the clauses of our model dispensing, when appropriate, with those components that make reference to attitudes such as "*believe/conceive* etc that...", and considering the content of these attitudes only):

> There are several individuals and myself; there is a state of affairs the bringing about of which is constituted by me and all the others performing certain actions and displaying certain attitudes: our intending to follow, and following, some rule(s) for a significant period of time, namely the rule(s) most of us have agreed to follow; I intend to follow the rule(s),

and hence to fulfil the agreement, and follow the rule(s), and this is no secret; the same applies to the rest of us; we are bringing about the state of affairs, which purports to be valuable in relation to individuals other than us and in relation to some aspect(s) of the life of the community as a whole; in short, we form a group which acts, and I am a member; this means, in particular, that I satisfy a special property: I have agreed to perform some actions that are partly constitutive of (together with certain attitudes) the bringing about of this state of affairs; and since there is a normative consideration according to which agreements should be kept, I ought to perform the relevant actions (to follow the rule(s)).

As you can see, the way in which participants see their situation does not differ significantly with the way in which members of a group with a normative unity of type (I) understand their situation, as shown in the previous section. After all, to insist, these institutions *are* particular kinds of groups with a normative unity of type (II). So the same considerations apply.

The only point worth stressing here is this. As said, when there is an institution of the kind we are interested in, participants believe that they have a duty qua members of a particular group (not necessarily qua members of an institution). Our model captures this feature. According to it, these properties, as seen by members, are those which add up to being members of a group defined by conditions (a)–(d) and whose activity purports to be valuable in the way described. Of course, participants are normally aware that conditions (a)–(f) obtain, and normally they have the concept of an institution. Put otherwise, they are normally aware that there is an institution; and that is why, normally, they believe that they have a duty because they satisfy certain properties, i.e. those which add up to their being members of the institution. But these are more complex cases which can be captured, in accordance with the minimalistic strategy, by adding further conditions to the model.

In short, the model construes these self-understandings thus: "as a member of a group which acts – defined by conditions (a)–(d) – whose activity purports to be valuable in relation to individuals other than us and to (some aspect(s) of) the life of the community as a whole, I have a duty to do my part", while not denying that, in more complex cases – where members are aware that conditions (a)–(f) obtain – they appear as having the form "as a member of this institution I have a duty to do my part". Notice that, in these more complex cases, it is also their satisfying some of the properties that add up to their being members of the institution (i.e. those mentioned in the previous paragraph) which account for their thinking that they have a duty qua members.

It is easy to see how participants would conceive of their situation when the scenario is different (e.g. when most have purposively led others to expect that they will perform the relevant actions, or have been ordered to perform the relevant actions by a particular authority), so I shall not consider these possibilities here.

Given that our clauses are needed to capture the presence of this self-understandings, they are necessary. And they are, I think, also sufficient for there to be an institution of this type.

To illustrate the model I shall alter somewhat our example of a *non*-developed institution, so as to highlight the differences. Suppose that, as happened in the original example, an individual notices that children from a poor background need to be nourished adequately. He thinks that, given this and other circumstances (*inter alia*, he has free time and he is relatively well-off), he is under a duty to remedy this situation. But he cannot remedy it alone. The situation is so bad that he needs several individuals acting, and being disposed to act, in concert for a significant period of time. He therefore designs a plan, i.e. a set of rules to be followed by several individuals, including him, for a certain period of time (how meals are to be cooked, served, and so on). He conceives of the scenario where the to-be-recruited partners abide by his plan as a state of affairs the bringing about of which is constituted by the actions (and attitudes) of all of them, and as a state of affairs which, if obtained, would be valuable in relation to the children, and indirectly to the life of the community as a whole. In our original scenario several individuals showed up spontaneously. But here, unfortunately, this does not happen. So our entrepreneur sets out to recruit people. He notices, nevertheless, that all the possible would-be partners, for a variety of reasons and despite being in principle interested in helping the children, need some incentive. So he offers them a small salary. And he agrees with them that he will pay the salary in exchange for their following his plan. Each thinks that the actions and attitudes of all (their intentionally following the plan they have agreed to follow) are constitutive of the bringing about of a state of affairs which purports to be valuable in relation to individuals (the children) other than themselves, and indirectly to the society as a whole. And their conceptions of this state of affairs overlap. So clauses (a) and (b) of our model are met. In fact, they think that it is their duty to perform their parts, for they have agreed and there is a normative consideration according to which agreements should be kept. But this group does not act yet. Suppose now that they begin to follow their parts of the plan, that this situation persists for many years, and that they are all aware of this. Naturally, since all thought, before executing their intentions, that they have a duty to perform their parts, they still think that they are under a duty. So clauses (c)–(f) of our model are met. There is now a particular type of group which acts with a normative unity of type (II). We have arrived at a point in the story where it is clear, I submit, that there is an institution in this neighbourhood. Say, a charity. And it is a point where conditions (a)–(f) are met. (This example shows clearly, I think, that members need not be aware that there is an institution of this type, i.e. a group defined in terms of conditions (a)–(f), for them to belong to one.)

So the model seems adequate. These institutions, of course, might become more complex, just as other-regarding, non-developed institutions can become more complex.

Suppose that, just as happened with our example of the charity as a non-developed institution, in the charity mentioned one paragraph above (i.e. in our developed institution) members want to feed more children than the group has managed to nourish so far, and more adequately. But to do this they need more individuals participating. They need more members. So they conceive of a second, more complex state of affairs. It is a state of affairs the bringing about of which will be constituted by the performance of certain actions and the display of certain attitudes by *all* the relevant individuals (the initial members, and the new would-be members): their following, and intending to follow, the plan. But the situation is such that, if the new would-be members do not follow the plan, this will not hinder the achievement of the first state of affairs, i.e. the state of affairs which is being obtained now, which is still acceptable. So suppose that they adopt a special rule to incorporate new members. For instance, a rule according to which, if an individual agrees to perform his part, he will count as a member. Here this simply means: "we will see his actions and attitudes as partly constitutive of the bringing about of the second state of affairs; and he has now acquired a duty to do his part". Suppose that some individuals show up, and that they are incorporated. Here this simply means that everyone, the new individuals included, understands that the actions and attitudes of these individuals will be seen as partly constitutive of the bringing about of the second state of affairs, and that they have acquired a duty to perform their parts.[219] They are not active members yet, for they do not perform the relevant actions. They are, so to speak, "formal" members. So the first state of affairs is being obtained. But the second state of affairs would be obtained if (and only if) the formal members did their parts, i.e. if (and only if) they became active members.

Notice that, just as happened with our example of the charity as a non-developed institution, when the new individuals have just been incorporated but not performed the relevant actions yet, there are two groups which are inter-related: there is a set of individuals who satisfy conditions (a)–(f) of the model (the initial members) which is related in a particular way to another set of individuals (the formal members). Due to the incorporation of new members, we can say that both groups form the non-developed, other-regarding institution. This idea is not captured by the model, for according to it an institution of this type is a set of individuals who satisfy conditions (a)–(f). And here there are two sets of individuals (two groups) which are interrelated, and only of one of them satisfies conditions (a)–(f). Moreover, according to the model the new individuals are not members of the institution, for they do not satisfy our test of membership: they do not execute their intentions.

But as claimed before this does not represent any particular problem, for this case is more complex. The model, which focuses on the simplest cases, can be expanded to capture more complex cases. It can be expanded to capture the sense in which all these individuals form the institution. The expanded model should simply claim that, in this sort of complex case, "institution" refers to a complex group formed by two sub groups. One of them is a set of individuals described in terms of conditions (a)–(f) suggested by the minimalistic model, the other is a set of individuals who, due to the adoption of special rules, have been incorporated in the sense described. This is simply an expanded model, for it employs clauses (a)–(f). And from this expanded model we can extract an expanded test of membership. An individual is a member of this sort of institution if, and only if, there is a set of individuals such that he: (i) either satisfies the conditions mentioned in our test of membership above, or (ii) has been incorporated in the sense described (he is a formal member); but (iii)

---

[219]Cf p 112 above, where the charity was a non-developed institution. The new individuals were not seen as acquiring any duty when becoming members.

most of these individuals must satisfy our test of membership above; otherwise the institution would disappear.

It should be clear why the foregoing remarks are relevant. The model sketched above entails that an other-regarding, developed institution is a group which acts intentionally only if *all* its members follow, and are disposed to follow, some rule(s). And it entails that an individual is a member of this sort of institution only if he follows, and is disposed to follow, the relevant rule(s). Yet in my initial approximation to developed institutions, I claimed that one of their pre-analytical features (see the first feature) is that they are groups which act intentionally only if (most of) its members follow, and are disposed to follow, some rule(s). The "most" (which is intentionally vague) appears between brackets because, in some cases, there is an institution of this type (and hence a group which acts intentionally) where not all its members follow, or are disposed to follow, the relevant rule(s). In these cases certain individuals count as members of the institution (and hence as members of the group which acts intentionally) even if they are not disposed to follow, or even if they do not follow, the relevant rule(s). These cases seem not to be captured by the model.

These cases are, nevertheless, more complex cases. Our charity is one of them. The new individuals count as members because of a special rule to that effect, even if they have not followed the plan yet. And we can claim that here there is an institution (and hence a group which acts intentionally) where only *most* of its members are following some rule(s). But this case can be captured by expanding the model. Here "institution", I have suggested, refers to a complex group formed by two subgroups which are inter-related, namely the sub group of the initial members plus the sub group of formal members. Only the first sub group acts intentionally, the second has not acted intentionally yet. So the claim that here there is an institution (and hence a group which acts intentionally) where only most of its members are following some rule(s) simply means: there is a complex group (formed by two sub groups which are inter-related, i.e. the initial, active members, and the new, formal members) part of which acts intentionally (namely the first subgroup); so only most members of the complex group (namely the initial members) are following the relevant rules.

I think that we can generalize, just as we did when considering non-developed institutions: all cases where we claim that there is an other-regarding, developed institution (and hence a group which acts intentionally) and where only most (not all) members (are disposed to) follow some rule(s) – and hence cases where an individual counts as a member regardless of whether he is disposed to follow, or follows, the rule(s) – are more complex cases, where "institution" refers, in part, to a complex group (a set of individuals defined in terms of certain properties) part of which (a sub group of the complex group) acts intentionally. So these cases can be captured by expanding the model. And the fact that an individual counts as a member of the institution (the complex group) even if he does not follow, or is not disposed to follow, the rule(s), can be captured by extracting from the expanded model an expanded test of membership.

The minimalistic model seems, therefore, adequate. It captures all the simplest cases of other-regarding, developed institutions, and can be expanded to capture more complex cases.

Of course, these institutions can become even more complex, just as non-developed institutions can become more complex. For instance, in our charity participants might adopt a rule that establishes when an individual is a member of the institution (and hence they might adopt a rule that makes reference to the institution itself). Suppose that the rule states something along these lines: "an individual count as a member of this institution only after procedure X, which involves his agreeing to do his part, is followed". Assume that all the former members have left, that they have been gradually replaced by others through the procedure, and that all the individuals who belong to the institution (the formal members) are also are doing their parts (i.e. they are active members too). Suppose now that some of them have left, and that new individuals are incorporated to replace them. They count as members (as formal members) that very moment, even if they have not followed the plan yet. This case is even more complex, in part because participants have adopted a rule that makes reference to the institution itself, a possibility that the minimalistic model does not contemplate. But here, again, "institution" refers in part to a complex group (a set of individuals defined in terms of certain formal properties) part of which (namely the sub group of active members) acts intentionally. So this sort of complex case can be captured by expanding the model. And from it we can extract an expanded test of membership. Notice that the expanded test of membership should state that an individual is not a member of a complex group of this sort unless most of the other individuals of the set: conceive of a state of affairs the bringing about of which is constituted by their actions and attitudes (their following the plan they have agreed to follow); have overlapping conceptions of the relevant state of affairs; intend to do their parts (i.e. to follow the plan); execute their intentions; think of the state of affairs that is being obtained as purporting to be valuable in the way described; think that a normative consideration of the type described above is applicable to them. For if these conditions were not met the whole group would not be an other-regarding, developed institution; and hence an individual could not count as a member of the institution.

These institutions might become more complex in other ways. Participants might assign to certain members an authoritative position. They might adopt rules to expel members. They might designate representatives. The account I have deployed does not capture complex cases of this sort, but it could be further developed to do so.

Notice why these institutions are developed. They are developed because they can survive the possibility of alienation. Recall our thought-experiment. When envisioning an institution, suppose that most of its members think of the activity as actually valuable in the way described. Suppose now that each of the relevant members stops thinking, individually, of the activity in this way. If, for that reason, each of them would stop thinking of himself as under a duty, then the institution is a non-developed one. (In fact, we should say that the institution *was* an institution, for a necessary condition for the existence of any institution is that most of its members think of themselves as under a duty.) If, on the contrary, the relevant individuals continue to think of themselves as under a duty, then it is a developed one. This is what happens in our model. If most members realized that the activity of the group is not in fact valuable in the way described, they would still think of themselves as under a duty qua members, and hence the institution would survive. The remaining duty might be seen as of very little weight, but they would still consider themselves as under a duty.

9.4 Developed Instances of the Judiciary

We have at our disposal, I think, enough material to sketch a model of developed instances of the Judiciary, for most of the work has already been done. On the one hand, we can avail ourselves of the results of our previous inquiry on other accounts. Raz's views are particularly relevant in this respect. When inspecting his model we concluded that at least this partial characterization of the Judiciary could be attributed to him: there is a group of individuals (most of) whose members follow some rule(s) requiring them to evaluate conduct by applying norms identified by criteria contained in it, norms that form a system (they are internally related norms) which is open, comprehensive and supreme. We also claimed that there is reason to think that these conditions are necessary for there to be an instance of the Judiciary. On the other hand, we can avail ourselves of the model of other-regarding, developed institutions sketched above, which provides the conditions that are individually necessary and jointly sufficient to characterize other-regarding, developed institutions in general.

So consider the following proposal:

> There is a developed instance of the Judiciary if, and only if, there is a set of individuals (defined extensionally or intensionally) such that
>
> a) each conceives of a state of affairs the bringing about of which is constituted by the performance of certain actions and the display of certain attitudes by all of them: their following, and intending to follow, some rule(s) for a significant period of time, *which require that the conduct of members of the community be evaluated according to norms that satisfy certain criteria, such that a system of internally related norms which is open, comprehensive and supreme exists*; the relevant actions are the actions which, together with certain facts (e.g. the fact that they are the rule or rules which all –or most – of them they have agreed to follow), appear in the antecedent of a content-independent normative consideration applicable to all (or most) of them;
> b) their conceptions of this state of affairs overlap;
> c) each intends to perform the relevant actions, and conceives of these actions as related in the way described to the state of affairs; his intentions are publicly accessible;
> d) each executes his intention for a significant period of time and, as a result, the state of affairs mentioned in (b) obtains;

e) each believes (or most believe) that the previous conditions obtain, and that the state of affairs that is being achieved purports to be valuable, primarily, in relation to individuals other than themselves, and in relation to (some aspect(s) of) the life of the community as a whole;
f) each believes (or most believe) that the content-independent normative consideration mentioned in (a) is in effect applicable to them.

The model is just a more specific version of the model of other-regarding, developed institutions sketched in the previous section. The only difference (which is highlighted in italics) lies in the particular characterization of participants' conceptions of the state of affairs. So each of the clauses, putting aside the particular way of describing the state of affairs, should be understood accordingly. Besides, if the Judiciary is an other-regarding institution, if there are developed instances of the Judiciary (and I claimed that most actual instances are), then the clauses, putting aside the particular way of describing the state of affairs, must be individually necessary and jointly sufficient to capture developed instances of the Judiciary.

It should also be clear what the particular characterization of participants' conceptions of the state of affairs, or of the relevant rule(s), are. These ideas are, essentially, the same as Raz's, and I have already described what Raz's idea of a system of internally related norms, etc, which appears in our description of participants' conceptions of the state of affairs, involves.

This model is adequate to capture some of the cases mentioned in my initial characterization of non-developed instances of the Judiciary. It does not capture those cases where (most) members think of themselves *as under a duty qua members of the institution* (and not merely qua members a particular type of group which acts). But these cases are, I have argued above, more complex cases, and they can be captured by expanding the model just sketched. Besides, in some cases there is a developed instance of the Judiciary and yet *only most* (not all) members (are disposed to) follow the relevant rule(s). But these are more complex cases too, and they can also be captured by expanding the model just sketched, which is minimalistic, in the way I suggested in the previous section. For instance, there might be rules stipulating that an individual is a member of the Judiciary only after procedure X, which involves his agreeing to do his part, is followed, and until he is removed. In this scenario, there is an instance of the Judiciary and yet not all members satisfy conditions (a)–(f) of the model. But this is a more complex case. The Judiciary is here a complex group (a set of individuals defined in terms of certain formal properties) part of which (namely the sub group of formal members who are active members too) acts intentionally. So the model can be expanded to capture this case by following the same strategy employed before, when expanding our test of membership.

So before concluding let us return to some issues I left open.

Firstly, compare our account with the Hartian account (as deployed in the Postscript) and the conventionalist account. Our model allegedly overcomes all their difficulties, but it retains one aspect of them that seems correct. Roughly, both Hart and the conventionalists claim that, when there is an instance of legal practice, members follow the relevant rule *only if others do so*. This seems, in effect, correct. For if members followed the relevant rule with complete disregard of what others do (i.e. even if they thought that nobody else was following the rule), they could not think of themselves, in so doing, as members of a group. And officials do conceive of themselves as members. Our model retains, then, this aspect of Hart's and the conventionalist account in relation to non-developed instances of legal practice.

Secondly, I claimed that one reading of the simplified Razian model would not contain sufficient conditions in relation to developed instances. The reading in question is this: there is a developed instance of the Judiciary if there is a set of individuals who follow some rule(s) (which require them to evaluate conduct by applying norms identified by criteria contained in it, norms which form a system which is open, comprehensive and supreme) out of purely prudential reasons. I argued that this does not account for participants' self-understandings to the effect that they are under a duty qua members. But I suggested that these conditions are not sufficient for another reason, namely because we would not treat a set of individuals so described as an institution, i.e. as a group which acts intentionally. We can now see why. For our model shows that several elements, those which are needed to show that there is a group which acts intentionally, are absent from the picture. The requirements that members conceive of their following the rule(s), and of the system, as a state of affairs the bringing about of which is constituted by their actions and attitudes, that they intend to follow the rule(s), and that they conceive of these actions as related in that way to the state of affairs in a way which is publicly accessible, are absent. So a host of elements, those which explain in part in what sense the Judiciary is an institution, i.e. a group which acts intentionally, are missing from this reading of the simplified Razian view.

Finally, I claimed that under one plausible reading Shapiro's model (which claims that a developed instance of the Judiciary exists if, and only if, there is a set of individuals who satisfy the conditions of his model – they intend to contribute by way of meshing subplans, etc, out of purely self-interested considerations) would not be sufficient to capture developed instances, for it would not capture participants' self-understandings to the effect that they are under a duty qua members. But I also suggested that these conditions are not sufficient either for another reason. We can now see what this reason is. For several elements are absent from this picture. The model so understood employs the idea of a unified system, a group of norms that satisfy the same criteria, but not the idea that these norms form a special kind of system which is open, comprehensive and supreme. And it does not require that members conceive of their following the rule(s), and of the system, as a state of affairs the bringing about of which is constituted by their actions and attitudes either.

9.5 Conclusion

From this account of developed instances of the Judiciary we can extract a particular view of the content and structure of legal practice, when legal practice is understood as the practice of members of a developed instance of the Judiciary.

The *content* of the practice is this: there is a group which evaluates the conduct of members of a community by applying norms that satisfy certain criteria, norms that form a particular type of normative system. The *structure* of the practice, i.e. the attitudes that participants display, is quite complex: they see their doing this (where "their doing this" is tantamount to "our group doing this" or "our joint activity") as constituted by a complex set of attitudes and actions, and they think that a normative consideration that does not make reference to the value of such state of affairs (a content-independent normative consideration) requires that they perform the relevant actions.

We have already considered the structure and content of legal practice when the Judiciary is a non-developed institution, in Chapter 6. Given that the Judiciary is either a non-developed or a developed institution, these two views about the content and structure of legal practice are exhaustive of all the possibilities. So we can put the result of our inquiry in this respect in the following way. The *content* of legal practice *simpliciter* is this: there is a group which evaluates the conduct of members of a community by applying norms that satisfy certain criteria, norms that form a particular type of system. The *structure* of the practice *simpliciter* is quite complex: they see their doing this (where "their doing this" is tantamount to "our group doing this") as constituted by a complex set of attitudes and actions, and they think that, *either* a normative consideration that makes reference to the value of such state of affairs requires that they do their parts, *or* that (in addition) a normative consideration that does not make reference to the value of such state of affairs (a content-independent normative consideration) so requires.

We should now establish whether our account of developed instances of the Judiciary, and more generally, whether our account of the Judiciary *simpliciter*, meet our tests. This will be the task of our final chapter.

Chapter 10
Developed Instances of Legal Practice. Meeting the Tests

10.1 Overview of the Chapter

I shall claim that our account of developed instances of legal practice and, more generally, our account of legal practice *simpliciter* (which is composed by the accounts of non-developed and of developed instances of legal practice) meet our three tests (Sections 10.2–10.5).

10.2 Meeting the First Test

The first test requires from a theory that claims that legal practice has the same structure, although a distinct content, as collective intentional activities, that it provide an account that captures the main features of collective intentional activities. Our account of legal practice *simpliciter* meets this test. For it is based on a general account of collective intentional activities which is composed by three general models: the model of the activities of groups with no normative unity deployed in Chapter 5, the model of the activities of groups with a normative unity of type (I) suggested in Chapter 6, and the model of the activities of groups with a normative unity of type (II) proposed in Chapter 9. I have already argued, in each of these chapters, why each model captures the relevant features of the relevant type of collective intentional activities. And since the three models are exhaustive, as far as I can see, of all the possible configurations of collective intentional activities, our account meets this test.

10.3 Meeting the Second Test

This test demands that a theory of legal practice should provide a characterization of its content and of its structure in terms of the favoured category of practices, such that conceiving of the practice in those terms captures its main features, namely that it is the practice of members of an institution (a group with special features).

R.E. Sánchez Brigido, *Groups, Rules and Legal Practice*, Law and Philosophy Library 89, DOI 10.1007/978-90-481-8770-6_10,

I have already claimed, in Chapter 6, that our account of *non-developed* instances of legal practice meets the relevant aspects of this test. But legal practice can be either non-developed or developed. Accordingly, our general account of legal practice *simpliciter* would be correct if our account of *developed* instances met this test.

It seems to me that it does. It meets the standard requirements (consistency, clarity, etc.). In particular, the favoured category of practice (the practice in terms of which legal practice should be understood) is not characterized using the notion of an institution in an un-analyzed way. In fact, I have attempted to propose an analysis of that notion. Besides, it seems to me that the conditions mentioned in the account are, in relation to developed instances, necessary. And they also seem sufficient. The theory entails that, if there is a developed instance of legal practice as characterized by it, there is an instance of the practice of members of an institution, a (complex) group of individuals (part of) which acts intentionally (it evaluates the conduct of members of the community by applying certain norms). It also entails that (most of) its members follow some rule(s). And it entails as well that (most) members of the institution think that they are under a duty qua members regardless of whether they consider the activity as particularly valuable in the way described. That is, even if they are alienated. These beliefs are not absurd. The explanation of why this is so is contained in the explanation, proposed in the previous chapter, of why members of developed institutions in general conceive of themselves as under a duty qua members even if alienated, so I shall not repeat the argument.

In short, the model of developed instances of the Judiciary seems to meet our second test. Before concluding this section let me make some final remarks in support of the account.

From the model of developed instances of the Judiciary (as defined by clauses (a)–(f) in the previous chapter) we can extract a test to establish when an individual is a member (an official). Deploying the test is tedious but, I believe, it is helpful in order to assess the explanatory power of the account. Naturally, the test varies depending on whether the relevant instance of the Judiciary is one where all or most members think of themselves as being under a duty qua members. I shall consider the case where most do so first. An individual is here an official if, and only if, there is a set of individuals (defined intensionally or extensionally) such that: (i) he conceives of a state of affairs the bringing about of which is constituted by the performance of certain actions (and the display of attitudes) by him and by the other members of the set: their following, and intending to follow, some rule(s) for a significant period of time requiring them to evaluate the conduct of members of their society according to norms that satisfy certain criteria, norms that form a system (they are internally related) which is open, comprehensive and supreme; the relevant actions are the actions which, together with certain facts (e.g. the fact that the rule or rules in question are the rule(s) which most have agreed to follow), appear in the antecedent of a content-independent normative consideration applicable to most; (ii) his actions (and attitudes) are seen by the others, together with their own actions (and attitudes), as related in the way described to the state of affairs; (iii) his conception of the state of affairs overlaps with the conceptions of the others; (iv) he intends, publicly, to perform the relevant actions, and so do the others; (v) he executes his intentions, and so do the others, and the state of affairs configured by their overlapping conceptions is being obtained; (vi) he either (a) believes that the foregoing conditions obtain and that the state of affairs being achieved purports to be valuable in the way described or (b) does not so believe; (vii) he either (c) thinks that the normative consideration mentioned in (i) is applicable to him or (d) does not think that; but (viii) most of the individuals of the set who satisfy conditions (i)–(v) must also satisfy conditions (vi)(a) and (vii)(c). In turn, when the institution is such that *all* members think of themselves that they are under a duty, a similar characterization can be construed. Here an individual is a member (an official) if, and only if, there is a set of individuals such that: (i)' he conceives of a state of affairs with the same characteristics as described above; the only difference is that the relevant actions are the actions which, together with certain facts (e.g. the fact that the rule or rules in question are the rule(s) which *all* have agreed to follow), appear in the antecedent of a content-independent normative consideration applicable to *all*; (ii)' his actions (and attitudes) are seen by the others, together with their own actions (and attitudes), as related in the way described to the state of affairs; (iii)' his conception of the state of affairs overlaps with the conceptions of the others; (iv)' he intends, publicly, to perform the relevant actions, and so do the others; (v)' he executes his intention, and so do the others; the state of affairs configured by their overlapping conceptions is being obtained; (vi)' he believes that the foregoing conditions obtain and that the state of affairs being achieved purports to be valuable in the way described; the same applies to the others; (vii)' he thinks that the normative consideration mentioned in (i)' is applicable to him; the same applies to the others.

The test seems quite complex and perhaps too detailed. But, as said, it should be helpful to see the explanatory power of the model. Consider, in effect, its implications. When there is an instance of legal practice, a complex state of affairs obtains. This state of affairs is not something that one can bring about on one's own. It is constituted by the actions and attitudes of several individuals. In addition, when there is an instance of legal practice, the relevant individuals believe all this to be the case.[220] Our test captures these aspects of the situation, for according to them an official is an individual who conceives of his actions (and attitudes), together with the actions of the others, as constitutive of the bringing about of the relevant state of affairs. This is in part what conditions (i) and (i)' require.

Naturally, these conditions are not enough. Suppose that John thinks that he satisfies the foregoing properties (he sees his actions and attitudes as partly constitutive of the bringing about of the relevant state of affairs). This does not yet make him an official. He could be a bogus member. In order not to be so, the other relevant individuals should, at least, see John's actions as contributions. Our test (conditions (ii) and (ii)') captures this aspect of the situation too.

---

[220] Recall that, when referring to attitudes such as "believe/conceive/think etc", I mean actual or counterfactual attitudes.

Yet still the aforementioned conditions are not sufficient. The notion of overlap (there must be overlap in participants' conceptions of the state of affairs) is, I have argued, also needed if we are to conceive of the Judiciary as an institution, and hence of the relevant agents as members. This is what our conditions (iii) and (iii)' require.

It is quite clear, however, that the foregoing conditions are still insufficient. Suppose there is a set of individuals who satisfied the foregoing properties but have not formed any intention yet, and consequently have not acted so far. This set, clearly, would not qualify as an instance of the Judiciary. So officials, those individuals who form the Judiciary, must form the relevant intentions and execute them. This is what our conditions (iv)–(v) and (iv)'–(v)' demand.

Besides, in some cases, an individual might not be an official unless he thinks that the activity purports to be valuable. For instance, there might be cases where all the others would not consider him a member of the group unless he did so. This is captured by condition (vi)' of our test. But in many other cases the fact that he does not think of the activity in this way does not deprive him automatically of his status as an official. When this is so, nevertheless, most of the other relevant individuals must be in the opposite position. Otherwise the acting-group would not be an other-regarding institution. This aspect of the situation is captured by conditions (vi) and (viii).

Finally, there might be cases where an individual is not an official unless he thinks that he has a duty in part because of certain facts (e.g. his having agreed). For instance, cases where, if he had not agreed, or if he did not consider the agreement valid, the rest would not consider him a member. This is captured by conditions (i)' and (vii)'. But in many cases not all have agreed, and not all consider the agreement they have reached as really creating obligations, and this does not deprive them of their status of officials. Nevertheless, in the agreement-case, most must have agreed and consider the agreements they have reached as actually creating obligations. Otherwise they would not conceive of themselves as under a duty in the way required. And if that were the case, the Judiciary would be unrecognizable. Conditions (i), (vii) and (viii) capture this aspect of the situation.

Some may be tempted to claim that the test requires too much, and hence that the account is incorrect. Officials, the objection goes, simply apply, and intend to apply, certain rules, which they treat as rules of law. However one characterizes "officials", they need not display all the attitudes I have mentioned.[221] Consider, however, the "epistemic" attitudes that appear in my characterization of officials (such as believe/think/conceive etc). Recall that I mean actual *or* counterfactual attitudes. I claimed that, both in developed and non-developed instances, there is a set of individuals who believe (or *would* believe if they thought about the matter), among other things, that there is a complex state of affairs the bringing about of which is constituted by their following, and intending to follow, some rule(s) requiring them to apply norms that satisfy certain criteria, norms that form a system. It seems clear that a number of individuals would not be "applying certain rules *as*

[221] Cf Gardner (2002, 495, 500).

rules of law" (as the objection claims) in any relevant sense unless they recognized, upon reflection, that these rules form a system, and that "their applying these rules as rules of law" is a complex state of affairs the bringing about of which is constituted by those (their) actions and attitudes. If that were not so it would not be a recognizable instance of legal practice, and hence these individuals would not be officials in any relevant sense. So officials must be characterized, in part, in those terms. The same can be said of the rest of the content of the epistemic attitudes I mentioned. Consider now "conative" attitudes. I claimed that, both in developed and non-developed instances, there is a set of individuals who intend to follow some rule(s) requiring them to apply norms that satisfy certain criteria, but that they see their doing as "my doing my part of our obtaining this state of affairs". It seems also clear that each would not be "intending to apply certain rules as rules of law" in any relevant sense if each followed the rule(s) containing the criteria even after realizing that his doing so does not fall under the description "my doing my part of our bringing about this state of affairs" ("our applying certain rules as rules of law"). So this attitude must also appear in the characterization of officials.

So our test contains, I think, conditions that are sufficient to characterize officials. And they are also necessary. Of course, there are more complex cases, such as the case mentioned in the last chapter, where there are rules of the form: "an individual is a member of the Judiciary only after procedure X, which involves his agreeing to do his part, is followed, and until he is removed". Here an individual count as a member (i.e. as an official) even if he does not intend to follow the relevant rule(s), and even if he does not follow it. In fact, he might count as a member even if he does not meet any of the conditions of our test of membership. But this, I have argued above, is a much more complex case, where the Judiciary is a complex group (a set of individuals defined in terms of certain formal properties) part of which acts intentionally. So this sort of case can be captured by expanding the model. And from the expanded model we can extract an expanded test of membership. The latter must require that, of most of the individuals of the set (of most of those individuals who form the complex group), it be true that each satisfies conditions (i)'–(vii)'. Otherwise there would be no developed instance of the Judiciary, and hence an individual would not be a member of a developed instance of the Judiciary.

In short, the model contains a characterization of officials that, it seems to me, is correct, and this is a reason in favour of its adequacy.

The most important test in support of the model, nevertheless, is whether it can capture and explain some prominent aspects of actual instances of the Judiciary. For example, contemporary instances of the Judiciary in the western world. So let us see whether the model is successful on this count.

According to it, developed instances of the Judiciary can be normatively structured around voluntary undertakings, or authoritative commandments, or the purposive creation of expectations, among other possibilities. My impression is that the most familiar cases are those where most participants have voluntarily undertaken the obligation to follow some rule(s). Most actual instances are, I think, of this sort.

Consider a hypothetical story to illustrate this. Suppose that there is a small-scale, non-developed instance of the Judiciary. That is, suppose that the clauses of the model deployed in Chapter 6 are met. There is a set of individuals, defined intensionally or extensionally, each of whom conceives of a state of affairs the bringing about of which is constituted by all of them intending to follow, and following, a set of rules (or more generally, a plan) requiring them to evaluate the conduct of members of the society by applying norms that satisfy certain criteria, norms that form a system which is open, comprehensive and supreme. Their conceptions of the state of affairs overlap. They intend, publicly, to follow the plan, and execute their intentions for a significant period of time, such that the state of affairs is being obtained. They believe that all this is so, and that this state of affairs is valuable, primarily, in relation to the individuals other than themselves, and to the life of the community as a whole, and that a normative consideration which makes reference to the value of the state of affairs is applicable to them.

Now suppose that each of them foresees a difficulty. Each reasons as follows: "I have thought about the matter thoroughly, and I have concluded that this state of affairs is actually valuable in relation to individuals other than us, and for the community as a whole. It is unlikely that I change my mind. But what would happen if one us changes his mind? Most likely, we will attempt to persuade him of his mistake. This would demand time and effort, and persuasive skills, but it could be achieved. Nevertheless, what would happen if others begin to change their minds as well? They would most likely opt out. Here the strategy of attempting to persuade them of their moral error would be more difficult to implement. This situation is fairly unstable".

If they voluntarily undertook the obligation to follow the plan this lack of stability would be overcome. In fact, agreements seem particularly suitable in this type of setting, where not many individuals are involved, and participants might well arrive at this conclusion. For once valid agreements are reached, duties arise that are independent of the question of whether the action one has agreed to perform is particularly valuable. If members agreed to follow the plan this lack of stability would be surmounted. For participants would recognize that they are under a duty to follow the rule regardless of whether doing so is in effect particularly valuable. Besides, agreements create a special right to demand compliance, and compensation eventually. This is the price to pay if one agrees. For one might in effect come to realize that the activity is not particularly valuable, and despite this one will be under a duty to follow the plan. One can decide not to follow it, but then one will face claims demanding compensation. Each of them is, let us suppose, willing to pay this price, for as said they think that it is unlikely that they will change their minds as to the value of the activity. So assume that they agree to follow the plan they have been following so far.

The institution is now in a phase of transition, from being a non-developed instance of the Judiciary to becoming a developed one.

In effect, each still conceives of a state of affairs the bringing about of which is constituted by their following, and intending to follow, a plan. The only difference is that, now, the plan is that which they have agreed to follow. So clause (a) of our model of developed instances of the Judiciary is met.

Clause (b) is also met. Their conceptions of the state of affairs overlapped when the Judiciary was non-developed, and they still overlap now. But the overlapping conceptions refer now to a state of affairs the bringing about of which is partly constituted by certain actions under the general description "our following the plan we have agreed to follow".

Clause (c) is also fulfilled. Participants publicly intended to follow the plan when the Judiciary was non-developed, and they still can be said generally to intend that now. But strictly speaking their intentions are now tantamount to their intending to fulfil the agreement they have reached, i.e. to follow the plan they have agreed to follow.

One aspect of clause (e), that members conceive of this state of affairs as *purporting* to be valuable, primarily, in relation to individuals other than themselves, and in relation to the life of the community as a whole, is also met. For here a stronger condition is fulfilled (i.e. they conceive of the state of affairs as being *actually* valuable in the way described), and hence the weaker condition just mentioned is also satisfied.

Clause (f) also obtains. For now participants think that a content-independent normative consideration, which requires that agreements be kept, is applicable to them. This is not to claim, of course, that they have stopped thinking that the normative consideration they considered applicable to them when the Judiciary was non-developed (namely that everyone who is in a position to bring about, together with others, a state of affairs which is valuable in relation to others, should perform the relevant actions) is no longer applicable. Now they think that the two considerations apply.

The transition, i.e. from being a non-developed instance of the Judiciary to becoming a developed one, would be completed if they executed their intentions for a significant period of time and, as a result, the relevant state of affairs were being obtained, and if they believed that this is the case. That is, if clause (d) and the other part of clause (e) of our model were met. Suppose that this is so. We have now a developed instance of the Judiciary.

The situation might become more complex. Suppose that members now recognize that further problems jeopardizing the maintenance of the relevant state of affairs might appear. They reason as follows: "A member might change his mind and think of opting out. We would now have a special right to demand compensation from him, and this might be an incentive for him not to opt out. But it might not. He might be willing to face these demands. The situation would not be terrible nevertheless. His opting out will hinder our project, but not significantly. The situation would be fairly different, however, if most decided to opt out and pay the price of breaching the agreement. The whole enterprise would be doomed".

So members foresee mechanisms of replacement. The mechanisms might be simple, such as adopting a rule requiring any new, would-be member to agree with all. But this might be seen as impractical, and members might decide collectively to require of any new would-be member to agree with one of the members only, say,

John, whose accepting the proposal counts as accepted by all. This, though better, might be seen not to be as far-reaching a strategy as it could be. For John might well opt out in the way described above. This flaw might be overcome by making the rule somewhat more sophisticated. For instance, the rule might refer to any individual who is already a member and who satisfies certain properties. So we have now formal conditions of membership.

The situation might become even more complex. New members might be incorporated, others might opt out, and others might be replaced. With all these changes the (alleged) normative relations among members become in a sense depersonalized. Talk of duties owed to the institution as a whole, and indirectly to its (alleged) beneficiaries, begins to take place. Other changes might well occur. Participants might collectively decide to consider some members, due to their personal qualities, as being in an authoritative position in relation to others. And this in turn could be further changed by mechanisms that describe members with authority over others in terms of other, impersonal qualities.

With all such changes several modifications would have taken place which the account, as deployed, does not capture. But these changes need not occur and, besides, the account can be extended to capture them if they do.

The story could further evolve in many other ways. In fact, it could have started otherwise, i.e. not from the transition from a non-developed instance of the Judiciary towards a developed one. For instance, participants might form a revolutionary group and think of the common goal of establishing a new normative system as desirable. But they might think that this could be achieved more smoothly, in virtue of considerations such as those mentioned above, if they voluntarily undertook the relevant obligations in advance, and if some of them were assigned an authoritative position in relation to the others. This group is, at this stage, a "prospective" institution (a group which can become an institution if, and only if, several additional conditions are met; among other things, they must perform their parts). It is structured, from scratch, by voluntary undertakings, and authoritative positions are assigned from the very beginning.

Most of the foregoing characteristics (the adoption of rules stipulating impersonal conditions of membership, mechanisms of replacement, and the creation of authoritative relations among members) are instantiated in actual instances of the Judiciary in the western world, and to capture them the account should be extended accordingly. But they need not. It is, I think, in this last feature, and in the minimalistic character of the account (which makes it flexible enough to be expanded), where its explanatory power in part lies.

In fact, actual instances of the Judiciary have several further traits. The state of affairs is normally seen by most members as being actually valuable in the way described for particular reasons, i.e. because it embodies particular political values (communism, capitalism, democracy, political freedom, equality, fairness, etc). Accordingly, the relationship that obtains among officials itself (a meshing set of attitudes and actions) is seen as particularly valuable. Content-independent normative considerations are then brought to bear in different ways. Officials are normally hired for the performance of certain tasks. That is, normally they are linked by normative relations created by their having agreed, agreements that, because they take place in the impersonal way coarsely described above, are seen as if the relevant individuals have agreed with the institution as a whole. But normally officials make also certain vows. These voluntary undertakings are not only symbolic in character. They are thought of as actually creating an obligation (and when valid they do create an obligation). They are, it seems to me, expressive in character: they are a form of manifesting or expressing what is deemed an appropriate attitude towards the value that the relationship (allegedly) embodies. The account can be refined to capture these possibilities as well.

In short, our account of developed instances of the Judiciary meets our second test. And our account of non-developed instances of the Judiciary, as shown in Chapter 6, meets it as well. So our account of legal practice *simpliciter*, which is built up by these two accounts, is adequate in relation to our second test.

10.4 Meeting the Third Test

Recall that the problem is to provide a characterization of legal practice that explains why in D, a conceivable instance of legal practice where the criteria of legality are (conceived of as) properties that pick out sets of norms which do not overlap, officials disagree about what some of the criteria are. When they disagree, they count their practice as grounding their assertions about what the criteria are. Each believes that his or her view is sounder, and disagreement is pervasive.

I want to argue that, if D were a developed instance of legal practice as construed by our account, this type of disagreement could obtain and be explained. To show this one has to see what type of configuration legal practice has in D. For, as the account purportedly shows, these instances of legal practice might be structured, *inter alia*, around voluntary undertakings, authoritative commands, or acts of purposive creation of expectations.

(a) Consider the latter type of setting. According to the account, here participants conceive of a particular state of affairs: one the bringing about of which is constituted, in part, by their performing certain actions – their following some rule(s) requiring them to evaluate the conduct of members of the community according to norms that satisfy certain criteria – which they have led others, purposively, to expect that they will perform. Which actions they have a duty to perform, and hence which rule(s) they have a duty to follow, depends on what expectations they have purposively created. Thus, if they have created, purposively, expectations to the effect that they will follow a rule requiring them to evaluate by applying norms that satisfy criteria C1 and C2, then this is what their duty amounts to. Can the type of disagreement in which we are interested obtain in this type of scenario?

This depends on what reading of "purposively" one settles on, a question that, among others, I have left open in relation to the normative principle of expectation-creation. But insofar as it involves the idea that, for the relevant individuals to have an obligation to do A, they must have had acted in a certain way having in mind that, because of this, others will expect that they will do A, if disagreement about their duties obtained it would be different in character. Their disagreement as to whether norms that satisfy criterion C3 or C4 should be applied should be reconstructed as a disagreement as to whether most have led most others to expect, purposively, that they will follow a rule requiring them to apply norms that satisfy criterion either C3 or C4 (in addition to C1 and C2). So here the disagreement could not be as pervasive or as deep as the objection points out. The question can be settled, under this reading of "purposively", by simply asking the parties whether they had in mind that they were leading the others to expect that they will apply these norms too or not.

(b) Suppose now that D is a developed instance of legal practice structured around voluntary undertakings. For simplicity, I shall assume that there are few members and that agreements have taken place. But the considerations I shall mention apply, *mutatis mutandis,* to other types of voluntary undertakings (promises, vows, oaths, etc).

Suppose that these agreements have been reached, as it happens normally, within the framework of agreeing practices. That is, in their community there are agreeing practices, and the agreements into which this small subset of individuals have entered have been reached within the framework of these practices.

Agreeing practices are, as said, rules of a special kind that require that certain acts count as agreeing, when agreeing is understood in the idealised sense. They might have different contents. Suppose that they demand that certain acts count as agreeing to do A when these acts can reasonably be interpreted as if the relevant individuals intended to bind themselves to do A, regardless of whether they actually intended to bind themselves to do A. What the practice exactly demands depends on how the larger community in which this practice obtains understands this. We can imagine, for instance, that they all understand that it demands that the relevant actions be interpreted assuming that the person who performed them is reasonable. And that this amounts to interpreting them assuming that the person is an individual who has a relatively good grasp of how the applicable reasons bear on the context of the interaction.

This type of agreeing practice is, I take it, fairly common. Something like this is what takes place in contractual commercial practices. What tradesmen have agreed to normally depends, not on what they intended to bind themselves to do, but on whether they have performed certain actions that can reasonably be interpreted, in the broader context of commercial practices, as if they intended to bind themselves to do that thing. And what it is normally meant by this is that the relevant actions be interpreted assuming that the person who performed them is a reasonable tradesman, that is, a person who has a relatively good grasp of how the applicable reasons bear in the broader context of commercial practices. Broader commercial practices are normally constituted by shared understandings and by certain rules, which are taken to promote certain values. Rapidity, security and fairness in profitable transactions seem to be the prominent ones. A reasonable tradesman is a person who is acquainted with this context and who understands it. He is a person who has a relatively good grasp of how these reasons (I am assuming of course that the values I mentioned are considered abstract reasons) bear on this context. Tradesmen many times agree (in the sense that they have the same opinion) as to whether a particular agreement has been reached. To re-adapt an example mentioned before, if a tradesman signs a document that he had every reason to believe was a form of contract but negligently failed to acknowledge as such, almost every actor in the field would understand that he has bound himself to do what the document provides for, even if he did not intend to do so. Tradesmen would argue in favour of such a view by claiming that this is what the contractual (i.e. agreeing) commercial practice requires, that this is so because his actions can reasonably be interpreted, in the broader context of commercial practices, as if he intended to bind himself to that. Other times tradesmen disagree as to whether an agreement has been reached. Cases of mistakes, blunders, and ambiguities as to the thing agreed to are but examples. And when they disagree as to whether an agreement has been reached, almost every actor in the field would defend his view by appealing to what he deems is the reasonable interpretation of the relevant actions, a disagreement that runs deep because this depends on how the values in play (rapidity, security, and fairness in the transactions), which sometimes are in conflict, bear on the matter.

These agreeing practices are, I think, very common in many other contexts. In fact, I would say they are the normal case. Adapting a well known example, suppose that Matthew agrees with John that he (John) will teach Matthew's six-year old son a game. If Matthew discovers that John has taught his son how to play poker for money, he would quite sensibly claim that John has breached the agreement. And the fact that John intended to bind himself to teach him how to play poker for money (let us suppose that this is the case) is irrelevant. Matthew argues in that way because there is a practice of agreeing of the sort described, according to which what they have agreed to depends, not on what John intended to bind himself to, but on a reasonable interpretation of his actions. Matthew interprets John' actions assuming that he is a reasonable person, that is, a person who understands what reasons bear on the broader context of teaching games to children (more abstractly, assuming that he is a person who understands what values teaching games to children is supposed to promote). I take it that most would submit that Matthew is right, that John has violated the agreement because he had to teach him a non adult-game. This is what he could reasonably be taken to have committed himself to. But other times the reactions, I think, would diverge. If John had taught him how to play a table-game whose theme is warfare many people might react in different ways. (And some may demand that the example be filled in much more to determine whether the agreement has been breached: When the child is learning to conquer the world as the game progresses, does he get a sense that people are being killed? Or is it a more abstract idea of "conquering"? Is conquering the only aim of the game, or is conquering understood, in the game, as something designed to enhance the lives of those who lose the battles?) But their reactions would be grounded on an argument that appeals to the agreeing practice, and hence an argument that involves establishing, *inter alia*, what the reasonable interpretation of John's actions is, a question the answer to which depends, in turn, on what it is important and valuable in the context of teaching games to children.

So let us suppose that in D our individuals have reached an agreement within the framework of this particular (and very common) type of agreeing practice.

Our account entails, among other things, that the following situation obtains. Participants conceive of a particular state of affairs: one the bringing about of which is constituted, in part, by their performing certain actions which most have agreed to perform. Which obligations they have validly undertaken is for them an objective question, in the sense that it depends on what the agreeing practice (which they deem valuable) requires, regardless of whether the parties actually intended to undertake such and such obligations. As they see it, if this agreeing practice requires that certain actions count as having agreed to do A and B, then this is the agreement they have reached. So for them which concrete actions they have acquired an obligation to perform depends on what the valuable agreeing practice requires.

It seems clear that there could be disagreement about what the rule requires, i.e. about which are the criteria that the norms they should apply are. Which actions they have agreed to perform, and hence which rule they have agreed to follow, depends for them on what the (in their view valuable) agreeing practice requires. Half of them might think that it requires that the relevant actions count as having agreed to follow a rule according to which they should evaluate conduct by applying norms that satisfy criteria C1, C2 and C3. They think this because, they claim, the relevant actions can reasonably be interpreted as if they intended to bind themselves to follow such a rule. Put otherwise, they claim that the relevant actions can be seen, assuming that they were acting as reasonable individuals at the time the interaction took place (i.e. assuming that they had a relatively good grasp of how the applicable reasons bore in the context), as if they intended to bind themselves to follow such a rule. And some of them might think that the agreeing practice requires that the relevant actions count as having agreed to follow a rule according to which they should evaluate conduct by applying norms that satisfy criteria C1, C2 and C4. They argue in a similar way, but towards different conclusions. And they can significantly disagree about this matter. For it is an objective matter in the sense described: the question of what their duties are depends on what they have agreed to; what they have agreed to does not depend on what they think they have agreed to, nor does it depend on what they intended to bind themselves to; it depends on what the agreement really amounts to; this is determined by what the agreeing practice requires; and what the practice requires depends, in turn, on what the reasonable interpretation of the relevant actions really is.

Thus, they could appeal, in part, to one aspect of their practice (to one aspect of their *legal practice*) to ground their assertions as to what the criteria that the norms they should apply are: they appeal to the agreement they have actually reached. And they might disagree about this endlessly. For what the reasonable interpretation of the relevant actions is might be a highly controversial matter, an issue on which, since it depends on the question of how the applicable reasons bore on the context in which the interaction took place, participants might debate time and again.

The story could be fleshed out more. For example, suppose that the agreement was reached in order to promote certain values more effectively, and that this was clear to all. In fact, assume that participants had a common conception of the relevant values, although most acknowledged that these conceptions were revisable if further normative considerations, the existence of which they were unaware of at that moment, pointed in a different direction, and that all this was in the public domain. In fact, we can suppose, the situation is roughly the same now. In this context, what the purpose of the agreement was (indeed, what the purpose of the agreement is) is seen as bearing on the question of what the reasonable interpretation of the actions is. Most participants might argue as follows: "Assuming that we were reasonable individuals who together wanted to promote these values, it is clear that our actions count as having agreed to follow a rule that requires that we evaluate conduct according to norms that satisfy criteria C3 (or C4) as well". The "clear" is intended to convey the idea that participants have here an immediate sense of what their actions count for. But the situation could be different, for they might not have an immediate sense of this issue. This might be something that they can discover later, after hard normative reflection on the values they wanted to promote. Suppose that each reasons: "Now that I think about it carefully and thoroughly, it is clear that our actions count as having agreed to follow a rule that requires that we evaluate conduct according to norms that satisfy C3 (or C4) as well; I wasn't aware of this, but now I recognize it clearly". Here the "clear" conveys the idea that the conclusion of a normative chain of reasoning is clear. Note in passing that this chain of reasoning – "think carefully again of what you have actually bound yourself to in this particular" – is the chain of reasoning in which each side of the debate expects the other side to engage.

Consider now a setting in D where the agreements have been reached, not within the framework of agreeing practices, but within the framework of special relationships. These relationships, I claimed, are constituted in part by norms (which are deemed valid insofar as they promote certain values) which may also require that certain acts count as agreeing to do A, when agreeing is understood in the idealised sense.

We considered some examples of this. Recall the case of James, who is confused about dates (he thinks that his five-year old niece's birthday is on the 19th when in fact it is on the 18th). After making the offer he takes notice of his confusion, and he acknowledges that, despite his intention to bind himself to go with her on the 19th, he should go with her on the 18th. He claims that that is so because he has agreed to this. Yet James did not intend to bind himself to go on the 18th. James thinks that his intention to go on the 19th is actually irrelevant because he conceives of his relationship with his niece as having certain features (it requires that the uncle should attach special importance to the birthdays of his niece, and that he should conduct himself in such a way that her niece learn that agreements are not to be made without thinking carefully). The relationship as such, James think, requires that his act count as having agreed to go on the 18th. Notice that normally this type of relationship is not only constituted by norms stipulating that certain acts count as agreeing (which are deemed valid insofar as they promote certain values within the relationship), but also by shared understandings and practices that evolve with time. Depending on the complexity of his relationship, James might think that other questions as to what he has agreed to (e.g. to which zoo? for how long?) are also answerable by establishing what his particular relationship with his niece requires in this respect.

The example is simple, but its lessons can be extended to more complex relationships. For instance, let us assume that, in D the group was, when the institution was a prospective one, a revolutionary group. Its members were linked by a special relationship then. We could label it a relationship of "political fellowship". It is constituted by norms which regulate the actions of its members, which are deemed valid because they are oriented to the promotion of certain political ideals (democracy, political freedom, equality, or what have you), by shared understandings and by previous practices (they have been together in countless meetings, public protests, complots, etc). Now, in D, there is an institution in the proper sense, but participants are still linked, let us suppose, by essentially the same relationship.

In this scenario, our account entails that the situation is in part this. Participants conceive of a particular state of affairs, one the bringing about of which is constituted in part by their performing certain actions they have agreed to perform: their following a rule requiring them to evaluate conduct by applying norms that satisfy certain criteria. Which particular actions they have agreed to perform, and hence which rule they have agreed to follow exactly, depends on what the relationship that links them (which in their view is valuable) requires. They are all aware of this. Half of them might think that this relationship requires that the relevant actions count as having agreed to follow a rule according to which they should evaluate conduct by applying norms that satisfy criteria C1, C2 and C3. And the rest might think that this special relationship requires that the relevant actions count as having agreed to follow a rule according to which they should evaluate conduct by applying norms that satisfy criteria C1, C2 and C4. They disagree about this issue because they have different conceptions of what this particular instance of political fellowship requires in this respect. And they disagree about this, let us suppose, in part because they have different conceptions of the particular political ideals. All recognize that an answer to the question of which actions they have agreed to perform depends on what the relationship requires. It is an objective matter, in the sense that it does not depend on what they think in this respect, but rather on what the relationship, properly understood, really amounts to and demands.

Thus, they could appeal, in part, to one aspect of their practice (to one aspect of their *legal practice*) to ground their assertions as to what the criteria that the norms they should apply are: they appeal to the agreement they have actually reached. And they can disagree about this endlessly. For what they have agreed to depends on what the relevant relationship that links them requires in this respect; and this might be a controversial matter, a normative issue on which participants might debate time and again.

The foregoing remarks are sufficient to show, I hope, that the type of disagreement we are interested in could intelligibly obtain in these settings. I have already argued that the theories we have assessed, as they stand, do not entail that conclusion, so I shall not return to the issue again. But we can make a general diagnosis of why, as they stand, they fail.

Putting details aside, these theories agree that there is an instance of legal practice only if there is (at least) one rule (or plan) in the relevant group (a rule of recognition) which requires that its members evaluate conduct by applying norms that satisfy certain criteria C1...Cn. And we can safely claim that they share the view that such a necessary condition is met only if two conditions are met. First, members must judge conduct by applying norms satisfying C1...Cn. Second, they must display convergent attitudes towards their actually doing that. Of course, each theory construes these attitudes differently (very roughly: they must at least be disposed to apply norms satisfying C1...Cn, on Hart's account; each must at least prefer and expect that the others apply norms that satisfy C1...Cn, on the coordinative-convention approach; they must believe that applying norms satisfying C1...Cn is something required by a rule, on Raz's account; and they must intend to apply norms satisfying C1...Cn, on Shapiro's account), but this is unimportant for present purposes. The point is that the question of what the content of rule (or plan) of the group is, and hence the question of what the criteria are, depends on what members do and on their displaying convergent attitudes towards that: only if they are applying norms that satisfy criteria C1, C2 and C3 (or C4) and are displaying convergent attitudes toward their doing that, do C1, C2 and C3 (or C4) count as criteria specified in the rule (or plan) of the group. Accordingly, in D participants could not appeal to the practice itself, which in part is appealing to the rule (or plan) of the group, in order to ground their assertions as to whether C3 or C4 is the criterion that the norms they should apply must satisfy. For according to this view in D there would be no rule (or plan) in the group to that effect. The conditions required by the view for that to be the case are not met in relation to C3 or C4: neither C3 nor C4 have been employed so far and the convergence of attitudes does not obtain.

According to the account I have sketched, it is true that there is an instance of legal practice only if there is (at least) one rule (or, if you prefer, a plan, i.e. a set of rules) in a group (a rule of recognition) which requires that its members evaluate conduct by applying norms that satisfy certain criteria C1...Cn. But the account claims that this idea, i.e. that there is such a rule (or plan) in the group, should not be interpreted in the way the general view suggests, for there is no reason to understand it in that way necessarily. Consider two alternative possibilities.

If members of a group have agreed, within the framework of larger agreeing practices or special relationships of the type described above, to follow a rule (or plan) that requires that they evaluate conduct by applying norms that satisfy C1...Cn, there is a clear sense in which there is a rule (or plan) in this group now. And it is clear that, for that to be the case, it is not necessary that members judge conduct by applying norms that satisfy C1...Cn or that they display convergent attitudes toward their doing that. Whether there is a rule (or plan) of this sort in the group depends on whether there is an agreement to that effect. So the question of what the content of the rule (or plan) of the group is, and hence the question of what the criteria are, depends, not on how participants are judging conduct or on convergent attitudes towards that, but on what the agreement they have actually reached (as to what rule – or plan – should be followed is) really is. And this is an objective matter in the sense described above. Thus, only if the larger agreeing practices or the special relationships require that the relevant actions count as their having agreed to follow a rule (or plan) that requires that conduct be evaluated by applying norms that satisfy criteria C1, C2 and C3 is there such rule (or plan) in the group. Only if that is the case do C1, C2 and C3 count as the criteria. This is precisely, in part, what might happen in D according to the account I sketched.

On the other hand, if members have entered into that type of agreement, if they intended to follow the rule (or plan) – the one they have agreed to follow –, and if they followed the rule (or plan) at least in part (e.g. because the occasion for abiding by all its requirements has not obtained yet), there is also a clear sense in which there is a rule (or plan) in this group. But this is a different sense. Here "there is a rule (or plan) in this group" means that the rule (or plan) which they have agreed to follow is by and large followed, at least in part, and that they intend to follow it. Thus, members might have entered into an agreement to follow a rule (or plan) that requires that conduct be evaluated by applying norms that satisfy C1, C2 and C3 (or C4). Since this is an objective matter in the sense described, participants might fail to see that this is exactly the content of the rule (or plan) which they have agreed to follow. For instance, they might fail to see that C3 is one of the criteria. Besides, they might intend to follow the rule (or plan) they have actually agreed to follow, even if they fail to see what its content is exactly. Thus, some might not intend, e.g., to employ C3, for as said they might fail to see that C3 is one of the criteria specified in the rule (or plan) they have agreed to follow; but if it were shown to them that the latter is in effect the case they would, for as said they intend to follow the rule (or plan) they have actually agreed to follow. Finally, they might judge conduct by applying norms satisfying C1 and C2 (e.g. because the occasion for applying norms that satisfy C3 – or C4 – has not arisen yet). If these three conditions were met, there is a clear, but different, sense in which there is a rule (or plan) in this group (and here the two conditions that the general view requires for that to be the case are not satisfied). Here this means that the rule (or plan) they have agreed to follow is by and large followed, at least in part, and that they intend to follow it. This is precisely, in part, what might happen in D according to our account too. In D the practice might be in part of this sort: they might be following, at least in part, the rule (or plan) they have agreed to follow and intend to follow that rule (or plan). Accordingly, in D participants can appeal to one aspect of this practice itself, to one aspect of their *legal* practice, to ground their assertions as to what the disputed criterion really is. They appeal to the rule (or plan) they have agreed to follow, and what the content of the agreement is exactly (and hence what rule or plan they should follow exactly) is an objective matter in the sense described: it depends on what the larger agreeing practices or the special relationships, within the framework of which the agreement has been reached, require. And this might be controversial. But they are still appealing to the same rule (or plan), i.e. to the rule (or plan) of the group: that which they have agreed to follow.

These considerations are applicable, *mutatis mutandis*, to other forms of voluntary undertakings, such as promises, vows, oaths, etc, for there are practices of promising, vowing, etc, with similar contents, and promising, vowing, etc, obtain in special relationships with similar contents too. Of course, practices of agreeing (and of promising, vowing, etc), or special relationships, might have many other different contents, and hence disagreement might acquire other forms. But those which I have focused on represent, it seems to me, the familiar cases. Normally the question of what their duties are is a question of what obligations they have voluntarily undertaken, and this is normally, for the reasons mentioned, an objective question in the sense described.

(c) Similar considerations apply, finally, to the authoritative context, which I shall consider very briefly. Suppose that D were a developed instance of legal practice of this sort. According to our model, this entails that the members conceive of the relevant state of affairs as something the bringing about of which is constituted in part by their performing certain actions which an authority (be it an individual, or another group, or another institution) has commanded them to perform (following a rule which requires that conduct be evaluated by applying norms that satisfy certain criteria). And they might disagree as to what their duties are, i.e. as to whether, according to the authority, they should apply norms that satisfy, in addition to criteria C1 and C2 (there is no disagreement about the content of the orders in this respect), criteria C3 or C4 in certain cases. They might disagree about this because they might have different conceptions of the concept of authority. Questions such as "is the content of an authoritative command determined by considering the actual mental states of the authority, or by considering its counterfactual mental states, or by ...?" are typically controversial in this connection. And one could imagine debates among participants as to whether they have a duty to apply norms that satisfy C3 or C4 in the relevant cases by putting forward arguments that advocate different answers. Each side might appeal to one aspect of the practice itself (to one aspect of their *legal* practice) to justify in part their views, namely to the fact that the authority has commanded so. But each side might argue that its view is sounder, for it is grounded on the best construal of the notion of authority that is available so far. In short, the type of disagreement in which we are interested might well obtain if legal practice were configured in this way too. The theories we have assessed, as they stand, could not account for this type of disagreement, for they subscribe to the general view described above.

Before concluding let me clarify three things. Firstly, there is no denial that these theories could reformulate their proposals to explain this type of disagreement. For instance, by incorporating in some way the idea of voluntary undertakings created within the framework of special practices or special relationships of the sort I considered. The only point I have urged in this respect is that they should do so, that the general view upheld by them which I described above should be revised.

Secondly, it is important to notice what the scope of the account is. Recall the disagreement between two individuals over the concept of "table" (assuming that it is a criterially explicable concept).[222] These individuals did not agree as to what the criteria for something to qualify as a table are. I claimed, following Raz, that they could not disagree about that if they took the question of what the criteria are as something determined by a personal, individual rule, and not as something governed

[222] See Chapter 1, p. 21

by a common rule (even if they are not fully aware of its content, or cannot make it explicit). The latter is, in effect, a pre-condition of genuine disagreement.

This is precisely what happens in D. Consider again, to illustrate, the case of voluntary undertakings. Here participants take the question as to what the criteria of legality are as a question to be answered by a common standard, namely the plan they have agreed (or promised, or taken vows) to follow (if even if they are not fully aware, or cannot make explicit, its content). For participants have agreed (or promised, taken vows, etc) to follow the plan within the framework of larger agreeing (or promising, etc) practices or special relationships, which are constituted by norms and which determine the content of the plan. For instance, I claimed, they could have agreed to follow a plan within a larger agreeing practice according to which certain acts count as agreeing to do A when they can be reasonably interpreted as if the relevant individuals intended to bind themselves to do A, regardless of whether they actually intended that (a reasonable interpretation being an interpretation that assumes that the relevant individuals are individuals who have a good grasp of the reasons that bear on the context of the interaction). Everyone understands that the content of the plan they have agreed to follow depends on what the larger agreeing practice requires, and hence they may not be fully aware of what the common plan is, or may not be able to make it explicit before thinking of the matter thoroughly. And when attempting to make it explicit they may arrive at different conclusions because they may have different views on the reasons that bear in the context. There is, accordingly, genuine disagreement about the content of the common plan. Naturally, there could not be massive disagreement about the rules that are constitutive of the larger agreeing practices or the special relationships. For if that were the case genuine disagreement at the level of the plan would be impossible. For instance, participants could not disagree about the fact that the larger agreeing practice requires that certain acts count as agreeing to do A when they can be reasonably interpreted as if the relevant individuals intended that, a reasonable interpretation being one that assumes that the individuals are reasonable, i.e. that they a good grasp of the reasons that bear on the context. As said, they may have different ideas of the reasons that bear on the context. But they must agree about what the content of the larger agreeing practice is.

Some may tempted to object that the account only pushes the problem of disagreement out one step further without solving it, or something along those lines. After all, the objection would go, in the example just proposed there is still some disagreement at the level of the larger agreeing practice; otherwise participants could not disagree about the reasons that bear on the context. But the objection is misguided in several ways. On the one hand, there is disagreement on what the reasons that bear on the context are, but not about the fact that the larger agreeing practice requires to take those reasons into account. The former kind of disagreement is not a problem for our account. It would be a problem if disagreeing about the reasons were incompatible with agreeing about the content of the larger agreeing practice. But this is not the case. So long as participants believe that the question of what the reasons are is an objective question in the sense explained (something that does not depend of what the two parties in the dispute think of the applicable reasons, but on what the reasons really are), the disagreement is perfectly intelligible.[223] So it is not the case that the account "pushes out the problem one step further" in any relevant sense. On the other hand, the objection ignores the scope of the account. The account is not proposed to explain disagreement at any level, or disagreement of any type. Thus, the account is not designed to explain moral disagreement, or religious disagreement, or scientific disagreement. It should explain disagreement in legal practice. Some general considerations about disagreement, of course, are needed if the account is to be successful. But the fact that there should be a common rule in the sense explained, and that the questions should be taken as objective in the sense explained, are, I think, sufficient in that respect.

The foregoing remarks also help to show more clearly why there cannot be genuine disagreement in *non*-developed instances of legal practice. When examining that issue, I claimed that a necessary condition for that sort of practice to exist, according to the model, is that there is one shared rule or plan in the group that makes reference to certain criteria such that, if participants disagree about the criteria, there is no shared rule or plan. So there could not be disagreement. The reason for that is rooted in the fact that, in non-developed instances, duties are grounded on content-dependent normative considerations (not on content-independent normative considerations, as happens in developed instances). Each participant thinks that he or she (and the others) should follow the plan for certain normative reasons that depend on its content. Participants could realize, of course, that the normative content-dependent consideration no longer applies. But then the institution would disappear (for participants' thinking that they are under a duty is, in any institution, a condition for its existence). They could also realize that a new normative content-dependent consideration that makes reference to the value of a different plan is applicable, and decide to follow the new plan. But then we would have a new, different institution, and hence they could not argue that this is what their practice always required. In short, the structure of non-developed instances of legal practice is too simple to leave room for the kind of disagreement we envisaged.

The third and final consideration is also related to the scope of the account. The explanation is not designed to explain any kind of disagreement. It does not claim, for instance, that any disagreement among legal actors over specific legal provisions, or about the scope of a constitutional clause, can be explained in the terms proposed. It does follow from the account, nevertheless, that disagreement at those levels is genuine only if there is a common rule and if the questions are taken as objective in the sense explained.

Besides, it is true that I have considered a special scenario only (D). It is artificial because of the way in which the criteria of legality are construed. But as said before the scenario is not as artificial as it may seem. For instance, in Argentina it is indisputable that norms enacted by Parliament are law, and that officials are required to

---

[223] This is not to claim, of course, that the only possibility for disagreement at this level is of that sort (for disagreement may occur for many different reasons) As Raz claims, complexity and non transparency of criterial explanations, and the relatively interdependence of concepts, may be some of the reasons that originate disagreement (*TVNLP* 266–270).

apply those norms. This is, in our artificial language, a criterion of legality (C1). Yet in this legal system there is an intense, and relatively recent debate, as to whether certain decisions by the Supreme Court (the holding of certain cases) should be followed by lower tribunals (or, to be more precise, whether lower tribunals should follow these decisions when unable to find new and compelling arguments to the contrary). So there is a dispute as to whether certain decisions by the Supreme Court are a criterion of legality (call it C2). And the debate is of importance, in part, because (or to the extent that) C1 and C2 have no norms in common. Of course, perhaps this is not the best reconstruction of the dispute. My only point is that it resembles D, the scenario described above, in many respects. And when one considers the arguments put forward by judges to the effect C2 should or should not be employed, one notices that they are the kind of arguments that we considered above. Thus, for instance, judges sometimes claim that the decisions should be followed because not doing so would demand time and effort pointlessly (for the Court will overrule the decision that does not abide by its doctrine), thus hindering the constitutional value of procedural economy; or because following the holding of the case would further the constitutional value of legal certainty; or because following the doctrine promotes the constitutional value of equality. In turn, those who deny that the holding of the case should be followed claim either that those constitutional values would not be promoted, or that promoting them is not a sufficient reason to generate the relevant duty, for other constitutional values (such as the judges' independence, or respecting citizens' expectations that judges adjudicate according to their own view) have more weight. Naturally, those claims are not put forward as if judges were free to choose among the constitutional values in conflict (procedural economy, legal certainty, etc). Judges have committed themselves (by accepting their role, which is a special form of voluntary undertaking) to promote those constitutional values, and they have done so within the framework of a special, political relationship. Everyone would agree, I would say, that this relationship requires that their accepting their role counts as having accepted to apply norms that satisfy certain criteria such that all (and only) the constitutional values mentioned above (procedural economy, legal certainty, independence, etc) are promoted in a reasonable and balanced way. Thus, judges may well argue that these commitments, properly interpreted by considering what the relationship requires, demands that they apply norms that satisfy C2 as well, or that it does not. In fact, as the debate evolves, new questions appear (e.g.: What happens when the Court changes its members? And when the Court changes its opinion? Is the decision by the Court in one case enough, or does one need a line of decisions? Is the Court itself bound by its own decisions?). And in all cases those questions are answered by considering the scope of the commitments, which in turn depend on what the relationship requires, an issue that is considered objective in the sense explained.[224]

Naturally, the explanation I have just suggested is provisional only. To make it good a detailed study of the arguments put forward by judges should be proposed,

[224] For the best explanation of the state of the debate, see n 35.

among other things. But this is beside the point. The point is that the general account, despite its abstracter character, seems to have enough resources to explain actual instances of disagreement in contemporary legal systems.

So, to conclude, our model of developed instances of the Judiciary meets the third test. Accordingly, our account of legal practice *simpliciter*, which is built up by this model and by our model of non-developed instances, is adequate in this respect. And since it satisfies the other two tests too, it is adequate.

10.5 Conclusion

I have attempted to deploy an account that answers two questions: What is the structure of legal practice? And what is its content? The account is continuous with the doctrines I have assessed in many ways. It describes the content of legal practice in roughly the same way (it consists, essentially, of evaluating the conduct of members of a community by applying norms that satisfy certain criteria). Besides, its view about its structure incorporates many of the elements that these doctrines deem necessary to understand it. But it focuses on some other elements that they have failed to consider. These elements explain the possibility of a particular type of disagreement. More importantly, these elements explain that possibility within a general explanatory framework of the sense in which legal practice is the practice of members of an institution.

Bibliography

Abercrombie, Nicholas. *The Penguin Dictionary of Sociology* (2nd ed). London: Penguin, 1988
Ardal, Pall S. "And that's a Promise." *Philosophical Quaterly* 18 (1968): 225
Atiyah, Patrick. *The Rise and Fall of Freedom of Contract.* Oxford: Clarendon Press, 1979
Atiyah, Patrick. *Promises, Morals and the Law.* Oxford: Clarendon Press, 1981
Atiyah, Patrick. *Essays on Contract.* Oxford: Clarendon Press, 1986
Bach, Kent, and Michael Harnish. *Linguistic Communication and Speech Acts.* Cambridge: MIT Press, 1979
Baltzer, Ulrith. "Joint Action of Large Groups." In *Social Facts & Collective Intentionality*, edited by G Meggle. Frankfurt: Dr Hansel-Hohenhausen AG, 2002
Brandt, Richard. *Theory of the Good and the Right.* Oxford: Clarendon Press, 1979
Bratman, Michael. *Intention, Plans and Practical Reason.* Cambridge: Harvard University Press, 1987
Bratman, Michael. *Faces of Intention: Selected Essays on Intention and Agency.* Cambridge: CUP, 1999
Burge, Tyler. "On Knowledge and Convention." *The Philosophical R* 84 (1975): 249
Coleman, Jules. "Incorporationism, Conventionality, and the Practical Difference Thesis." In *Hart's Postscript: Essays on the Postscript to The Concept of Law*, edited by J Coleman. Oxford: OUP, 2001a
Coleman, Jules. *The Practice of Principle.* Oxford: OUP, 2001b
Coote, Brian. "The Essence of Contract." *Journal of Contract Law* 1 (1988): 91
Dworkin, Ronald. *Taking Rights Seriously.* London: Duckworth, 1977
Dworkin, Ronald. *Law's Empire.* Cambridge: Harvard University Press, 1986
Dworkin, Ronald. "Hart's Postscript and the Character of Political Philosophy." *Oxford Journal of Legal Studies* 24 (2004): 1
Endicott, Timothy. "Objectivity, Subjectivity and Incomplete Agreements." In *Oxford Essays in Jurisprudence* (4th Series), edited by J Horder. Oxford: OUP, 2000
Endicott, Timothy. "Are There Any Rules." *The Journal of Ethics* 5 (2001): 199
Finnis, John. *Natural Law and Natural Rights.* Oxford: Clarendon Press, 1980
Gardner, John. "Reasons for Teamwork." *Legal Theory* 8 (2002): 495
Gauthier, David. "David Hume, Contractarian." *The Philosophical R* 88 (1979): 3
Gilbert, Margaret. *On Social Facts.* London: Routledge, 1989
Gilbert, Margaret. *Living Together: Rationality, Sociality and Obligation.* Lanham: Rowman & Littlefield Publishers, 1996
Gilbert, Margaret. *Sociality and Responsibility: New Essays in Plural Subject Theory.* Lanham: Rowman & Littlefield Publishers, 2000
Gilbert, Margaret. "Acting Together." In *Social Facts & Collective Intentionality*, edited by G Meggle. Frankfurt: Dr Hansel-Hohenhausen AG, 2002

R.E. Sánchez Brigido, *Groups, Rules and Legal Practice*,
Law and Philosophy Library 89, DOI 10.1007/978-90-481-8770-6,

Gilbert, Margaret "Considerations on Joint Commitment: Responses to Various Comments." In *Social Facts & Collective Intentionality*, edited by G Meggle. Frankfurt: Dr Hansel-Hohenhausen AG, 2002
Goddard, David. "The Myth of Subjectivity." *Legal Studies* 7 (1987): 263
Hacker, Peter. "Hart's Philosophy of Law." In *Law, Morality, and Society: Essays in honour of H.L.A. Hart*, edited by P Hacker and J Raz. Oxford: Clarendon Press, 1977
Hart, Herbert Lionel Adolphus. "Legal and Moral Obligations." In *Essays in Moral Philosophy*, edited by AI Melden. Seattle: University of Washington Press, 1958
Hart, Herbert Lionel Adolphus. *The Concept of Law* (2nd ed). Oxford: Clarendon Press, 1994
Kolodny, Niko, and R. Jay Wallace. "Promises and Practices Revisited." *Philosophy & Public Affairs* 31 (2003): 119
Kutz, Christopher. *Complicity: Ethics and Law for a Collective Age*. Cambridge: CUP, 2000
Kutz, Christopher. "The Judicial Community." *Philosophical Issues* 11 (2001): 442
Lagerspetz, Eerik. "A Conventionalist Theory of Institutions." *Acta Philosophica Fennica* 44 (1989)
Lamond, Grant. "Commitments and Practical Reason." DPhil thesis, University of Oxford, 1996
Langille, Brian, and Arthur Ripstein. "Strictly Speaking – It Went Without Saying." *Legal Theory* 2 (1997): 63
Lewis, David. *Convention: A Philosophical Study*. Cambridge: Harvard University Press, 1969
MacCormick, Neil. "Voluntary Obligations and Normative Powers." *Proceedings of the Aristotelian Society* Supp 46 (1972): 59
MacCormick, Neil. *H.L.A.Hart*. London: Edward Arnold, 1981
MacCormick, Neil, and O Weinberger. *An Institutional Theory of Law*. Dordrecht: Reidel Publishing Company, 1986
Marmor, Andrei. "Legal Conventionalism." In *Hart's Postscript: Essays on the Postscript to The Concept of Law*, edited by J Coleman. Oxford: OUP, 2001
Morton, Peter. *An Institutional Theory of Law*. Oxford: Clarendon Press, 1998
Murphy, Liam. "Promise and Practice." http://www.law.nyu.edu/clppt/program2002/readings/murphy/murphy-ch1-promise0802.pdf (accessed July 17, 2006)
Narveson, Jan. "Promising, Expecting and Utility." *Canadian Journal of Philosophy* 1 (1971): 207
Pratt, Michael. "Scanlon on Promising." *Canadian Journal of Law and Jurisprudence* 14 (2001): 143
Postema, Gerald. "Coordination and Conventions at the Foundations of Law." Journal of Legal Studies 11 (1982): 165
Rawls, John. *A Theory of Justice*. Cambridge: Harvard University Press, 1971
Raz, Joseph. *The Concept of a Legal System* (2nd ed). Oxford: Clarendon Press, 1980
Raz, Joseph. "Voluntary Obligations and Normative Powers." *Proceedings of the Aristotelian Society* Supp 46 (1972): 79
Raz, Joseph. *Practical Reason and Norms*. Oxford: OUP, 1990
Raz, Joseph. "Promises and Obligations." In *Law, Morality, and Society: Essays in Honour of H.L.A. Hart*, edited by P Hacker and J Raz. Oxford: Clarendon Press, 1977
Raz, Joseph. *The Authority of Law: Essays on Law and Morality*. Oxford: Clarendon Press, 1979
Raz, Joseph. "Promises in Morality and Law." *Harvard Law Review* 4 (1982): 916
Raz, Joseph. "On the Nature of Rights." *Mind* 93 (1984): 194
Raz, Joseph. *The Morality of Freedom*. Oxford: Clarendon Press, 1986
Raz, Joseph. "Facing Up: A Reply." *Southern California Law Review* 62 (1989): 1153
Raz, Joseph. "Two Views of the Nature of the Theory of Law: A Partial Comparison." *Legal Theory* 4 (1998): 249
Rivera, Julio, and Santiago Legarre. "La obligatoriedad de los fallos de la Corte Suprema de Justicia de la Nación desde la perspectiva de los tribunales inferiores." IV LexisNexis Jurisprudencia Argentina, Suplemento de Jurisprudencia de la Corte Suprema de Justicia de la Nación (2006): 1333

Rivera, Julio, and Santiago Legarre. La obligatoriedad atenuada de los fallos de la Corte Suprema y el *stare decisis* vertical. (2009): La Ley 1
Robins, Michael. *Promises, Intending and Moral Autonomy.* Cambridge: CUP, 1984
Sartorious, Rudolph. "Positivism and the Foundations of Legal Authority." In *Issues in Contemporary Legal Philosophy*, edited by R Gavison. Oxford: Clarendon Press, 1987
Searle, John. "Collective Intentions and Actions." In *Intentions in Communication*, edited by P Cohen, J Morgan and M Pollack. Cambridge, MIT Press, 1990
Searle, John. *Speech Acts: An Essay in the Philosophy of Language.* Cambridge: CUP, 1969
Scanlon, Thomas. *What We Owe to Each Other.* Cambridge: Harvard University Press, 1998
Scanlon, Thomas. "Promises and Practices." *Philosophy and Public Affairs* 19 (1990): 199
Scott, Richard. *Institutions and Organizations.* London: Sage Publications, 1997
Shapiro, Scott. "Law, Plans, and Practical Reason." *Legal Theory* 8 (2002): 387
Stoljar, Samuel. "Promise, Expectation and Agreement." *Cambridge L R* 47 (1988): 193
Treitel, Guenter. *The Law of Contract* (11th ed). London: Sweet & Maxwell, 2003
Tuomela, Raimo. *The Importance of Us.* Standford: Standford University Press, 1995
Vermazen, Bruce. "Objects of Intention." *Philosophical Studies* 71 (1993): 223
Warnock, Geoffrey. *The Object of Morality.* London: Methuen, 1976

Index

A
Action
acting qua member of an institution, 3–15, 95, 141–161
acting qua member of a group, 89, 91–109, 141–161
intentional, 57–78, 79–89
Agreement(s), 121–139, 146
Ardal, 125
Atiyah, 122, 137
Attitude, 6, 18, 31–34, 37, 39, 42, 49, 58, 65–67, 92–94, 96–98, 100, 103–104, 106–107, 114, 117, 130, 141–142, 144–147, 149–150, 152–155, 157–158, 160, 164–167, 170, 177

B
Bach and Harnish, 133
Baltzer, 114
Brandt, 125
Bratman, 61–70, 79, 82, 113, 115, 147
Burge, 50

C
Coleman, xvii, xx–xxi, 18–19, 30, 33, 37, 40–41, 57
Collective intentional activities, xxi–xxv, 1, 57–89, 113, 119, 163
Commitment, 62, 68, 72, 97, 111–118, 182
Convention, xviii–xxiv, 18, 25–44, 50, 52, 54–55, 105–106, 159–160, 177
Conventionalism, xix, 33, 105–106, 159–160
Custom, 19, 26, 28

D
Disagreement, xxii–xxiv, 17–23, 29, 40, 43, 54–55, 63, 73–74, 77–78, 108, 171–174, 176, 178–181, 183
Duty (duties), xxiii–xiv, 5–18, 20, 32–33, 35–39, 42–43, 45, 52–53, 58–60, 62, 69, 74–77, 87, 89, 91, 93–96, 98–99, 103, 105, 108, 112–118, 127–129, 144–148, 150, 152–155, 157, 159–160, 164–166, 168, 170–172, 174, 179, 181–182
Dworkin, xvii, xxii, 17–18, 21, 33

E
Endicott, 50, 138

F
Finnis, xvii

G
Gardner, 166
Gauthier, 50
Gilbert, 26, 59, 111–119, 122, 134–135
Goddard, 138
Group(s)
which acts intentionally, 57–89
with a normative unity of type (I), 91–109
with a normative unity of type (II), 141–161
with no normative unity, 79–89

H
Hacker, 30, 32
Hart, xix–xx, xxii–xxiv, 17–18, 25, 29–34, 36–38, 123, 159

I
Institution(s)
developed, 141–161
member(s) of an, 2–3, 11, 16, 36, 39, 42–43, 51–52, 99, 107–108, 153, 163–164
non-developed, 14–15, 95–105, 151, 153–156, 161
other-regarding, 4, 6, 13–16, 91, 95, 101, 104, 155, 159, 166

Institution(s) (*Cont.*)
  self-regarding, 5–6, 95
Intention(s), 57–89, 124–133

J
Judiciary, 2–3, 14–15, 17, 29, 36, 38–39, 42–43, 51–53, 74, 78, 91, 95, 103–107, 141–161, 164, 166–171, 183

K
Kolodny and Wallace, 123
Kutz, xxi, 37, 40, 57, 66, 68–69, 79–89, 109, 113, 147

L
Lagerspetz, xx, 50
Lamond, 131, 133, 147
Langille and Ripstein, 138
Legal system, xxiii, 3, 21, 29–32, 37–38, 41, 45–49, 52, 70–71, 182–183
Lewis, 40–41, 50, 122

M
MacCormick, xvii, 2, 30, 32, 125
Marmor, xvii, xx, 33–34, 40, 43
Moral, 18–19, 29, 43, 47, 49, 69–70, 125, 128–129, 131, 147–148, 168, 181
Morton, 3
Murphy, 123, 127

N
Narveson, 125

O
Officials
  norm-applying, xvii–xix, 30–33, 41, 71
  norm-enforcing, 46

P
Plan(s), 67, 71–72, 75–77, 81, 84, 99–100, 102–103, 125, 154–157, 168–169, 176–178, 180–181
Postema, xvii, xx, 40–41, 50
Practice
  content, xviii–xix, 16, 30, 32–33, 39, 49, 72, 107, 137–139, 161, 183
  conventional, xviii–xx, xxiii, 1
  coordinative, xx, xxii–xxiii, 1, 25–44, 52, 54–55, 177
  institutional, xxiv–xxv
  legal, 70–72, 91–109, 163–183
  social, xvii–xix, xxii, 2–3, 18, 20, 32, 54, 108, 123
  structure, 172
Pratt, 127
Promise(s), 9–12, 27, 34, 37, 63, 69, 109, 121–137, 139, 146–148, 172, 178, 180
Promising principle, 130, 136

R
Rawls, 123–124
Raz, vii, xxi–xxiv, 1, 11, 13, 18, 21–22, 25, 37, 45–55, 103–106, 127–132, 147–148, 158–160, 177, 179–181
Reason(s)
  cancelled, 12
  conflict, 12
  ordinary, 12–13, 27, 34–35, 39, 42–43
  special, 13, 27–28, 34–36
  strength, 11–12
  weight, 11–12, 34, 126–127
Regularity, xviii–xx, xxii, 18, 34, 40–43, 49
Requirement
  categorical, 11–12, 16, 38, 53, 59, 75–76
  teleological, 38, 53, 76
Rivera and Legarre, 21
Robins, 122, 147
Role, xx, 10, 37, 48, 63, 67–69, 80, 82–83, 182
Rule(s)
  of adjudication, 29–31, 37, 42, 77
  of change, 29–31
  to follow, 8, 12, 174–178
  of recognition(s), xix, 18–20, 29–33, 36–43, 47, 49, 53–55, 75, 176–177
  social, vii, xix, xxi, xxiii, 1, 17–20, 25–44, 45–55, 131

S
Sartorious, xvii, 26, 50
Scanlon, 119, 125–128
Scott, 3
Searle, 58, 123
Shapiro, vii, ix, xvii, xxi–xxiv, 1, 40, 57–80, 82, 106–107, 113, 160, 177
Stoljar, 125

T
Tradition, xviii, 28
Treitel, 137
Tuomela, 50, 109, 119

V
Vermazen, 82
Voluntary undertaking(s), 130, 139, 146–149, 167, 170–172, 178–180, 182

W
Warnock, 34

MIX
Papier aus verantwortungsvollen Quellen
Paper from responsible sources
FSC® C105338

If you have any concerns about our products,
you can contact us on
ProductSafety@springernature.com

In case Publisher is established outside the EU,
the EU authorized representative is:
Springer Nature Customer Service Center GmbH
Europaplatz 3, 69115 Heidelberg, Germany

Printed by Libri Plureos GmbH
in Hamburg, Germany